Free Burma

. . . The whole house with its manifold and graded activities must be a house of prayer. It does not mean keeping a Quiet Room to which we can retreat, with mystical pictures on the walls, and curtains over the windows to temper the disconcerting intensity of the light; a room where we can forget the fact that there are black beetles in the kitchen, and that the range is not working very well. Once we admit any violent contrast between the upper and lower floor, the 'instinctive' and 'spiritual' life, or feel a reluctance to investigate the humbling realities of the basement, our life becomes less, not more, than human; and our position is unsafe. Are we capable of the adventure of courage which inspires the great prayer of St Augustine: 'The house of my soul is narrow; do thou enter in and enlarge it! It is ruinous; do thou repair it'? Can we risk the visitation of the mysterious Power that will go through all our untidy rooms, showing up their short-comings and their possibilities; reproving by the tranquillity of order the waste and muddle of our inner life? The mere hoarded rubbish that ought to go into the dustbin; the things that want mending and washing; the possessions we have never taken the trouble to use?

Evelyn Underhill

Evelyn Underhill, *Concerning the Inner Life with the House of the Soul* (London, Methuen, 1947), p. 70.

Of the Woman and the Hen

A woman was sitting
before her gate, watching
as her hen scratched
and gathered her food.
The hen worked hard all day with great steps.
The woman spoke to her with great love:
'Beauty', she said, 'let it be,
you don't have to scratch so much.
Each day I'll give you
a full measure of grain to your desire.'
The hen replied:
'Why do you say this, lady?
Do you think I like your wheat better
than what I have always had?
Not at all, not at all,' said the hen.
'If there were half a bushel before me,
every day, full, I would not stop
nor would I delay
to seek more every day

according to my nature and my custom.'
By this example, it is shown
that many people can find
goods and whatever they need,
but they cannot change
their nature or their habits;
every day their courage revives.

Marie de France

The *Fables of Marie de France*. Tr. Joan M. Ferrante in *Medieval Women Writers*, ed. Katharina M. Wilson (Manchester University Press 1984), pp. 26–7.

I am convinced it is a great art to know how to grow old gracefully, and I am determined to practise it . . . I always thought I should love to grow old, and I find it is even more delightful than I thought. It is so delicious to be done with things, and to feel no need any longer to concern myself much about earthly affairs . . . I am tremendously content to let one activity after another go, and to await quietly and happily the opening of the door at the end of the passage way, that will let me in to my real abiding place.

Hannah Whitall Smith

Hannah Whitall Smith, *A Religious Rebel, the Letters of H. W. Smith* (1949), pp. 156–7. Quoted in *Christian Faith and Practice in the Experience of the Society of Friends* (London Yearly Meeting of the Religious Society of Friends 1960), no. 519.

Read, Reader, the Little Verses of this Epitaph
Dhuoda's body, formed of earth,
Lies buried in this tomb.
Immense king, receive her!
Here the earth has received in its bowels
The all too fragile clay which belonged to it.
   Benign King, grant her pardon!
Under and over her are the opaque depths
Of the grave, bathed in her wounds.
   O King, forgive her sins!
O you of all ages and sexes who come
And go here, I beg you, say this,
   Great Hagios, unlock her chains!

Free Burma

Transnational Legal Action and Corporate Accountability

John G. Dale

University of Minnesota Press
Minneapolis
London

Portions of chapter 1 were previously published in Anthony M. Orum and John G. Dale, *Political Sociology: Power and Participation in the Modern World*, 5th ed. (New York: Oxford University Press, 2009); reprinted by permission of Oxford University Press. Portions of chapter 6 were previously published as "Transnational Conflict between Peasants and Corporations in Burma: Human Rights and Discursive Ambivalence under the U.S. Alien Tort Claims Act," in *The Practice of Human Rights: Tracking Law between the Global and the Local*, ed. Mark Goodale and Sally Engle Merry (Cambridge: Cambridge University Press), 285–319; copyright 2007 Cambridge University Press; reprinted with permission.

Published by the University of Minnesota Press
111 Third Avenue South, Suite 290
Minneapolis, MN 55401-2520
http://www.upress.umn.edu

Library of Congress Cataloging-in-Publication Data

Dale, John G.
    Free Burma : transnational legal action and corporate accountability / John G. Dale.
        p.   cm.
    Includes bibliographical references and index.
    ISBN 978-0-8166-4646-3 (hc : alk. paper) — ISBN 978-0-8166-4647-0 (pb : alk. paper)
        1. United States—Foreign relations—Law and legislation. 2. United States. Alien Tort Claims Act. 3. Burma—International status.
    4. Burma—Politics and government—1988– . 5. United States—Foreign relations—Burma. 6. Burma—Foreign relations—United States.
    I. Title.
    KF4651.D35   2011
    341.5'82—dc22   2010051603

Printed in the United States of America on acid-free paper

The University of Minnesota is an equal-opportunity educator and employer.

18 17 16 15 14 13 12 11   10 9 8 7 6 5 4 3 2 1

*To my children, Lotte and Elijah,
with the hope that this book may one day inspire
their own transnational imaginations
and pursuit of social justice*

Contents

Preface

This book examines how Burma's pro-democracy movement, beginning in the 1990s, became increasingly transnational in scope, organization, and strategy. Burma's activists incorporated new actors from outside Burma to join in its struggle to reclaim from the military some form of democratic civilian governance. As it did so, Burma's once state-centered movement became increasingly and simultaneously influenced by campaigns promoting human rights and corporate accountability. It is important to clarify from the outset that I have not written this book to serve as a history of the pro-democracy movement and its many diverse campaigns. Rather, I am trying to draw attention to the history of this movement's focus on corporate accountability, giving special (although not exclusive) attention to its struggle with corporations from the United States.

The Free Burma campaigns focusing on corporate accountability have been unusually creative and, I argue, have much to teach us about democracy, human rights, and the politics of globalization. At the very least, they offer new understandings of Burma's relations to states, markets, and civil societies around the world. Indeed, other movements operating in contexts that are different from Burma's have also adopted the transnational political and legal strategies and discourses informing these campaigns.

But my focus on the campaigns struggling to rein in corporate abuses of human rights in Burma, and the critique of market fundamentalism that I assert in this book, targets only a small (however important) part of the problem facing Burma's engagement with globalization. Economic isolation—a quarter century of the "Burmese way to socialism" promoted by the ruling military elite—contributed mightily to the destruction of the country's economy and society. Substituting an equally extreme market fundamentalism along the lines of that which U.S. corporations have pedaled as "constructive engagement," particularly at this historical moment when Myanmar (Burma's name since 1989) is considering how to reorganize its markets, would serve only to produce new forms of destruction for the economy and society of Burma.

This book does not offer a comprehensive alternative economic policy vision for surgically removing the military's harmful "protectionist" strategies while promoting beneficial market protections. But it does attempt to show, contrary to market fundamentalism, why certain protections are necessary and why corporate self-regulation (even, and perhaps especially, in heavily regulated markets like Myanmar's) is not a sustainable alternative for anyone interested in promoting democracy and human rights in Burma. Transnationalist discursive strategies, like the ones deployed in the Free Burma campaigns that I examine in this book, help us to begin reconceptualizing both the relations through which we institutionalize economic globalization and the ways that we imagine the possibilities for participating in its institutionalization.

Transnational Legal Ethnography

The methodological approach that I have taken in producing and analyzing these case studies of transnational legal action in the Free Burma movement might be referred to as a form of institutional ethnography, yet it is one that takes an archaeological approach to representation. Institutional ethnographers of development, like Arturo Escobar, have taught us how academics are embedded in disciplinary institutions whose conceptual boundaries and practices threaten to reinscribe the very discursive distinctions that facilitate the institutionalization of neoliberal politics.[1] To avoid deterritorializing the transnationalist legal meanings and transgressive political subjectivities that I have uncovered in the discursive legal sites that I mine requires a suspension of positivist judgment.

This kind of ethnographic approach does not ask about big correlations between the specifics of laws or policies and the effectiveness of specific institutional mechanisms. Instead, it looks to the logics of particular contexts as a way of illuminating complex interrelationships among political, legal, historical, social, economic, and cultural elements. The goal of such an ethnography is to better understand, and thus provide a mapping of, how transnational legal space operates by identifying the mechanisms through which governance is accomplished and the strategies through which governance is attempted, discussed, experienced, resisted, and revised, taken in historical depth and cultural context. The theoretical ambition of this view is not well characterized by the term "hypothesis testing." Instead, theory building comes from noting complex relationships in one setting and then seeing how well other settings can be understood in those terms. Such comparisons produce modifications that result from considering the next case. In the end, this comparative methodological process produces not one nomothetic (or universal, one-size-fits-all) theory, or an elegant model that abstracts away from the particular and the distinctive, but instead produces a set of repertoires that can be found in real cases and that provide insight into how the emerging institutional mechanisms of transnational legal space shaping global markets operate. Learning the repertoires that such an ethnography reveals enables us to see more deeply into particular cases. While this certainly provides us with a better sense of what to expect in the future, such understanding cannot immunize us from the historical contingency of particular settings. The goal of this ethnographic approach is not prediction but comprehension, not explained variation but thematization.

I have found sociologist Michael Burawoy's description of the "ethnographic archaeologist" to be an appropriate representation of my ethnographic self in relation to the subjects of this study. "The ethnographic archaeologist," writes Burawoy, "is one who seeks out local experiments, new institutional forms, . . . who places them in their context, translates them into a common language and links them to one another across the globe."[2] An ethnography of transnational legal space, however, represents not only an excavation of new legal terrains but also one of "globalized" territory, i.e., a space of hegemonic discursive flows that threatens to strip mine such new legal terrains of the opportunities they provide for debating, confronting, and negotiating political, legal, and moral norms and values.

An ethnography of transnational legal space, then, is the study of the central legal elements of the polities mediating the construction of globalization using methods that are capable of recovering the lived detail of the politico-cultural legal landscape. It is the interpretive project of a transnational legal ethnographer who seeks to understand a temporally unfolding location of relations among contingent and conflicting representations before their discursive resolution within the fixed boundaries of any particular institutionalized outcome. It is only in recovering the political, legal, and moral representations of these alternative rules and institutional arrangements that have been overruled and underwritten by hegemonic discourse on globalization that such transnational legal space may be preserved as a meaningful place to begin constructing more democratically institutionalized market arrangements.

Of course, there are certain limitations that come with such a focus on transnational legal discourses. In my subsequent research, I have been taking a different approach that delves into struggles within the Free Burma movement to thicken the social relations through which they have been constituting their transnational solidarity. I have been exploring the efforts of various organizations within the movement to develop grassroots human rights training programs that are self-reflexively working to democratize the collective process through which NGOs (nongovernmental organizations) and other entities in the global North and global South are producing understandings of the practice of human rights in Burma.

In this book, I explore the *transnational legal action* of the Free Burma movement, a concept that I develop in detail in the Introduction. My aim is to demonstrate the transformative potential of engaging politico-legal institutions of the state. This, in my opinion, is important to establish. Although I fully embrace current efforts to identify the ways in which unequal relations of power among activists across the global North/South divide operate to silence or marginalize certain voices, identities, framings, and discourses of human rights abuse in Burma, I am also concerned by arguments suggesting that institutionalizing democratic relations among civil societies will "trickle-up" to politico-legal institutions of the state. To my mind, this is the mirror image of the problem with the "trickle-down" assumptions of politico-legal institutionalism.

In some ways, these competing approaches to understanding the development of global justice are analogous to the debates of the 1980s between political process theorists in North America and new social movement theorists of Western Europe. The former focused predominantly on citizens collectively targeting the state to achieve political inclusion; the latter eschewed engagement with the (hegemonic) state, focusing more on how to transform civil society from within through identity politics. Neither school of thought gave much attention to engaging the state through a politics of influence. In the Introduction, I develop this point further. Here, I want to suggest that it may be productive for scholars of transnational social movements to consider how a politics of influence may be a useful concept for thinking through how to bridge top-down and bottom-up practices of institutionalizing transnationalist and progressive cosmopolitan discourses for effecting more equitable and just social change.

But this book will not build that bridge. Rather, it seeks to demonstrate that engaging the hegemonic discourse of globalization that so greatly influences the legislative, administrative, and judicial processes of the United States, while fraught with perils, is not necessarily a course devoid of political opportunities for progressive transnational social movements. My hope is that the cases of transnational legal action that I present in this book may serve to assist those who are working to build more cosmopolitan forms of transnational solidarity, and also to identify creative ways of rearticulating and transnationally influencing their relations to states and corporations that dominate the practice of national and international law, foreign policy, and human rights.

Burma or Myanmar?

I have been self-reflexive and deliberate in my use of the names Burma and Myanmar. A brief explanation of the rationale behind my use of one or the other names at different points in this book may be helpful to the reader. The name Burma is derived from the Burmese word "Bamar," which also is the colloquial form of "Myanmar." Historically, "Bamar" referred to the ethnic majority *Burmans* (or the Bamar). British colonial rule introduced the name Burma, and it remained the dominant name of the country after it gained independence in 1948 and until 1989.

In the wake of international condemnation for its violent repression of the pro-democracy movement in 1988, the military's ruling party in Burma—the State Law and Order Restoration Council (SLORC)—initiated a series of measures intended to sublimate any collective memory of the illegitimate means by which it had secured its political domination over the state. One of the first measures that the SLORC took was to change the name of the country that it ruled from Burma to Myanmar. The political act of renaming the country is a contested issue to this day, even outside the country.

The name Myanmar more closely resembles the country's pronunciation in the Burmese language than does the name Burma. The country's military generals argue that dispensing with the name Burma is simply another step toward greater national independence from its legacy of colonial control. Yet many opposition groups, including those supporting the pro-democracy movement on which this book focuses, resist using "Myanmar" when writing or speaking the name in English. To these groups, retaining the British name Burma is an act of political protest against the ruling military's claims to legitimate authority, including its authority to officially rename the country. In other words, using the term "Burma," despite its colonial legacy, is upheld by some of these opposition groups as a stance for democracy. Many non-Burman ethnic groups also reject the name Myanmar because it has historically referred to only the dominant, majority ethnic group, thus marginalizing the multitude of other ethnic identities embraced within the country. The military generals argue that such thinking is further evidence of the nationally divisive and politically intrusive influence of Western cultural neocolonization.

The name is contested by and within different countries as well. The United Nations (UN) recognizes the name Myanmar, but this does not prevent member countries of the UN that do not recognize the name from referring instead to "Burma" during its General Assemblies, even when the Myanmar ambassador to the UN is present and repeatedly registers his protest. The United States, the United Kingdom, France, Canada, and Australia still officially use the name Burma instead of Myanmar. China, Russia, India, Japan, and Germany, as well as the

Association of Southeast Asian Nations (ASEAN), officially recognize the country as Myanmar.

Media organizations are similarly divided in their policies about how to identify the country, and these lines of division do not simply reflect the policies of the states within which they reside. For example, although France uses the term Burma, the *Agence France-Presse* refers to the country as Myanmar. Within the United States, the *New York Times* and CNN use the name Myanmar, but the *Washington Post* and *Time* magazine use the name Burma.

Any author who wishes to write about the conflict in the country first must make some inevitably contentious choices about how to refer to it. In this book, I use "Myanmar" to refer to the post-1990 military government. Yet, to resist playing too easily into the questionable intentions of this regime's project of collective forgetting, and in some measure as a stance for the ideals of democracy and human rights that Burma's opposition movement seeks to institutionalize, I retain "Burma" to refer to the country and its civil society.

I am aware that this does not resolve the contradictions that I have raised and risks playing into the Myanmar government's claims regarding neocolonialism. But I would add that it should be clear to readers by this book's end that I do not spare the United States and other Western governments, or their transnational corporations operating in Burma, from critical analysis of their role in sustaining the military's exercise of illegitimate authority and undermining democracy and human rights in Burma.

Relating to the Subject

Finally, my relationship to the Free Burma movement: I first became interested in this movement as a resident of Berkeley, California. Our city council at the time passed a resolution barring corporations from anywhere around the world from doing business with Myanmar if under contract for the provision of goods and services with Berkeley. The city council reasoned that such corporations were financially sustaining a military regime that abused human rights with impunity and that Berkeley, as a market participant, did not want to further facilitate such a process. I discuss Berkeley's place in this much broader campaign in chapter 3

("Free Burma Laws"). But here I want only to emphasize how this transnational thinking immediately impressed me. As a graduate student already studying what was then a nascent literature on transnational collective action, I decided at that moment that I wanted to make this the topic of my dissertation research, and subsequently this book.

I had many questions concerning just how transnational was the organization underlying the strategy of this campaign. In 1997 and 1998, I conducted my first fieldwork and more than one hundred tape-recorded formal interviews in Burma. I wanted to know if people living there were actually contributing to the organization of this campaign or if this was simply the work of progressive activists in the United States. This was essentially a political question. And in Burma, discussing politics is a dangerous undertaking.

Assembling publicly in groups of five or more people is unlawful in Burma. It is not that this does not occur fairly regularly, and without resulting in arrest; the point is that people gather cautiously, keeping a watchful eye for military intelligence and always with the understanding that they *could* be arrested for doing so. Bringing a personal laptop computer into the country is also illegal, and at the time I was there e-mail was restricted to military personnel and those who had connections to them. Since then, these restrictions have changed dramatically. Internet access abounds, although Burma has only three Internet service providers, all state-owned, and all e-mail correspondence that travels through them is heavily monitored and often censored. I did not break or test these rules in Burma. But I did violate the cardinal principle around which these laws were designed: I did discuss politics with people in Burma.

Securing each interview entailed a great deal of planning, especially with the people whom I was interviewing: officers and other members of the main political opposition party (the National League for Democracy, or NLD) in their modest offices throughout the country; student opposition movement leaders of former and current generations, as well as students who supported the military regime; active members of ethnic minority rebel groups; directors of unregistered NGOs; former politically active monks and novices; Burmese journalists, political cartoonists, comedians, and authors; book collectors (a political bunch if ever there was one); village religious leaders (not only Theravada Buddhist, the dominant religious affiliation in Burma, but also Christian and Muslim);

unemployed professors and teachers; physicians; leaders of Burmese and ethnic minority political organizations who were promoting democratic interethnic and gender relations; ex-military officers; and "ex-pat" Western as well as Burmese businesspersons and attorneys. I also carefully interviewed, and employed, several trustworthy translators.

Meeting someone for an interview was like performing a careful dance through time and space. The assumption in most cases was that I was being followed by "MI" (military intelligence). I would often have to meet some stranger in a public place who would then silently escort me to another location, where I would be introduced to another escort who would lead me, or direct me, to another location. I would often have to meet several strangers, sometimes over the course of several days, to land my interview. Some days I was juggling up to three such scavenger hunts at one time, hoping that I would not have to cancel one of them after all the hard work I had put into getting that far. Sometimes it was my interviewee who would cancel, despite my having followed all of his or her instructions. Securing my interviews required me to learn the local politics of discussing politics.

To protect the names and contact information of the people I interviewed, I created a code based on Thai and Burmese recipes, which I made a point of collecting throughout my travels. Combining measurements, sequences of ingredients, and certain letters within each ingredient, I became pretty good at coding important information in a way that actually made culinary sense on paper. One recipe became the equivalent of an encrypted business card. My concern was that I might have my notes confiscated at any time by Myanmar authorities and that they would be able to determine with whom I had spoken and then arrest them. This was a real fear throughout my research in Burma.

I discovered that, indeed, many people in Burma, particularly individuals and groups from the cities of Rangoon (Yangon) and Mandalay, as well as Shan State, Kayin (Karen) State, and Kayah State, were contributing in essential ways to this transnational campaign. Furthermore, I discovered that this was not the only transnational campaign targeting the relationship between foreign corporations and Myanmar that they were helping to organize. Thus began a rather long process of framing the book before you.

These interviews, and the cultural and political experience that I gleaned from my research in Burma and Myanmar, greatly informed but ultimately did not serve as the focal data for this book. To reiterate, this is not a traditional ethnography. It is not even a typical transnational ethnography. It is an ethnography of relationships and practices that are introduced through transnational legal discourse. It is a study of how the meanings of these relationships and practices shift and change as they confront powerful institutional contexts. And, I argue, it has every bit as much to do with Burma, its people, and their struggle for democracy and human rights as does the subject matter of more traditional ethnographies. Indeed, they could prove to be compatible approaches.

Since my first research trip to Burma, I have cultivated a long and extensive list of contacts and friends there. I have returned twice to Burma to conduct research (most recently in 2010), and throughout that time I have continued to research the development of the movement and the changing politics of the country. But I also have developed relationships with many Burmese and ethnic minority citizens (and some former citizens) of Burma living in exile around the world. Many of them are very active in the Free Burma movement, but there are many who are not. I also have interviewed people who, like me, are not from Burma, yet who deeply care about, and devote their energy and resources to, the country and its people.

In the process of this research, I have observed how I have gradually become a part of the movement. My role has been not so much as an activist but more as a scholar and advocate. I am often introduced by those who know me within the movement to those who do not as a "professor and friend of the movement." It is precisely because I am a longtime friend of this transnational movement that I am not reluctant to offer my constructively critical insights on the practices and relations, or decisions and strategies, of the activists and others supporting it. In this small way, I hope that my own practices will contribute to a freer Burma.

Abbreviations

ABC	American Broadcasting Company
ABFSU	All Burma Federation of Student Unions
ABSU	All Burma Students' Union
AFL-CIO	American Federation of Labor and Congress of Industrial Organizations
ALP	Arakan Liberation Party
ASEAN	Association of Southeast Asian Nations
ATCA	Alien Tort Claims Act
BBC	British Broadcasting Corporation
BSPP	Burma Socialist Program Party
CCR	Center for Constitutional Rights
EC	European Commission
ERI	EarthRights International
FBC	Free Burma Coalition
GATT	General Agreement on Tariffs and Trade

HEED	(International Law Project for) Human, Economic, and Environmental Defense
ICC	International Criminal Court
ICID	Institute for Community and Institutional Development
ILO	International Labor Organization
IMF	International Monetary Fund
INGO	international nongovernmental organization
IOC	International Olympic Committee
IR	International Rivers
KIO	Kachin Independence Organization
KMT	Kuomingtang
KNLP	Kayan New Land Party
KNPP	Karenni National Progressive Party
KNU	Karen National Union
LNUP	Lahu National Progressive Party
MI	military intelligence
MOGE	Myanmar Oil and Gas Enterprise
NAFTA	North American Free Trade Agreement
NCGUB	National Coalition Government of the Union of Burma
NDF	National Democratic Front
NFTC	National Foreign Trade Council
NGO	nongovernmental organization
NLD	National League for Democracy
NLG	National Lawyers Guild
PLA	People's Liberation Army
POCLAD	Program on Corporations, Law, and Democracy
PSLO	Palung State Liberation Organization
PTT	Petroleum Authority of Thailand Exploration and Production

RIT	Rangoon Institute of Technology
RUSU	Rangoon University Student Union
SLORC	State Law and Order Restoration Council
SPDC	State Peace and Development Council
SSPP	Shan State Progressive Party
TSMO	transnational social movement organization
TVPA	Torture Victim Protection Act
UN	United Nations
UPNO	Union Pa-O National Organization
WTO	World Trade Organization

Map 1. Myanmar. From Wikimedia Commons, modified United Nations map
of Myanmar.

Introduction

Theorizing Transnational Legal Action

Preamble for a Novice

He is frustrated, yet hopeful, as he joins the long march of ten thousand, maybe one hundred thousand, others like him. He is defiant, yet willfully peaceful, as he raises his alms bowl upside-down toward the sky above his head. He is no more than eighteen years old, but he is the moral conscience of the people of Burma who have suffered for forty years under military rule—and much longer under the lingering effects of ethnic conflict caused by British colonization. Don't let his saffron-colored robes fool you; he is not protesting merely on behalf of Burma's monks. This line of people extends across the country and spreads far beyond the territorial borders of Myanmar. For him, as for everyone in his country, the past few months have been especially difficult. The price of cooking fuel and other basic staples has skyrocketed, drawing even the most timid of citizens to the streets to voice their anger. But even this is not why the novice monk leads the march.

Behind him is another person, also with hands raised above his head, holding a handwritten sign in English that prioritizes some of their demands: sufficiency of food, clothing, and shelter, freedom for political prisoners. National consolidation, the military's number-one priority, is at the bottom of this list. There can be no national consolidation without political freedom.

Our young novice may not know that his country has one of the worst human rights records in the world, nor that both the United States and China have historically played a significant role in creating and arming the authoritarian military government that he suffers today. He may not even know that both countries in different ways still help to sustain his government. But he knows well the stories of his grandparents who were imprisoned and tortured for doing exactly what he is about to do. He has friends who have been conscripted into serving as porters to construct natural gas pipelines for U.S. and Chinese corporations near the seashore where his family once spent a vacation during the dry season. He remembers the puppet shows that he attended as a child, which magically sprinkled the rich heritage of Burmese drama with silent gestures of political comedy until humorless undercover military intelligence began attending as well and sent the great artists to prison for seven years. He has received a bowl of rice when he was hungry from ethnic minority villagers who themselves had nothing more than that after fleeing the soldiers of the State Peace and Development Council (SPDC),[1] Myanmar's ruling military regime, which destroyed their village along with more than three thousand other villages, more than the number of villages destroyed in the genocide of Darfur. Just as he is about to do, all of these people have publicly denounced the military's authoritarianism. They all have demanded the restoration of the civil and political rights that generations before them once had secured.

Our young novice may not know that his country historically has played an influential role in promoting democracy and human rights in struggles throughout the world. But he does know that, on this very street in the largest and most populated city in the country, the dust beneath his flip-flops and between his toes has been mixed with the blood of students younger than he for more than forty years because they refused to accept the idea that they had no right to form an independent student union. And when the military closed their universities over and over again, they walked the same streets, proclaiming their rights to an education and facing the same bullets. Walking down this street today, he is connected to these same students, these same ethnic villagers, these same political prisoners, and these same forced laborers. Their stories have sustained his hope for, and inspired his courage to participate in making, a freer Burma.

He is also connected to you and me. He is very far away, as I watch him walking, just hours after his death, on YouTube. As I sit at my desk in Arlington, Virginia, halfway around the world, I think about his friend, whom he met only that day while they risked their lives together to tell us something. His friend smuggled to the Thai-Myanmar border a digital photo in the camera of his cell phone. It was an image of the young dead monk's bloodied flip-flop, laying in the street. Because the military pulled the plug on the country's four Internet servers to prevent the escape to foreign news media of any information about their violent crackdown on the peaceful "Saffron Revolution," he smuggled the cell phone through a complicated network of contacts to ensure that we could witness what the Myanmar state had done to his friend, to him, to all of us.

Our Buddhist novice may not have known the names of the hundreds of companies—like Heineken, PepsiCo, Macy's Federated Department Stores, Apple Computer—who did business with his military government. But I do. I doubt that our young monk, nor even his friends who were forced to work at gunpoint on the gas pipelines, knew that the "foreign" corporation profiting from their slavery was chartered in California, where I spent most of my life. But I know. And I am fairly certain that this young man died without knowing that you and I have the legal power to strip a U.S.-chartered corporation of its right to exist when it commits egregious violations of his, and our, human rights. Few of the most educated friends that I have, even the ones who are lawyers, know this.

This novice monk was, and is, part of something much bigger than this demonstration, or his generation, or even his Buddhist monastery. He is the face—one among millions—of Burma's long struggle for democracy and human rights. As this book explains, his struggle is connected to our own. Our young novice has joined the march to teach us about how we can make a better world for ourselves. Listen to the lessons that he has for us.

Transnational Legal Space

Before 2007, to most observers outside of Burma, the Burmese pro-democracy movement seemed like a comatose patient. The activists outside of Burma who continued campaigning for a "Free Burma" seemed like a life-support system barely sustaining an essentially dead patient. After all, even after four decades of struggle, the Myanmar state holds power as firmly as ever. The vast majority of Burma experts had long since dismissed the vitality of the pro-democracy movement and, even if only grudgingly, declared it a failure. Even some influential activists in exile from Burma concluded that the pro-democracy movement has been politically hijacked by nongovernmental organizations of the global North that see in Burma only an opportunity to advance their particular human rights agendas. The so-called Saffron Revolution has not necessarily changed the assessments of these critics.

However, in this book, I argue that this movement has not only kept alive the hopes and aspirations of the people for a free and democratic Burma, but also challenged how we should understand and assess social movements. The domestic pro-democracy movement that first emerged in 1988 in Burma transformed itself over the decades into a transnational social movement. In doing so, it built a new model. At a simple level, it took advantage of new forms of communication, like satellite phones and the Internet, to get information in to and out of the closely censored nation. The movement cultivated new relations of transnational solidarity with other pro-democracy movements, as well as movements for human rights, women's rights, and environmental, labor, and indigenous rights, changing the Free Burma movement and its sister movements in the process.

What I focus on in this book is how the Burmese pro-democracy movement built on these new transnational networks to initiate innovative campaigns that used legal mechanisms to not only bring attention to the gross violations of human rights, but also to expose how democratic states and multinational corporations were sustaining and supporting the repressive regime. Through what I call "transnational legal actions"—three of which I examine in detail in this book—the movement created transnational legal spaces in which the movement challenged neoliberal conceptions of justice and democracy.

The three campaigns, which I examine in greater detail in Part II of this book, encompass the passage of a selective purchasing law that restricted the state of Massachusetts from doing business with any company that also did business with Burma and the ensuing lawsuit over the statute; a petition to decharter the Unocal Corporation on the grounds

Figure 1. Oil painting by Burmese artist S.K.H., displayed in border town restaurant in Thailand, depicting a Burmese monk confronting the *tatmadaw* (military) during the Saffron Revolution in 2007. Photograph by author, 2009.

that its projects in Burma supported a corrupt and repressive regime; and an Alien Tort Claims Act (ATCA) suit brought by peasants who claimed to have been used as slave laborers and subjected to human rights abuses while working on a Unocal pipeline in Burma. I use each campaign to illustrate *transnational legal action*. I use the term to signify the cultural (discursive) practices of actors in legal contexts when they invoke a transnationalist discourse to transform the legal meaning and legal identification of practices and relations in ways that influence state action. Typically, this action targets state actors or others in political society attempting to influence other state actors who are attempting to colonize or deterritorialize within a nationalist, internationalist, or globalization discourse the legal meaning and identification of the same practices and relations. The transnational legal actions organized by Burmese pro-democracy activists, unlike the previous protests inside Burma, were not centered directly on the Myanmar state. They instead targeted democratic states (such as the United States) and the transnational corporations chartered by those states that sought to profit from Burma's opening market after 1988.

This discursive struggle produced what I call transnational legal space, i.e., the shifting and contested terrain of legal discourse within and through which state actors, global elites, and social movement actors and advocates struggle to shape the legal practices and legal meanings of the rules and relations that are currently being institutionalized to facilitate and constrain the process of globalization. The cultural production of transnational legal space therefore provides opportunities for mediating how the emerging rules of global markets are politically, legally, and morally constructed.

Transnational legal space is now an important battlefront in the effort to shape the process of globalization. This book presents a case study of the Free Burma movement to demonstrate the potentially transformative movement politics of transnational legal action. I present an analysis of the transnational legal action and legal space of the Free Burma movement to examine how it has struggled to get its alternative discourse into the mix of predominantly neoliberal arguments on globalization. In doing so, I argue for the contemporary viability of Burma's pro-democracy movement, explaining that appreciation for such a claim begins with understanding the campaigns that its participants and supporters have organized outside of Burma since 1994, as well as the discursive struggles they have waged within the transnational legal space that these campaigns have helped to produce.

Locating Power in the Free Burma Movement

Most researchers analyze social movements within a framework that is explicitly or implicitly national, whereby constituencies from within a presumed national, bounded "society" confront national elites and/or the state. Burma's pro-democracy movement emerged *initially* within a national scope of collective action. The repressed "people power" uprising in 1988 indeed targeted the state directly, although unsuccessfully.

A state-centered social movement framework also allows for the analysis of an *international* context in which relations are maintained between governments (or their agencies) that invoke the nation-states that they are supposed to represent within a mutually reinforcing "international system." Current scholarship examining the prospects for political change in Burma acknowledges that the context of the struggle for democracy in Burma since 1990 has increasingly stretched beyond the state's borders. However, I agree with Daniel Mato that

this conventional usage [of the term "international"] equates the notions of "nation" and "state," and thus further legitimates state hegemony and activities and the practices of ruling groups and state bureaucracies through state agencies.[2]

The bulk of state-centered social movement research has been influenced by a common set of structural concepts, such as "political opportunity structures," "mobilization networks," and "cultural framing," that were originally developed to explain social movements taking place within Western democratic states during the 1960s and 1970s.[3] This work has focused primarily on the modes and consequences of interaction over time, specifically through a state-bounded temporality. That is, researchers analyze the movement within temporal boundaries that are determined on the basis of collective action taking place within the territorial boundaries of the state.

This way of understanding social movements has heavily influenced Burma experts' analysis of the prospects for democratic change in the country. Some of this state-centered analysis focuses on the inter-state relations between Myanmar's military regime and foreign nation-states.[4] This scholarship offers mixed conclusions, but it generally claims that, if democratic change is to occur, it will come from the influence of foreign nation-states through the engagement, rather than isolation, of the military, coupled with foreign economic investment in the country.[5] The present influence of the pro-democracy movement, within this framework, is portrayed as a "domestic" actor or process.

Less optimistic state-centered analyses suggest that the movement is not so much in a condition of abeyance as arrested development.[6] They represent the movement as having become an ultimately marginal factor in a political process dominated by international economic interests and balance-of-power nation-state politics.[7]

This kind of methodological nationalism has consequences for how we assess the success and potential of social movements. One consequence is that, when historical comparisons are made, it is states as contexts of interaction that serve as the units of comparative analysis. Another consequence of this state-centered framework is that it provides no conceptual space for analyzing any transnational networks that may be influencing the social movement. Seen through the lens of such a state-centered perspective, the prognosis for Burma's pro-democracy movement looks bleak.

Yet the actual analysis informing such observations has devoted little sustained attention to how transnational networks created by the pro-democracy movement activists in particular have influenced this process. In part, this is because most research on Burma's pro-democracy movement has been conducted within a state-centered analysis.

Some state-centered analyses identify the Myanmar military's relations with transnational actors (for example, corporations, regional trading blocs, international nongovernmental organizations, and transnational social movements), but relegate these transnational relations to background discussion, while reserving empirical analysis for the unfolding relations between the military and its domestic opposition.[8]

Although the national context in Burma has remained extremely important, we cannot understand the dynamics of the Free Burma movement solely in terms of a national-level or "domestic" nation-centered politics. The overlapping and sometimes changing boundaries of political identity and alliance, choice of targets, and power within the Free Burma movement render analysis of the construction of actors and meanings, as well as analysis of the sources and exercise of power and persuasion, more complex than in movements typically depicted in the state-centered movement literature.[9]

The Free Burma Movement as a Transnational Social Movement

I explore in this book how this traditional social movement transformed itself into a transnational social movement. Transnational social movements are sustained contentious interactions with opponents by networks of actors that have common purposes linked across nation-state boundaries, and that demonstrate a capacity to generate coordinated social mobilization in more than one country to publicly influence social change.[10]

During the 1990s the Burmese pro-democracy movement began to organize transnational campaigns. I examine three of these campaigns in this book. In the first, which I refer to as the "selective purchasing campaign," activists convinced thirty municipal governments and Massachusetts to enact "Free Burma" laws. These laws stated that no entity that did business with the Myanmar state could also contract with the state or local entity that passed the law. These laws successfully influenced corporations to abandon their business operations in Burma. In practice, they were more effective at curbing business with the Myanmar state than was the economic sanctions policy discussed at the time (but not implemented) by many Western states. It is worth emphasizing that the Free Burma laws targeted all, not just U.S.-chartered, corporations that were doing business with Myanmar. This transnational strategy defied the neoliberal calculus of nation-states underlying conventional critiques of economic sanctions, which reasoned that preventing one nation's corporations from doing business with Myanmar only would create new business opportunities for competing nations' corporations. In response, a number of transnational corporations challenged the Massachusetts law in federal court.

The selective purchasing law campaign had successfully persuaded all but one U.S.-based corporation (and many foreign corporations as well) to quit doing business with Burma. The lone holdout was Unocal Oil Corporation (which is today owned by Chevron). From the outset of the selective purchasing law campaign, it had been also the largest U.S.-based corporate investor in Myanmar. The next campaign I examine targeted Unocal specifically, seeking to revoke its corporate charter on the basis of Unocal's reliance on forced labor in constructing its natural gas pipeline through Burma, severely undermining the corporation's claim that its investment in Myanmar was providing jobs for the people of Burma and that, in turn, its "constructive engagement" with the Myanmar state would likely promote democratic political change.

The final campaign focuses on a lawsuit filed by a dozen peasants from Burma against Unocal Oil Corporation, alleging its complicity in forced labor and other human rights abuses committed in Burma, under the U.S. Alien Tort Claims Act.[11] The First Congress of the United States adopted this act in 1789, but it remained largely unused for the next two centuries. The federal statute asserts simply that "the district courts shall have original jurisdiction of any civil action by an alien [non-U.S. citizen] for a tort [i.e., a harm or wrong] only, committed in violation of the law of nations or a treaty of the United States."[12] The *Doe v. Unocal* suit attempted to use the statute *for the first time* to hold liable in a U.S. court *transnational corporations*, not just state actors or private individuals, for their complicity in human rights abuses committed outside the United States in furthering their transnational joint ventures with states like Burma.

Transnational campaigns like these are strategies or sets of tactics to publicly influence social change that are coordinated and shared by sets of actors linked across nation-state boundaries.[13] The actors participating in transnational campaigns do not necessarily construct a unitary transnational identity, but often deploy a shared campaign discourse. They also frequently link a variety of different social movements. These campaigns may be organized around either institutionalized or noninstitutionalized political tactics. Activists from the Free Burma movement, as well as from the labor, environmental, human rights, and women's rights movements, banded together temporarily to coordinate a single transnational campaign—for example, the petition to decharter the Unocal Corporation in response to alleged human rights abuses in Burma and Afghanistan—only to later dissemble, scatter, and each reaggregate into separate transnational campaigns composed of new configurations of diverse social movements.

They waged these transnational campaigns in alliance with local state and municipal governments in the United States and Australia, as well as non-state actors, regional governing bodies like the European Union, nongovernmental organizations (NGOs) throughout East and Southeast Asia, international nongovernmental organizations (INGOs),[14] and voluntary associations on every continent and in more than thirty countries. The movement also attracted activists defending issues like human rights, women's rights, protection of the natural environment, labor rights, indigenous peoples' rights, and socially responsible corporate investment. They even created transnational advocacy networks—configurations of nonstate actors, based usually on informal contacts linked across nation-state boundaries who share common values, discourses, and a dense exchange of information[15]—including one formed around the international "right to know" about the labor conditions and environmental impact of proposed development projects that are financed through transnational corporations in partnership with the state.

These transnational campaigns all took place in the United States. Yet Burma's pro-democracy activists were involved in initiating each of these campaigns. They were neither conceived nor launched simultaneously, nor within the initial framework of an overarching, preconceived metadiscourse. These campaigns did, however, overlap in time, and each operated with an awareness of the others' strategies. Indeed, some of the actors participated significantly and simultaneously in more than one of these campaigns as they unfolded over varying durations.

It was in the process of organizing these campaigns in the early 1990s that the pro-democracy movement developed into a transnational social movement called the Free Burma movement. The pro-democracy movement's leaders came to realize that the Myanmar state was not its only obstacle to domestic political change. Transnational corporations and foreign states' investment in Burma buttressed the Myanmar state's power to repress the movement. The Myanmar state refused to acknowledge the victory of Burma's powerful opposition party in the 1990 democratic elections.[16] The military adopted a new economic liberalization policy in an effort to draw badly needed foreign direct investment, just as the cold war was ending and the neoliberal discourse on globalization was increasing its hegemony. Transnational corporations (such as Total and Unocal), seeking to build a natural gas pipeline through Burma, forged business partnerships with the military's state-owned oil and gas enterprise.

The movement increasingly started to migrate from a state-centered movement to one that targeted also the relationship between the

Myanmar state and its transnational corporate partners that were (intentionally or not) helping to sustain it. Critical to understanding the Free Burma movement is that it is not seeking a revolution (despite media descriptions of the statewide protest in 2007 as a "Saffron Revolution"), but instead radical reform through a *politics of influence*. To do so, it targeted the relationship between the transnational corporations sustaining the Myanmar state and the Western states (like the United States) that not only give them their legal right to exist, but also make policies and rulings and administer (or deliberately fail to administer) existing law in ways that promote or protect business ventures with the Myanmar state.

The Politics of Influence

Social movement theory has largely emphasized movements that target states for political inclusion or movements that target civil society through a politics of identity. However, the Free Burma movement helps illuminate a different dimension of contemporary collective action: a politics of influence. It is this dimension of contemporary movement politics—aimed at maintaining the link *between* civil and political society—that is missing from both political process theory and new social movement theory, and that may help us to avoid both the traps of democratic elitism and democratic fundamentalism.

Political process theory fosters democratic elitism—the idea that any change to promote democratic norms, values, relations, and institutions can come only from the elites who comprise political society. It typically appears in one of two forms: (1) when we think of social movements as capable of effecting significant change only when administrative or socioeconomic elites provide them with an opportunity; or (2) when we think that social movements must sacrifice democratic organization for more hierarchical and unequal forms of organization to gain acknowledgment from political society. In short, democratic elitism does not see social movement actors as *creating* opportunities, but only seizing those made available to them.

However, paying greater attention to how social movements interact with or attempt to influence civil society can help us to avoid the trap of democratic elitism. In the case of the Free Burma movement, this is an important concern. The movement itself struggles with democratic elitism when it questions the extent to which political change depends primarily upon the following: (1) the leadership of the main opposition party (Aung San Suu Kyi's National League for Democracy) versus the equal participation of Burma's nationalist ethnic minority group leaders; (2) the intervention of the international community or powerful individual states that can pressure the Myanmar state; and (3) the relations of power between the activists of the global North and the global South that constitute the kind of transnational solidarity underlying the collective action of the Free Burma movement itself. All of these relations, I argue, are important to the movement. Nevertheless, Burma observers themselves have a tendency to give greater importance to the more powerful actors in one or more of these relations and thereby risk introducing a democratic elitism that may blind us to empirically important sources of transformative agency.

In contrast to political process theory, new social movement theory[17] taught us that paying greater attention to civil society can help us to understand that contemporary social movements are concerned with not only a politics of inclusion but also a politics of identity. It can also help us to explore the *terrain from which* contemporary social movements wage their politics of inclusion and to answer questions about how social movement actors accomplish the task of constructing viable, relational social identities on which to base their collective action.

On the other hand, we must also be aware that a myopic focus on civil society, such as that underlying the new social movement theory's emphasizing identity politics, can as easily present another trap: democratic fundamentalism. Democratic fundamentalism is the idea that the only way to build a democratic society is through democratic means, norms, values, institutions, and forms of self-organization. In this view, to bureaucratize into hierarchical relations of authority, as many social movement organizations have, is not only to compromise democracy but also to reinforce antidemocratic values and can lead ultimately to only nondemocratic change.[18] In addition, democratic fundamentalism ultimately promotes a collective retreat from engaging political organizations and the state. All efforts at change remain focused on civil society. It fosters the notion that efforts to influence the state only lead to the domination or co-optation of civil society by the state.

Political society is that part of the political system that deals with how ideas and interests are aggregated into specific policy proposals.

The concept can be useful for examining the problem of how contending social classes and interest groups are connected to the governing process. This space of contention is usually referred to as *political society*—that is to say, the place where specific political institutions attempt to manage public demands. The institutions that make up political society can take many forms within a state, including administrative (such as in the petition to the California attorney general to decharter Unocal), legislative (such as in the Massachusetts selective purchasing campaign), or judicial (such as in the ATCA case heard by the U.S. courts). Social scientists often describe political society and civil society as having separate, although not necessarily disconnected, political cultures. Actors from each of these spheres may seek to influence the political culture of the other.

But the case of the Free Burma movement illustrates that civil society and political society do not exist in separate vacuums. They coexist in a complex and shifting set of relationships. Political society comprises people who manage the state. Members of civil society can at least attempt to influence the discourses and actions of people who are members of political society. When social movements convince members of the political elite—such as the legislators in Massachusetts convinced by the movement to pass the state's Selective Purchasing Law, despite the fact that there was no large constituency of Burmese in the state— to change not just what they think about a specific bill or proposal but how they think about a given topic, the social movement has altered existing boundaries of political discourse. In the best-case scenario they influence political leaders to create space for new identities, new norms, and new representations of need. Indeed, this attempt by members of civil society to influence members of political society is perhaps the key feature of contemporary social movements.

The sustained democratization of political and economic institutions is also critical to an effective politics of influence. It is not enough to convince a politician to vote in favor of the interests of a group just once. To effect change that is sustained over time and spreads to the culture at large, the social movement actors must effect a reform of the very centers and structures of power. Without this kind of reform, any gains within civil society would be much more vulnerable to the constantly changing political winds.

The challenge facing a movement that wanted to target the relationship between states and corporations was that, in a post–cold war environment, neoliberal free market discourses dominated thinking about the meaning of globalization and the power of states to rein in corporations—even those supporting regimes that violated human rights. In each of the three campaigns I examine, the movement deployed what Michael Peter Smith calls a "transnationalist discourse" of globalization that offers a different vision of what an increasingly globalized world could look like.[19]

Culture, Structure, States

Before exploring this concept further, however, we should consider how examination of the Free Burma movement and the discourses it deployed then helps us to examine how contemporary social movements exercise political influence and to rethink the relationship between culture, structure, and states. Culture is a set of practices, material as well as nonmaterial, that constitute meanings, values, and subjectivities.[20] William Sewell Jr., in his seminal article "A Theory of Structure, Duality, Agency, and Transformation," defines structures as cultural schemas that are invested with and that sustain resources. Structures also reflect and reproduce unequal power relations.[21] When structures take the form of discourses, rules, policies, methods, recipes, and the like, we can analyze how they enable or constrain action as subjects both intentionally and unintentionally appropriate and extend them to new contexts.[22] Culture in this sense is a dimension of all institutions—economic, political, and social.

Social movement analysis often dichotomizes culture on one side and political structure, that is, states or political society, on the other side. For example, Francesca Polletta points out that political process theory improperly conceptualizes culture as constraining action only when it impedes challengers' capacity to perceive the state's objective vulnerability.[23] In other words, despite the theory's emphasis on cultural framing,[24] and how culture enables challengers to represent their grievances as shared, and to construct their collective identity as a unified actor, and to perceive an existing political opportunity, the theory only considers culture's power to constrain challengers in cases when they fail to perceive what the theorist claims is an objective political opportunity. Furthermore, culture, in this sense, is only that which is inside the heads of challengers. In contrast, political process theory gives significantly less attention, if any, to culture that is inside the heads of state actors and, until recently, has given no attention to the cultural dimensions of political structures.

This happens because the theory implicitly conflates agency and culture, and results in a conception of culture as easily transformed.[25] Thus, culture becomes understood as subjective and malleable, whereas political structure becomes understood as objective and durable. Culture enables protest, but political structure constrains protest. The powerless (or actors in civil society) mobilize culture to challenge structure; but the powerful (or actors in political society) monopolize political structure to maintain power. By this logic, the term "cultural structure" is an oxymoron.

How then might we reconceptualize the relationship between culture and structures so that we better understand the politics of influence? Polletta offers a promising alternative approach when she suggests that "the task is not to abandon an emphasis on 'objective' political structures in favor of potential insurgents 'subjective' perceptions and valuations of political structures, but to probe the (objective) resources and constraints generated by the cultural dimensions of political structures."[26]

Mustafa Emirbayer and Jeff Goodwin have usefully pointed out that conceiving of the cultural dimensions of structures "as symbolic patterns possessing their own autonomous inner logic" is different than thinking of them as "substantively distinct 'domains' of social life."[27] Conceptually dichotomizing culture and political structures, and then reifying the boundaries between them, is to ultimately miss one of contemporary social movements' key insights: "Culture is political because meanings are constitutive of processes that, implicitly or explicitly, seek to redefine social power."[28] Political structures are also, though not only, cultural. To reiterate, culture is a dimension of all structures and practices, including political structures and practices.

So how does the politics of influence function, and why is it important to social movement theorists? The actions of the state are always embedded in culture. The actors of political society, the people who govern states, do not lack culture or morality, despite the tendency of political scientists and international relations theorists to define them as such. State actors are not immune to cultural or moral persuasion that draws upon salient cultural structures. Cultural structures—such as constitutional principles, rules of procedure, cultural traditions, conventional wisdom, institutional memories, political rituals like swearing an oath to uphold the political duties one is assuming, economic beliefs about the functioning of markets, understandings of legitimate rights, and moral values—can channel the choices and even imaginations of members of the polity as well as social movement activists. To the extent these cultural structures become institutionalized in the state, we can begin to analyze them as offering potential opportunities for social movements. Since there are often competing structures available, social movements can influence political society by getting their preferred structures into the mix. Note here that the emphasis is on political influence on the polity rather than political inclusion in the polity.

Free Markets and the Politics of Globalization

I noted earlier that to exert a lasting politics of influence, the Free Burma movement, in its transnational campaigns, challenged neoliberal conceptions of globalization. It did so by attempting to get into the mix an alternative discourse about the power of states and the responsibilities of transnational corporations.

In plain terms, the dominant features of contemporary globalization— the reorganization of production at the global level and the disproportionate growth of trade and finance that crosses the borders of nation-states—continue the nineteenth-century process that Karl Polanyi identifies in *The Great Transformation*.[29] They are reinforced by powerful transnational networks of actors, including corporations, states, social movements, and others, as well as a powerful economic ideology known as neoliberalism.

Writing during World War II, Polanyi produced his historical sociological analysis of the rise and decline of the market economy during the century between 1830 and 1930, which has a renewed relevance for understanding the contemporary globalization discourse on free trade. At the heart of this "great transformation," Polanyi observed the discursive power of the economic liberal creed: that is, the unshakeable belief in the possibility of constructing a self-regulating market on a world scale. Complete state deregulation, or free trade, it was then believed, would yield the "natural" conditions under which such a market was presumed able to regulate itself, and to do so better than could any amount of state planning.

Polanyi assumed that his generation was in a position to wish a final good riddance to this failed political economic experiment. The global rules, discourses, and networks currently being constructed around the interests of transnational corporations would suggest otherwise. Nevertheless, Polanyi's words seem prescient for contemporary transnational neoliberal political coalitions and their challengers:

> This, indeed, is the last remaining argument of economic liberalism today. Its apologists are repeating in endless variations that but for the policies advocated by its critics, liberalism would have delivered the goods; that not the competitive system and the self-regulating market, but interference with that system and interventions with that market are responsible for our ills.[30]

Polanyi does not equate globalization with the logic of either capitalism or modernity per se, but rather sees it as one possibility for a modern capitalist society, the realization of which requires conditions that are both contingent and political.[31]

Polanyi offered three propositions:

1. *Markets undermine social relations.* The organization of economic life, which historically has taken the form of complex, localized relations of reciprocal obligation, is usurped by markets in which transactions are mediated through monetary exchange and in which social relations are regulated by contract.
2. *State action is inherent to market formation.* Markets come into being through the activity of political organizations and, in the modern period, specifically through the actions of states. In short, markets are neither natural nor self-regulating. Markets do not arise spontaneously from our natural inclinations to "truck and trade," but instead through consciously planned political actions and choices. For Polanyi, the free market is a utopian conception. All markets are regulated in the sense that their parameters are established by state institutions.
3. *In order to protect itself society must ultimately delimit the space in which markets operate "freely."* Unless communities protectively

restrict and regulate markets in an effort to stem their socially disruptive effects, they will either collapse altogether or else develop authoritarian tendencies for the purpose of resisting the market's effects upon communities.

Looking at the rise of national markets, Polanyi argued that the socially unsustainable character of "self-regulating" markets generated a natural "protective" reaction on the part of a variety of social groups, including a portion of the elite. Unfortunately, in Polanyi's analysis this protective reaction was overwhelmed by the inability of the same protective reaction to prevail at the international level.[32]

Nevertheless, Polanyi's propositions remain relevant to what might be called the "second free market utopia," or a single global market as it is conceived by contemporary neoliberalism.[33] There are at least two implications of these propositions for analyzing contemporary globalization. First, neoliberalism is a cultural structure that enables (and constrains) state responses to markets. The human economy is enmeshed in historically contingent institutions, both economic and noneconomic. For Polanyi, "institutions are embodiments of human meaning and purpose."[34] Inclusion of the noneconomic is vital. Ideas, including the cultural dimensions of political structures that generate resources and constraints, are a constitutive source of globalization. Second, globalization necessarily remains a contested and ultimately unrealizable project.

The economic concept of free markets is the cornerstone of the neoliberal vision of the globe as a marketplace in which all trade and other economic action is freed from the "constraints" of law, politics, and morality—in short, freed from governance. The neoliberal "free trade" discourse presents itself as a neutral diagnosis rather than as a powerful contributor to the emergence of the very conditions it purports to analyze.[35] This discourse has been successful because many powerful economic actors believe and have convinced key politicians (and voters) that economic development *causes* the political response of deregulation, that neoliberal economic globalization is inevitable, and that states have no choice but to follow its logic or else be marginalized. In this sense, we can speak of neoliberalism as a cultural structure influencing political society. It is, at this point, an extremely powerful cultural structure, with many adherents.

Obviously, these processes are not the only ones shaping contemporary globalization. Globalization is a multifaceted set of processes. Equally important to note is that globalization is still "under construction," so to speak. While there are many ways to organize it, globalization still requires rules, policies, regulations, and enforceable contracts. The struggle over their content, working principles of justice and morality, and pragmatic institutionalization comprises a critical aspect of what I call the "politics of globalization."

Social movement actors who disagree with the premises or disapprove of the outcomes of a neoliberal version of globalization can seek to challenge it so that it does not remain dominant. The transnationalist discourse insists that the economy is always embedded in law, politics, and morality. In this discourse, the neoliberal vision of the self-regulating market, despite current efforts to construct such an elusive arrangement, is not only socially undesirable but, to echo Karl Polanyi, a "utopian impossibility."

It is important to note that "transnational" and "transnationalist" do not have the same meaning. Transnational refers to that which transcends nation-state boundaries and the *inter*national system of states. The transnationalist discourse challenges the binary distinction between globalization and the nation-state and "insists on the continuing significance of borders, state policies, and national identities even as these are often transgressed by transnational communication circuits and social practices."[36]

Moreover, this discourse does not treat the nation-state and transnational practices and processes as mutually exclusive social phenomena, nor even as binary conceptual categories. The transnationalist discourse depicts nation-states and transnational practices and processes as contributing to the constitution of each other. It sees nation-states as not only being transformed by transnational practices and processes, but as often participating in and even promoting those that are transforming nation-states. It is worth quoting at length Saskia Sassen's recent description of these phenomena:

> Although localized in national—indeed, in subnational—settings,
> these processes are part of globalization in that they involve trans-
> boundary networks and entities connecting multiple local or "national"
> processes and actors, or the recurrence of particular issues or dynamics
> in a growing number of countries or localities. Among these entities

and processes, I include, for instance, cross-border networks of activists engaged in specific localized struggles with an explicit or implicit global agenda, as is the case with many human rights and environmental organizations; particular aspects of the work of states—for example the implementation of certain monetary and fiscal policies in a growing number of countries, often with enormous pressure from the International Monetary Fund (IMF) and the United States, because those policies are critical to the constitution of global financial markets; and the fact that national courts are now using international instruments—whether human rights, international environmental standards, or WTO regulations—to address issues where before they would have used national instruments.[37]

This passage reflects Sassen's deliberate effort to build into her definition of globalization a transnationalist discourse.

What I wish to emphasize here is a discourse employed by social movements that seek to challenge "globalization from below," including the Free Burma movement. Peter Evans distinguishes between two types of globalization from below: (1) transnational networks that seek to *adapt to* the power of global elites, and (2) those that explicitly seek to *challenge* this power by "pushing for different rules and by building different ideological understandings."[38]

The first type of globalization from below refers to cases like those of ordinary citizens from poor countries who build transnational communities that link them to wealthy countries where they build assets while remaining engaged in their communities of origin. As Evans points out, while such collective action reflects the adaptive ability of these people facing the challenges and opportunities of globalization, it does not challenge the dominant global rules, nor even the economic ideology invoked to legitimate them.[39]

The collective actions of those in the first category are extremely interesting. However, the Free Burma movement represents a case of the second type: the social movements that are what Evans calls "counterhegemonic"—that is to say, challenge neoliberal globalization.[40] According to the transnationalist discourse, the question is not whether law, politics, and morality will shape our global economic future, but rather *whose* law, politics, and morality will shape it. All markets, including the global market currently under construction, depend upon rules and institutions to function. Who will shape their creation and how will they be arranged? These are the critical questions, from a transnationalist perspective, that the neoliberal globalization discourse does not address and, moreover, dangerously implies require no addressing.

The political opportunity to challenge neoliberalism and influence the discursive constitution of globalization arises in contexts of the political cultural struggle to influence which discourses do (and do not) become institutionalized through the politics of legislatures, the law enforcement of executive administrations, and the moral reasoning of judiciaries. To the extent that collective actors in civil society can continue to illuminate society's necessary role in regulating markets, they sustain the possibility of influencing the ideas around which we do organize such markets. As social theorist and Brazil's minister of long-term planning Roberto Unger argues:

> If we can change what free trade means and how it is organized, we can do the same, more generally to globalization. And if we can have globalization on our terms, rather than on those of the supposedly irresistible forces that its contemporary form is claimed to represent, all bets are off: we are freer than we suppose to rethink and to reconstruct.[41]

Many social movements and networks of transnational activists are trying to influence the politics of globalization. Examining the Free Burma movement as an example of a transnational social movement illuminates how the politics of influence might work in a globalizing world. It also highlights how social movement scholars will have to account for how globalization is changing social movements, while at the same time some of those movements seek to change globalization.

Significantly, the Free Burma movement began to develop a transnationalist discourse on corporate accountability by the mid-1990s. Free Burma campaigns used a transnationalist discourse to challenge several key neoliberal assumptions that Free Burma movement activists believed were propping up the repressive Myanmar state. For example, in the *Doe v. Unocal* suit, the movement challenged the notion that market participants cannot or should not select their business partners on the basis of their moral positions. In the selective purchasing campaign, they challenged the assumption that states are necessarily acting as market regulators when legislating sanctions, showing instead that states also can act as market participants who have the freedom to choose (and not choose) with whom they wish to procure goods and services in a global market.

Neoliberalism was not the only logic that Free Burma activists challenged. In the effort to decharter Unocal, they also used a transnationalist discourse to challenge the assumption that many global elites embracing neoliberalism would like us to believe, namely, that states are too weak under conditions of globalization to rein in transnational corporations. They even used a transnationalist discourse to challenge the *inter*nationalist logic of national sovereignty that corporations invoke to justify their abusive human rights practices. Corporations frequently claim that they are free to profit from the weak laws and enforcement practices of the states in which they operate and cannot be held liable for profiting even from local human rights abuses committed by those states. But the Free Burma activists creatively deployed and helped to institutionalize a transnationalist discourse that challenges this claim and the abusive human rights practices that this claim seeks to authorize.

One of the lessons that we can take from the case of the Free Burma movement is how transnationalist discursive strategies can empower and increase the effectiveness of movements. Transnationalist discursive strategies help to erode powerful nationalist concepts and ideologies that too often prevent citizens living in separate nation-states from being able to understand, see, or even imagine how their action (or inaction) affects or is affected by that of citizens living in other nation-states. At the same time, transnationalist discursive strategies render visible connections between citizens that transcend nationalist boundaries of difference, and thereby also reconfigure relations of community, class, race, ethnicity, and gender that the concept of nation mediates, to suggest new ways that citizens might more powerfully coordinate their action across national boundaries and generate meaningful identities, solidarities, and representations of their interests that have not been already circumscribed and subjugated by oppressive states and market arrangements.

Furthermore, transnationalist discursive strategies produce alternative spatialities and temporalities that can empower movements. Transnationalist discursive strategies create a new space—a transnational space—for socially constructing these alternative identities and representations, and project a new space for collective action. This transnational space enables people to perceive political opportunities for challenging repressive state and corporate power that exists outside of the cultural confines of nationalism and neoliberal globalism. Transnationalist discursive strategies also create new temporalities, re-narrating sequences of events and connecting the disparate histories of peoples whose experience and collective memory has been simultaneously yet separately interpreted through the cultural structures of competing nationalisms. By re-narrating the sequential unfolding of events, and thus the process of historical change, transnationalist discursive strategies also generate new understandings of what can be changed, by whom, and how.

Transnational movements that focus on influencing domestic policies in democracies are not necessarily less effective in enhancing representation of groups suffering under authoritarian rule. The case of the Free Burma movement illustrates how groups suffering under authoritarian rule may be repressed not only by the domestic policies of authoritarian states, but also by the domestic policies of democratic states that facilitate the undemocratic practices of the transnational corporations that they charter and which collaborate with authoritarian states in repressing for-profit groups that live there. We should recognize as well that these profits are often achieved through the lowering of costs of production subsidized by democratic states that its tax-paying citizens economically underwrite, although do not necessarily morally support.

When we pay closer attention to these transnational connections between democratic and authoritarian states, their domestic policies and their citizens, as well as the corporate practices and partnerships that span the boundaries of democratic and authoritarian states, it blurs the binary conceptual distinction between them. This provides the first step toward creating possibilities for imagining effective transnational legal action that challenges the hegemonic relations and discourses that sustain such a reified conceptual distinction between democratic and authoritarian states.

Why Transnational Legal Action?

Transnational legal action is primarily an act of cultural representation, that is, the discursive efforts of actors in legal contexts that invoke a transnationalist discourse to transform the legal meaning and legal identification of practices and relations in ways that influence state action. Typically, this action targets state actors or others in political society attempting to influence state actors who are attempting to colonize or deterritorialize within a nationalist, internationalist, or globalization discourse the legal meaning and identification of the same practices and relations. This discursive struggle produces transnational legal space.

Transnational legal space is a conceptual space of legal discourse that is shifting and contested. It is within and through this discursive contention that state actors, global elites, and social movement actors and advocates struggle to shape the legal practices and legal meanings of the rules and relations that are currently being institutionalized to facilitate and constrain the process of globalization.[42] The cultural production of transnational legal space therefore provides opportunities for mediating how the emerging rules of global markets are politically, legally, and morally constructed.

Transnational legal space is produced within the interstices of the international and national legal systems, often in discursive contestation between states and other norm-generating communities. Globalization produces and uncovers new practices and relations, the legal meanings and identities of which have not yet been institutionally "settled" and often not even (yet) identified or appropriated by states. Sometimes they have been settled by states long ago, but current state actors have forgotten about laws on the books concerning them, so they fall into disuse. And sometimes state actors know about them but have remained ambivalent about enforcing them. These lacuna of legal meaning, contested legal meanings, buried legal meanings, and ambivalent legal practices are often ripe for reinterpretation and representation within either a globalization or transnationalist discourse.

I do not use transnational legal action to refer simply to actors' attempts to make the legal meanings or practices of one national legal system actionable within another, although this may occur in the course of transnational legal action. Critical to transnational legal action, in the sense that I use the term, is the deployment of a transnationalist discourse, which challenges neoliberal prescriptions for the organization of relations among states, markets, and civil society. Thus, while Microsoft Corporation's "rule of law" project seeks to instantiate a common set of legal meanings and practices within national legal systems around the world in order to provide a globally enforceable legal context for its claims to intellectual property rights, it ultimately relies upon a hegemonic globalization discourse, rather than transnationalist discourse, to do so. The common political objective running through the examples of transnational legal action that I present in this book is to construct an enforceable regulatory regime of corporate accountability that is capable of transforming (or else severing) the market relations that link and sustain the Myanmar state and facilitate its repression of Burma's civil society.

The most common approaches to the study of the global development of human rights are *top-down* approaches. That is, they adopt a view of global justice *from above,* formulated through prescriptive or legislative means, which does little to supply a sense of how global justice is made from the ground up. These approaches largely ignore the significant role that social movements, transnational or otherwise, play in this process.

The most common approaches to the study of how transnational social movements shape the global development of human rights are more *bottom-up.* This kind of global civil society empiricism focuses on transnational networks of informal actors (social movements, NGOs, and activists) driving global justice from below. The emphasis here is on how such networks contribute to the formation of a transnational and politicized civic realm that represents progressive forces that can help counterbalance the role of hegemonic states and transnational corporations in national and world politics.[43] The focus of such approaches, however, is confined largely to the organizational dimensions of movement actors.

An emphasis on transnational legal action, and the transnational legal space that it creates, allows us to focus on the interstices between political society (the primary focus of politico-legal institutionalists' top-down approach) and civil society (the key organizational terrain of global civil society empiricists' bottom-up approach). What we need, and what this approach attempts to provide, is a conceptual space for analyzing the shifting and contested discursive terrain within and through which state actors, global elites, and social movement actors and advocates struggle to shape the legal meanings of rules and relations that are currently being institutionalized to facilitate and constrain the process of globalization.

Targeting the Business Partnerships Sustaining the Junta

The transnational network of relations that the Myanmar state created with corporations not only profited those corporations that sought to take advantage of a labor force whose state offered it no legal protection, but also buttressed the power of the Myanmar state, facilitating its efforts to repress pro-democratic activism within Burma. But these same transnational business partnerships also created new opportunities for the movement.

First, it is because transnational corporations are embedded in the politics, law, and morality of the states that have created them, and not only of the states with which they develop trade and investment ties, that relations like those between the Myanmar state and corporate partners have (unintentionally) provided their challengers with new opportunities.

Second, it is because transnational corporations bring with them histories to the less socially protected states with which they seek new, more profitable partnerships. Unocal brought with it to Burma its history of interaction with Californians whose oceanic coasts it had polluted in an oil-spill incident and for which it had failed to accept financial responsibility for cleaning up. Although most Californians could not locate Burma on a world map, and still fewer would recognize any reference to the Myanmar state, most of them know who Unocal is.

Transnational corporations not only span more than one nation-state, they link them. For their opponents in communities of one state, like Burma, they can provide an opportunity for mobilizing sympathetic opponents in communities of other states to which Unocal has links and a disreputable corporate identity.

In their path-breaking work on transnational advocacy networks, Margaret Keck and Kathryn Sikkink tell us that when channels between the state and its domestic actors are blocked, a "boomerang pattern" of influence characteristic of transnational networks may occur: domestic NGOs bypass their state and directly search out international allies to try to bring pressure on their states from outside. This is most obviously the case in human rights campaigns.[44] Keck and Sikkink's model illustrates an additional step in this process, whereby the domestic NGOs that have been blocked by their state activate the network *whose members pressure their own states* and, (if relevant) a third-party organization, which in turn pressures the blocking, i.e. target, state.

This model focuses almost exclusively on interactions between states and civil society. It provides no conceptual space for examining interactions between markets and society. Corporations and market relations do not appear in Keck and Sikkink's conceptual model of how transnational social movements or transnational advocacy networks exert pressure for changing the human rights conditions that motivated their action. Yet as we have seen in the case of the Free Burma movement, the trade relations between states and transnational corporations may constitute a very different kind of target and may require a different kind of pressure for effecting social change than that presumed by Keck and Sikkink's model.

Although Keck and Sikkink correctly emphasize the continuing significance of states, their reason for doing so betrays, in light of the empirical evidence presented in this book, a questionable assumption regarding human rights practices and their implications for transnational movements. They claim that governments are the primary violators of rights.[45] Upon this assumption they build the conceptual logic of their boomerang pattern: "When a government violates or refuses to recognize rights, individuals and domestic groups often have no recourse within domestic political or judicial arenas. They may seek international connections finally to express their concerns and even to protect their lives."[46]

Another lesson that we should take from the transnational campaigns of the Free Burma movement is that transnational corporations, as much as governments, may also be significant violators of human rights. In some cases, transnational corporations may even work together with states in violating them. Moreover, *Doe v. Unocal* and other cases filed against both corporate and state violators of human rights under the Alien Tort Claims Act reflect a transnational legal space where individuals and groups outside the United States may well find recourse within the judicial arenas of the U.S. District Courts. That is, the domestic state in which human rights victims hold their citizenship does not necessarily have a monopoly on their access to a judicial arena. Each of these points taken on its own may seem like trivial tinkering with Keck and Sikkink's model. Taken together, however, they begin to suggest an alternative pattern of transnational pressure that is distinctly different from the international pressure depicted in their model.

Keck and Sikkink's treatment of international pressure seems to suggest practices whereby foreign states are persuaded—via combinations of various types of politics (information, symbolic, leverage, and accountability)—to intervene in the affairs of the target state, either directly or through a mediating intergovernmental organization. However, the campaigns suggest a different pattern of pressure, whereby foreign states neither intervene directly in the affairs of the target state nor through a mediating intergovernmental organization. The various types of politics identified by Keck and Sikkink are still important to this alternative pattern of pressure, but they are deployed within a transnational legal space over legislative, administrative, and judicial matters of U.S. law that mediate how global markets (in this case, linking corporations chartered in the United States with the Myanmar state) become embedded in politics, law, and morality.

It is through these legislative, administrative, and judicial *dimensions* of state action, and at multiple spatial *scales* of state action (municipal, regional, and federal), that the United States exercises pressure—*transnational*, as opposed to international, pressure—on the transnational corporations that buttress the power of the Myanmar state. That is, Keck and Sikkink focus on international pressure that states exert on other states (sometimes mediated through international nongovernmental organizations), but they provide no conceptual space for considering the transnational pressure that states exert on transnational corporations. Such pressure may well contribute to social change within the blocking state that has forged business relations with the targeted transnational corporations. Only with substantial conceptual stretching might one suggest that this pattern of pressure represents a state exerting pressure on another state.

Organization of the Book

In chapter 1 ("Burma's Struggle for Democracy and Human Rights before 1988") and chapter 2 ("Locating Power in the Free Burma Movement"), I provide a basic history of Burma, as well as an introduction to the Democracy Summer of 1988 that led to the brutal repression of the domestic pro-democracy movement and the genesis of the transnational Free Burma movement. I explain how the movement started to adapt to the new transnational ties the regime sought with transnational corporations and its emergence as a transnational movement. In chapters 3, 4, and 5 ("Free Burma Laws," "Corporate 'Death Penalty,'" and "Alien Tort Claims"), I provide in-depth analysis of the three transnational legal action cases and the transnationalist discourses deployed in each.

The Transnational Campaigns: A Framework for Comparison

Each campaign targets specific neoliberal discourses that various net-works of actors (who eventually constitute a countermovement) invoke to promote continued investment and trade relations with Burma. I ini-tially approached the conflict generated by these campaigns as sites of discursive contestation through which a politics of representation is fought out. In the process, I came to see them more specifically as shifting and contested terrains of legal discourse within and through which state ac-tors, global elites, social movement actors, and advocates struggle to shape the meanings of rules and relations that are currently being insti-tutionalized to facilitate and constrain the process of globalization and its impact on the various local communities that these heterogeneous configurations of actors seek to empower.

These campaigns cumulatively and dynamically sought to transform the legal terrain upon which the new rules and institutional arrangements of global trade and investment are being constructed. These new rules and institutional arrangements, in turn, significantly bear upon eco-nomic, social, and political conditions in Burma and the pro-democracy movement's struggle to change those conditions. In short, the contexts that I examine are more than simply "windows" or perspectives from which to view this pro-democracy movement; rather, each represents how transnational legal space constitutes a significant contested terrain for institutionalizing the political, legal, and moral dimensions of the global market in ways that affect the relationship between the Myanmar state, its trade partners, and its opponents.

I have chosen to examine three campaigns, each of which represents struggles over U.S. law that have implications for the construction of global markets, but which simultaneously concern specific relations be-tween transnational corporations and the Myanmar state. In addition, each case highlights a different institutional dimension of law (legisla-tive, administrative, and judicial) to illustrate how these struggles bear upon the process by which global markets are embedded in, respectively, politics, law, and morality. Framing the cases in this way raises a fur-ther question for research. In focusing sociological inquiry on this trans-national legal space, what lessons might we learn about how the po-litical, legal, and moral dimensions of global markets are (or might be) institutionalized? Put differently, what might we learn about how trans-nationalist legal discourse impacts the process through which global markets become embedded in politics, law, and morality?

The Case Studies

I present a thick description of the various transnational campaigns waged by the Free Burma movement. What the case studies provide is a mapping of this contested legal terrain and its contingencies. The cases focus on the transnational legal action and politics of representation within these transnational legal spaces. I trace the shifting and contested legal strategies, identities, and targets deployed by the Free Burma movement and their opponents.

The data from which I have constructed these cases derive largely from a full range of legislative, administrative, and judicial legal documents, including opinions, transcripts, briefs, motions, petitions, appeals, treaties, statutes, memoranda, and commentaries. Legal documents are, of course, always an incomplete source of data for many reasons. Courts have strict rules of evidence, and they also impose page limits for making one's legal argument. Information that plaintiffs or defendants deem irrelevant to making their argument may not be included in these legal documents. Nevertheless, the materials provide us with access to political, legal, and moral discourses that assert a particular argument in dialogue with others and that are situated in particular transnational legal contexts.

Legislative Discursive Contention and the Politics of Global Markets

The first case (in chapter 3) focuses on the transnational legal space provided by selective purchasing laws, which I briefly describe above. The selective purchasing law campaign was initially successful at getting thirty municipal governments and the regional state of Massachusetts to legislate and enact "Free Burma laws." The case highlights *legislative* discursive contention over purchasing decisions by municipal governments and regional states over how they spend their money as market participants procuring contracts from transnational corporations. It illustrates how transnational legal space mediates the process through which global markets become embedded in *politics*. The selective purchasing law campaign deploys a transnational strategy through which the Free Burma movement attempts to get at the purse strings and leverage the purchasing power of municipal governments and regional states across the United States to force any transnational corporation, not just those headquartered in the United States, that does business with them to make a choice: either quit doing business with the Myanmar state or lose valuable contracts with these municipal governments and regional states.

Corporations immediately launched an effective legal countermovement to challenge the constitutionality of the selective purchasing laws. The central issue taken up by the U.S. Supreme Court concerned the constitutionality of local states conducting foreign policy.

The state of Massachusetts, the plaintiff in this test case for all subfederal Free Burma laws, argued that its selective purchasing law did not interfere with the intentions of the federal Burma law; rather, it was consistent with federal sanctions that had passed subsequent to the passage of the Massachusetts Burma law. Massachusetts also argued that it was not regulating the conduct of transnational corporations because it did not force them to quit doing business with the Myanmar state. Instead, Massachusetts argued, it was acting in its capacity as a "market participant" to procure goods and services in a manner that its constituency sees as morally fit. Like any market participant, Massachusetts explained, it was exercising its First Amendment right to do business with whom it chooses. Furthermore, its exercise of choice leaves open to other market participants a choice: do business with the Myanmar state or with us. Contrary to allegations of the corporations that filed the suit, Massachusetts asserted, the Massachusetts Burma law did not not infringe on the First Amendment rights of corporate market participants.

The Court struck down Massachusetts's (nonfederal) Free Burma law on the specific grounds that it interfered with the intentions of the federal Burma law. The Court interpreted the federal Burma law as legislation that was intended not simply to impose "blunt" sanctions, but rather to exert a "finely calibrated" amount of pressure on the Myanmar state *in combination with* economic incentives (akin to those offered under the existing policy of constructive engagement, which the U.S. government had publicly denounced as "soft on human rights abuse" when enacting its federal Burma law). In contrast, the Court explained, the selective purchasing legislation enacted by Massachusetts represented an extreme form of economic sanctions by comparison and offered the president too little room for diplomatic maneuvering in its effort to coax the Myanmar state toward democratic reform.

In principle, this ruling has not affected the legality of selective purchasing legislation more generally. It does not, for example, affect the use of selective purchasing legislation to hold Swiss banks accountable to Holocaust survivors and their relatives for the money that they stole from them during World War II. Nor does it call into question the constitutionality of the selective purchasing legislation that was used to influence corporations to sever their ties with South Africa's apartheid regime in the 1980s. Nor, for that matter, does it affect the Free Burma legislation enacted by several municipal townships throughout Australia. Rather, it affects only the Free Burma legislation enacted by local and regional governments throughout the United States. Therefore, the transnationalist legal discourse that the Free Burma movement deployed in this campaign may still be used in the future by other actors to challenge neoliberal foreign policy monopolized by nation-states to influence the process through which global markets are embedded in politics. The transnational legal space provided by selective purchasing legislation remains an open terrain for future political struggle.

Administrative Discursive Contention and the Law of Global Markets

For the Free Burma movement, the legislative struggle of the selective purchasing law campaign raised an important question: Under political conditions in which the federal government seems unwilling to challenge existing relations between U.S.-chartered corporations and the Myanmar state, what, if any, existing legal powers then are fundamentally vested in local and regional states that they can exercise to influence the conduct of transnational corporations operating in Burma? They found their answer in the transnational legal space provided by corporate charters.

The second case, which I discuss in chapter 4, involves a campaign specifically targeting Unocal to revoke its corporate charter on the basis of newly emerging evidence provided by NGOs that had documented Unocal's reliance on forced labor in constructing its natural gas pipeline through Burma. This case highlights *administrative* discursive contention over the enforcement of a long-forgotten law in California that emphasizes corporations as legal entities that owe their existence to the regional state that created them.

The law also specifies conditions under which corporations may be stripped of the charters that grant their right to exist. It provides a legal procedure allowing the people of California, acting through their attorney general, to initiate the charter revocation of any of its corporations that have violated existing law. Similar laws regarding the revocation of corporate charters exist on the books, yet remain unenforced, in most regional states throughout the United States.

The case illustrates how transnational legal space mediates the process through which global markets become embedded in *law*. The campaign to revoke Unocal's corporate charter deploys a transnational strategy through which the Free Burma movement attempts to get the California state attorney general to bring a lawsuit on behalf of the people of California that would decharter Unocal on the basis of "crimes against humanity," "environmental devastation," and other violations of international law that it has committed not only in California, but also in Burma and other foreign states.

The Free Burma movement's effort to petition the California state attorneys general Daniel Lungren and Bill Lockyer, respectively, to bring a lawsuit against Unocal that would revoke its corporate charter had mixed results. Neither attorney general was persuaded to bring such a lawsuit against Unocal. Then again, this campaign's organizers never really expected that they would. The primary goal of this campaign strategy was to challenge the apologetic claim of California's regional state actors that they had no power to regulate the conduct, however morally questionable, of corporations choosing to do business with the Myanmar state in Burma. The problem, these politicians frequently suggested, is that the conduct of corporations in Burma falls within the administrative jurisdiction of the Myanmar state; and the Myanmar state has greeted these corporations and their conduct with open arms, despite their domestic citizenry's outcry to the international community for economic sanctions.

This campaign sought to educate the public about the legal power that regional states in the United States have to challenge the misconduct of the corporations that they charter, regardless of where in the world those corporations conduct their business. It sought to show that Unocal's violations of human rights in Burma could be stopped by California's legal administrators—if they had the political and moral will to do so—because the state of California had chartered Unocal and

California's legal administrators have the legal grounds and power to revoke Unocal's charter.

The transnationalist discourse on corporate governance that emerged in this campaign then extends the one produced in the selective purchasing law campaign. In the selective purchasing law campaign, the Free Burma movement challenged the claim that only the federal government has the power to conduct foreign affairs. It did so by expanding the category "nonfederal entities" that the courts had used to distinguish and marginalize the foreign affairs power of municipal governments and regional states in its interpretation of the Constitution's foreign affairs clause. When the courts created this variable, they assumed that they were creating dichotomous categories that would be applied only to states. They failed to consider that nonstate actors also influence foreign policy. However, the Free Burma movement introduced a transnationalist discourse that compared the foreign policy activity of municipal governments and regional states with that of corporations— all of which, they pointed out, constituted nonfederal entities influencing the conduct of foreign affairs.

In the campaign to revoke Unocal's corporate charter, however, the transnationalist discourse is extended further to suggest that the very existence of these nonfederal entities called "corporations" is dependent upon the nonfederal (governmental) entities called "regional states," and thus could not exercise the influence that they do on foreign affairs without their ultimate nonfederal governmental authority. This transnationalist discourse that the Free Burma movement deployed in this campaign is, like that produced in the selective purchasing campaign, still serviceable as a potent tool for challenging, on a broadly coordinated scale in regional states throughout the United States, the political and moral choices of state actors who have the administrative power to enforce existing laws (and human rights norms) that directly affect the conduct, indeed the existence, of transnational corporations within the global market. The transnational legal space provided by corporate charters also remains an open terrain for future legal struggle.

Judicial Discursive Contention and the Morality of Global Markets

The third and final case (in chapter 5) focuses on the transnational legal space provided by the U.S. Alien Tort Claims Act (ATCA).[47] The First Congress of the United States adopted this act in 1789, but it remained largely unused for the next two centuries. The statute asserts simply that "the district courts shall have original jurisdiction of any civil action by an alien [non-U.S. citizen] for a tort [i.e., a harm or wrong] only, committed in violation of *the law of nations* or a treaty of the United States" (28 U.S.C. § 1350).[48] More recently, the statute has been invoked to hold states and their agents accountable for violations of international law committed *outside* the United States. The *Doe v. Unocal* suit, filed under ATCA, deploys a transnational strategy through which the Free Burma movement attempts to use the statute *for the first time* to hold liable in a U.S. court *transnational corporations*, not just state actors or private individuals, for their complicity in human rights abuses committed outside the United States in furthering their transnational joint ventures with states like Burma. The original legislators of this statute had never, nor could have, imagined using it for this purpose. Yet movement activists, deploying a transnationalist discourse, creatively appropriated this statute to address relations among states, citizens, corporations, and human rights that had significantly changed over the two centuries since ATCA's adoption. This suit illustrates how movement activists created a transnational legal space to shape the meaning and application of the ATCA for reining in the power of transnational corporations that violate human rights.

The *judicial* struggle of the *Doe v. Unocal* case, in itself, represents a stunning achievement for the Free Burma movement. This long shot of a transnational legal strategy soon became a landmark suit. The publicity from the suit brought stories of Burma's struggle for democracy into living rooms across the United States. Selective purchasing laws and corporate charter revocation had been used by others to challenge corporations even before the emergence of the Free Burma movement. But until *Doe v. Unocal*, the ATCA had never been used successfully to bring a lawsuit against a corporation. This transnational legal strategy has already disseminated to other movements that have also filed suits under the ATCA targeting different corporations in different contexts.

This institutionalization of what human rights lawyers term *jus cogens* (literally "compelling law") presupposes that some norms—such as those against slavery or genocide—are inherent and inalienable, reflecting the notion that there are ultimately fundamental moral choices to be made in law. Accordingly, there are noneconomic boundaries that market participants should not be permitted to transgress. This case illustrates how transnational legal space mediates the process through which global markets become embedded in *morality*.

The U.S. Supreme Court ruled that ATCA generally may be used to address jus cogens violations in cases predating *Doe v. Unocal*. But the question raised in *Doe v. Unocal* was whether a party specifically could sue a *corporation* for these jus cogens violations. Over the course of the nineteenth and twentieth centuries, U.S. courts increasingly granted corporations the rights of personhood, allowing them to be treated legally as private individual persons, separately from the individuals who own or operate them, and providing them with the same rights to due process under the law enjoyed by human persons.[49] The plaintiffs in *Doe v. Unocal* essentially argued that with the rights of personhood also come responsibilities. Thus, they argued, corporate violations should be held liable under the ATCA for jus cogens violations in the same way that individuals are. The federal district court ruled that the plaintiffs in *Doe v. Unocal* had a legitimate *cause of action* and agreed to hear the case. However, what remained at issue was whether Unocal should be held *liable* for the jus cogens violations suffered by the peasants who worked on the Burmese oil pipeline. But Unocal settled the suit before this question was ever decided by the courts, and it remains to this day a central question for ATCA claims against corporations.

In the conclusion of this book, I examine several important lessons from the transnational legal action of the Free Burma movement. I also examine the current limitations of this general type of collective action, at least as it has been practiced so far within the Free Burma movement. I conclude by proposing one way that we might begin to overcome these limitations to improve the transformative potential of transnational legal action.

Part I

The Emergence and Transformation of Burma's Democracy Movement

1

Burma's Struggle for Democracy and Human Rights before 1988

Burma today remains dominated by a military-ruled state that sees democracy and human rights as a grave threat to national security and treats proponents of democracy and human rights as enemies of the state. Accordingly, the Myanmar state has one of the worst civil and human rights records of any state in the world.[1]

Myanmar's fears of neocolonization, as well as social disintegration, are real. In its recent efforts to fend off democracy and human rights, Myanmar has adopted two discourses that are common throughout the non-Western world: authoritarian developmentalism and cultural relativism. The first discourse, on authoritarian developmentalism, asserts that a strong (authoritarian) governing hand is necessary to keep a lid on the bubbling cauldron of fractious, interethnic, nationalist rivalries within the country. It is only when the state has guided the country to a critical stage of economic development that it can afford the luxury of a more open (democratic) governing hand. In short, political democracy cannot precede, but rather must follow, economic development.

The second discourse, on cultural relativism, emerges in the form of a more particular regional variant that is often referred to as the "Asian values versus human rights debate." The Asian values discourse challenges the claim that human rights are universal and, furthermore, asserts that they are particularly Western values. Moreover, when the

West asserts its values as universal and attempts to foist them as universal (or international) standards upon Asian states like Myanmar, the West is in effect deploying human rights discourse as a political ideology that challenges the national sovereignty of these Asian states. It depicts Asian societies as having a different, particularly Asian, set of norms that conflict in important ways with Western human rights norms. Thus, human rights, Myanmar argues, are external to Burma's national culture. It characterizes activism inside the country that demands democracy and human rights as an expression of cultural neocolonialism (or the Western "brainwashing" of its citizens) and as a threat to the nation's cultural unity, social integration, and political security.

If there is one person that westerners today associate with Burma's struggle for democracy and human rights, it is Daw Aung San Suu Kyi.[2] She is the daughter of the country's revered military leader and political architect of their independence, General Aung San, who, in 1947, was assassinated with most of his cabinet members by a political rival in the months leading up to Britain's formal withdrawal from Burma. Like George Washington of the United States, Aung San is referred to as the father of his nation. Even among the people of Burma, Aung San Suu Kyi has become the face and symbolic leader of its movement for democracy.

Yet her immeasurably important role in sustaining the movement did not begin until after she returned to the country in 1988. After earning a B.A. degree in philosophy, politics, and economics at Oxford University in 1969, she spent three years in New York working for the United Nations. Later, she married a scholar of Tibetan culture with whom she had two sons, and in 1985 she completed a Ph.D. at the University of London's School of Oriental and African Studies. She returned to Burma on April 1, 1988, to care for her dying mother, who once had served as Burmese ambassador to India and Nepal. Although she did not know it at the time, the statewide conflict of "Democracy Summer" soon would command her attention.

Aung San Suu Kyi helped to forge a formal political opposition party to the military's SLORC government and was elected prime minister in a landslide democratic election in 1990 that the SLORC had been onfident it would win. The SLORC refused to transfer power. Instead, ·eated a military-led national convention to draft a new constitu- ·d renewed its campaign to suppress pro-democracy advocates, elected members of parliament. They also placed Aung San

Suu Kyi under house arrest, where she has spent most of her years since. Still, she has received numerous international honors for her efforts to resolve Burma's conflict, including the Nobel Peace Prize in 1991. Despite the military's restrictions on her communication, she still manages to exchange information with her first cousin, Dr. Sein Win, who serves from an office in Rockville, Maryland, as the prime minister of the National Coalition Government of the Union of Burma (NCGUB), also known as "the government in exile."

Myanmar's struggle for power often is viewed by outsiders as a process confined to its own territory, impervious to influences beyond its borders. But this is a fallacy. It is true that Myanmar, which spends 40 percent of its state budget on military expenditures, currently is at war with no external enemies, aside from those forces that it deems external to its national unity: the peaceful pro-democracy activists and armed ethnic national minority insurgents who live within Myanmar's borders. But even this characterization is problematic in light of the international and transnational nature of this political struggle. The Myanmar military does not act in isolation, nor is its struggle for power chiefly a matter of its own will. Rather, its struggle for power is embedded simultaneously in multiple, sometimes opposing foreign policies that at times facilitate, but at others constrain, its action.

Furthermore, Burma's struggle for democracy and human rights is embedded in transnational networks of activists, and it has influenced, as much as it has been influenced by, struggles for democracy and human rights well beyond its state's borders. Contrary to the military regime's "Asian values" discourse, human rights are not a foreign discourse that activists have appropriated in recent decades to challenge the Myanmar state. Burma's struggle for democracy and human rights is rooted in its first decade of independence from the British. Burma became an independent state with a parliamentary democracy in 1948, the same year that the United Nations (UN) enacted the Universal Declaration of Human Rights. Democracy and human rights discourse has come from within Burma ever since.

Exporting Democracy and Human Rights

Burma's struggle to institutionalize democracy and human rights in the early years of postcolonial statehood was not focused exclusively on domestic issues. During this volatile period of internal, nationalist, political turmoil, Burma's civilian government leaders embraced the Universal Declaration of Human Rights and played a leading role in promoting democracy and human rights around the world. Although World War II ended in 1945, conflict between the United States and the Soviet Union continued in other ways. Additionally, Western countries still maintained colonial domination over several regions of Asia and Africa, and their efforts to suppress anticolonial and anti-imperialist struggles within these regions led to new warfare in Indochina, the Korean Peninsula, Peninsular Malaysia (between Thailand and Singapore), Palestine, and many parts of Africa. Burma's civilian government leaders organized, hosted, and provided a leading voice in international and transnational conferences[3] that promoted an end to postwar Western and Soviet colonization and imperialism and an alternative vision of global development in which "newly emerging forces" in Asia and Africa were not marginalized by Western states from decision-making that affected them.

U Nu, the first prime minister of Burma, organized with Indonesia's president Soekarno (Sukarno) and India's prime minister Jawaharlal Nehru the 1955 Bandung Conference of delegates from twenty-nine Asian and African "Third World" nations.[4] Hosted in Bandung, Indonesia, this was the first large-scale Asian–African conference.[5] The "Spirit of Bandung" that the conference generated was a collective expression of unity in confronting superpower colonization and embracing the fundamental principles of human rights delineated in the Universal Declaration of Human Rights.[6] It also gave birth to the Non-Aligned Movement and represented a call for greater equality among nations in geopolitical decision-making that was shaping international development in the Third World.

Burma's contribution to the international development of democracy and human rights persisted even after 1962, when General Ne Win seized state power in Burma and ousted Prime Minister U Nu and his civilian government from office. This event marks the beginning of a long and dark period for democracy and human rights in Burma that continues to this day. Yet even while Ne Win was taking control of the state, Burma's U Thant was serving as secretary-general of the United Nations. He too had represented Burma at the Bandung Conference and, afterward, from 1957 to 1961, served as Burma's permanent representative to the UN. During this time, U Thant became actively involved in negotiations over Algerian independence. He served as the UN secretary-general for two consecutive terms before retiring at the end of 1971. During his time in office, he supervised the admission of dozens of new Asian and African states and sought to ease tensions between major powers. He maintained his steadfast opposition to apartheid in South Africa and received wide acclaim for his role in defusing the Cuban missile crisis, ending the civil war in the Congo, and publicly criticizing the United States' conduct of the war in Vietnam after the Johnson administration rejected U Thant's secret efforts to broker peace talks between Washington and Hanoi.

Ethnic Conflict in Burma

As of 2010, Myanmar is divided into fourteen administrative subdivisions, which include seven divisions (*pyi-ne*) and seven states (*tyne*).[7] The distinction between these two categories of administrative subdivisions betrays an ethnic division of power. Myanmar recognizes 135 "national races" (codified on dialectical variations), of which the major ones are Arakan/Rakhine (7 subgroups), Burman/Bamar (9), Chin (53), Kachin (12), Karen/Kayin (11), Karenni/Kayah (9), Mon (1), and Shan (33).[8] The Burman are the largest and dominant ethnic group in Burma.[9] They reside mostly in the central areas of the country, governed by Myanmar's seven administrative divisions.[10] This area includes the two largest cities, Yangon (formerly Rangoon) and Mandalay, as well as the newly designated capital city of Naypyidaw.[11] Other major ethnic nationality and minority groups occupy the seven states of the border areas.[12]

But the current relationship between central rule and the marginalized ethnic areas has not always been this way. Many ethnic nationalities have had their own kingdoms and principalities, and they still have their own languages, culture, and political identity. Indeed, before the British invaded and colonized it, Burma existed as a collection of territories that were ruled by different ethnic groups.

In 1885, the British forced into exile King Thibaw, the last monarch of the Kingdom of Burma's ruling Konbaung Dynasty. The British had already defeated the Burmese in two wars, in 1824–1826 and 1852–1853, and had annexed to British India what they mapped as Lower Burma, or British Burma, centered at Rangoon. This area was populated mostly by Mon, Karen, Bamar (Burman), and Anglo-Burmese. But

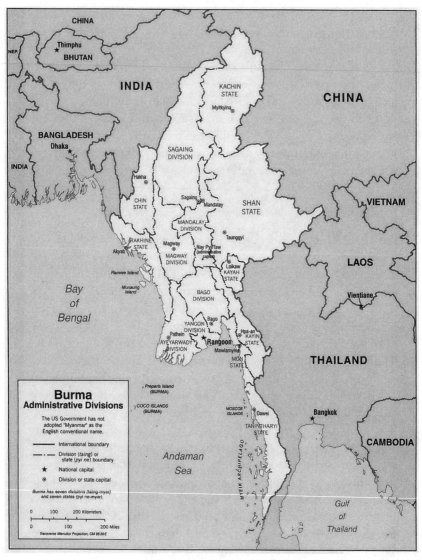

Map 2. Burma's administrative divisions and states. From CIA World
Factbook, 2007.

the Third Anglo-Burmese War, from 1885 to 1886, was a struggle for control over what the British projected onto the Court of Ava's royal city of Mandalay and surrounding region as Upper Burma (subsequently the central and northern administrative divisions of Myanmar). Upper Burma was predominantly Bamar.

As Burma historian Thant Myint-U explains, discussions of policy makers at the time reveal their perception that successive kings and governments in Mandalay had shown themselves incapable of accommodating British interests, permitting free trade, and keeping out unwanted rival European influences, like France, which was consolidating its hold over Vietnam, Laos, and Cambodia and receiving in Paris diplomatic missions of Burmese envoys.[13] There was organized resistance throughout the countryside to the colonial regime, and the British decided to abolish, rather than continue, its policy of collaboration with the monarchy.[14] Thant Myint-U describes the campaign of violent suppression through which the British "pacified" the countryside:

> Tens of thousands of villagers were forcefully relocated and suspected rebel sympathizers were summarily executed as the British army took the offensive. Over the next year, 40,000 British and Indian troops were poured into the old kingdom and harsh measures against civilians continued. Gradually, the colonial authorities gained the upper hand and, when the dust settled, very little of the old regime was left. The colonial state was born as a military occupation.[15]

This permanent military occupation superimposed a new colonial state and society that dramatically changed not only the economic, but also the political, social, and cultural organization of the country. The British initially annexed Upper Burma to British India, linking it conceptually (in their own minds, at least) to a contiguous territory that included Lower Burma. Rivalries, rules, and relations within and between the nobility and gentry were instantly banished, and the nobility and gentry themselves were evicted outside the city walls of Mandalay to dwell among the commoners, peasants, and bandits. Moreover, in ruling Burma's diverse population, the British favored certain ethnic groups over others.[16] By 1937, the British made Burma a separate crown colony.

During World War II, Japan trained the Burma Independence Army and fought with them against the British to take control of Burma. Still, as the war continued, many leaders of the Burma Independence Army focused on establishing an independent state.[17] It was at this time that they created the Anti-Fascist People's Freedom League and, under the leadership of General Aung San, shrewdly maneuvered to enlist the support of the British to liberate Burma from Japan in 1945.

After the war, Burmese nationalists demanded independence for Burma. When Burma resisted, leaders of the Anti-Fascist People's Freedom League sought the cooperation of Burma's ethnic nationality groups in forming a federal union of Burma.[18] As a result, Aung San and many (but not all) of Burma's ethnic nationality groups established the Panglong Agreement. As Burma expert Joseph Silverstein explains, this agreement established a "principle of equality" between Burmans and ethnic nationalities and provided a framework for a federal union with political autonomy for ethnic nationality areas[19] located now on the borders of what the British had constructed as modern Burma, and which today represent administrative states of Myanmar.

Just before independence was achieved, however, a new constitution became effective in September 1947 that, in Martin Smith's words, "was as lopsided and riddled with inconsistencies as any treaty drawn up in the era of British rule."[20] Instead of unifying Burma's diverse ethnic groups and political identities, it initiated an erosion of the trust in the principles of equality and political autonomy that the Panglong Agreement of February 1947 had established. The new constitution deemed states autonomous and gave certain ethnic nationalities, like the Karenni and Shan states, the right to secede from the union after ten years.[21] But it explicitly ruled out the right of secession for the Karens, who had historically been favored by the British and who were one of the largest and certainly most restive of the minorities.[22] More ambivalently, Aung San told Muslim and Rakhine nationalists of Arakan state, when they pressed him and the newly ruling Anti-Fascist People's Freedom League for constitutional rights of secession, that he in principle accepted their demands for statehood, but that pressing such demands before achieving formal independence might create an impression of disunity in the eyes of the British and delay their granting of independence.[23] Resolving the conflict between the central government and Karen and Arakan secession was to be settled after independence.

The Anti-Fascist People's Freedom League paid the price for sidestepping this ethnic conflict as a shortcut to establishing a formal democratic government. Civil war broke out from the start, and the Karen Nationalist Union insurrection, which by 1949 nearly seized control of

Rangoon, was the most formidable of the multiple rebellions fragmenting the newly independent Burma. By the time Ne Win seized power in the 1960s, numerous groups were in armed conflict with the Burmese Army. Indeed, civil war has been ongoing in Burma since its independence, and today represents the world's oldest active civil war. Ethnic conflict has remained at the root of this civil war.

However, since 1962, civil war in Burma has been perpetuated by different means. Ne Win's regime instituted a "Four Cuts" (*Pya Ley Pya*) policy aimed at cutting the main links—food, funds, intelligence, and recruits—between armed ethnic nationality groups and families and local villagers.[24] The Four Cuts policy caused thousands of civilian deaths and the destruction of food, crops, and numerous villages.[25] The main goal of the regime was to depopulate these regions.[26] As Burma expert Mary Callahan explains, "Since it was impossible to determine which Shans, Karens, or Arakanese were rebels and which were peaceful citizens, the easiest solution was to force everyone out of their homes, and in many cases across a flimsy border with a neighboring state such as Thailand or Bangladesh."[27] Evidence suggests that the Four Cuts policy is still the practice under General Than Shwe, the current leader of Myanmar.[28]

Between China and the United States

Observers of contemporary politics in Myanmar never fail to note that effective international influence on the country is complicated by relations between China and the United States. Worth pointing out, however, is that this has been the case since 1949, long before the military seized control of the state. Today, China is portrayed as Myanmar's silent protectorate from international intervention. The United States is depicted, even by the Myanmar state, as the most powerful threat to its sovereign affairs and stability. But China and the United States have been meddling in Burma's affairs ever since the British left. From 1949 to the mid-1950s, it was the spillover from the conflict between a divided China and the United States that most threatened Burma's civilian government and pushed its military toward a path of institutional transformation that soon would dominate permanently the governance of the country. In short, both China and the United States have contributed to the authoritarian turn and long-term stability of the Myanmar ruling military.

Concerned with developments in Indochina and the left-wing turn of nationalist regimes elsewhere in the region, President Dwight D. Eisenhower asserted U.S. influence in an effort to transform the region before the Soviet Union could gain political footholds.[29] When the United States invaded North Korea in 1950, it drew the People's Republic of China into the war.

In addition to fighting the threat posed by the Karen insurgency in 1949, Burma's military also had to contend with Chinese troops. Mao Tse-tung's People's Liberation Army (PLA) waged successful Communist military campaigns in China that year that forced weakened troops of Chiang Kai-shek's anti-Communist Chinese Kuomingtang (KMT) to retreat. Many of the KMT troops fled China's Yunnan Province into northeastern Burma's Shan states under the direct command of Chiang's General Li Mi. Over the course of the next several years, more disciplined and well-armed KMT troops followed, occupying by force (and even arson) many Shan villages.

In early 1951, as the People's Liberation Army chased General Douglas MacArthur's troops south of the 38th Parallel that divides North and South Korea, the Pentagon thought that the KMT could take some pressure off MacArthur by opening a second front. Under the direction of the Pentagon, and without the Burmese government's permission, the U.S. Central Intelligence Agency (CIA) covertly supplied these KMT troops in Burma with money, provisions, equipment, and weapons in an unsuccessful effort to retake Yunnan Province from the Communists.[30] The CIA began flying KMT soldiers into Thailand, training and equipping them and then delivering them, along with arms and ammunition, into northern Burma.[31]

Although the Burmese government tried to suppress their activities, the KMT defeated the Burmese National Army with relative ease. In protest, the Anti-Fascist People's Freedom League government refused to accept further U.S. aid and turned to the United Nations for support.[32] When the civilian government's diplomacy failed, the military stepped up its efforts. Beginning in November 1951, Burma's military launched a series of increasingly intensive operations, culminating in a full-scale, joint forces counteroffensive in February 1953.[33] But this too failed.

On the other hand, when the KMT attacked PLA forces in Yunnan Province, the PLA decimated them. However, many KMT remained in Burma, and in 1954, when Chiang Kai-shek ordered General Li Mi to withdraw from Burma, many Yunnanese in his army refused to leave and started the opium trade in the Golden Triangle region.

Throughout this crisis, more threatening to Burma's military than the U.S.-backed KMT was the concern that the People's Republic of China would take more aggressive measures to control the KMT and invade and ensnare Burma in global conflict in the process. Burma's army responded by undertaking its most significant structural transformation as a fighting force. As Callahan explains:

> The operational failures against a potentially formidable foreign threat made possible and necessary the overhaul of the armed forces. Field commanders, staff officers, and civilian government leaders alike acknowledged the need to transform the institution from its post-resistance, decentralized, guerrilla character into one capable of defending the sovereignty of the Union [of Burma]. In the 1950–53 period, staff officers hatched ambitious plans for the new army, but few came to fruition. Nonetheless, the negotiations, fights, and compromises that characterized the planning process established the broad outlines of a standing army with enormous autonomy to define what constituted "security" and who was an "enemy" of the state. The *tatmadaw* [Burma's military] never gave up this autonomy.[34]

Callahan's argument, which she supports with detailed archival evidence, is that, by the late 1950s, these guerrillas became state builders.[35]

When Prime Minister U Nu organized the Bandung Conference, the military already was pressuring his civilian government to relinquish to them greater responsibility and authority for state building. Therefore, another key concern discussed among the Bandung delegates was how to address the tensions between China and the United States. The United States did not recognize the authority of Mao's People's Republic of China, but rather backed the non-Communist KMT's Republic of China. U Nu, Soekarno, and Nehru invited the People's Republic of China's foreign minister premier Chou En-lai to attend the conference. The Eisenhower administration was suspicious that the conference signified a politically leftward drift among neutral countries and declined their invitation to participate.[36]

Moreover, the CIA, believing that China planned to use the conference to boost its image as a world power, seems to have covertly employed KMT operatives in Hong Kong to assassinate Chou en route to the conference.[37] The operatives planted explosives in the chartered airplane (Air-India's *Kashmir Princess*) that Chou was scheduled to take to the conference. The bomb killed sixteen passengers and crew. However, Chou somehow had intercepted intelligence regarding the assassination plot and never boarded the plane.[38] Instead, three days later, he flew to Rangoon to meet U Nu and Nehru and traveled safely to Bandung with them. But, as Wendell Minnick reported in the *Far Eastern Economic Review*,

> rumours of CIA and KMT involvement surfaced immediately. The day after the crash, China's Foreign Ministry issued a statement that described the bombing as a "murder by the special service organizations of the United States and Chiang Kai-shek," the head of the KMT government.[39]

Thus, this event reinforced for Bandung's delegates the seriousness of the tensions between the People's Republic of China and the United States.

But the Bandung Conference did not resolve these tensions, and Burma's military never sought to do so. Instead, they sought to exploit them. They secured resources for state building from arms manufacturers and superpower rivals: warplanes from Israel; expertise for establishing its first ammunition factory from Italy; and counterintelligence training from the United States.[40] Army leaders from Burma independently negotiated arms deals and military assistance, and were likewise courted by U.S. arms manufacturers who bypassed Burma's civilian government officials and political party leaders.[41] Ironically, therefore, the United States, almost from the outset of Burma's independence, played a significant role in promoting and strengthening the institutional development of the "pariah state" of Myanmar that it denounces today.

Sustaining the Struggle within Burma: The Role of Student Activists

Burma's struggle for democracy and human rights has also focused on the institutions of its own state and civil society. If there is one force in Burma that has remained as persistent and durable as the military in its struggle to shape the country's future, it is the university students. Collectively, they have struggled to defend (and occasionally advance) their "rights"—sometimes in the name of existing law, but also in the name of democratic or human rights principles that the current Myanmar state does not recognize. The collective action of these students over the years has served to preserve and periodically activate the collective memory of the country's struggle for democracy and human rights, providing a key resource for mobilizing other groups of supporters both inside and far outside Burma.

In the early 1930s, under British rule, Burmese nationalism flourished among the university students. They established the Rangoon University Student Union (RUSU), which quickly became the center of Burmese political activism. The RUSU encouraged students, through public speeches and its student-run *Oway Magazine,* to fight not only for student rights but also for colonial independence. In 1936, when British authorities attempted to censor the magazine and expel the student chair of the RUSU, the students went on strike and held a conference at which they established the All Burma Students' Union (ABSU). The ABSU formed additional student unions in secondary schools throughout the country that promoted anticolonial awareness and a collective vision for national independence. Government efforts to repress the union's activity by arresting its leaders only led to further protest demonstrations. At the end of the decade, many of these same students played a key role in the independence movement against the British and Japanese, joining the Burma Independence Army.

Even after Burma gained its independence, students continued to organize periodic small-scale demonstrations in the name of democracy. The ABSU changed its name to the All Burma Federation of Student Unions (ABFSU) and pressed U Nu's ruling civilian government, the Anti-Fascist People's Freedom League, for students' rights at every turn. By October 1956, the Anti-Fascist People's Freedom League attempted to abolish the student unions. Framing the state's action as a violation of their democratic rights, the students went on strike. About twenty-five students were imprisoned and ten times that number expelled. However, the Anti-Fascist People's Freedom League soon reversed its decision to abolish the student unions.

Two years later, in 1958, U Nu's civilian government transferred state power to General Ne Win's military "caretaker" government. The ABFSU denounced the transfer of power as an unconstitutional military coup and as a dangerous political precedent that would inevitably undermine democratic rights and practice in Burma. Their ensuing protest provoked a quick response from Ne Win. To constrain future student activism, he starved the RUSU of financial resources by terminating the collection of membership fees for student unions. Several months later, the state's University Council enacted a reform that abandoned the practice of including student union representatives on the hostel council. The ABFSU's protest resulted in the arrest of many students, and three of the union's leaders were banished to the country's harshest prison on Coco Island. Ne Win's caretaker government was voted out of office the following year, and U Nu was reelected as prime minister.

However, on March 2, 1962, Ne Win staged a military coup that permanently toppled civilian governance in Burma and weakened the effectiveness of civil society's efforts to leverage the state's legitimating ideology for defending and advancing democratic principles. Ne Win formed an authoritarian Revolutionary Council and appointed himself leader. One of his first steps as the effective dictator of Burma was to eliminate the University Council and transfer authority over all university affairs to the Revolutionary Council. On July 7, the students declared the RUSU building a "democratic fortress" and organized a demonstration to protest the Revolutionary Council's action. Military intelligence arrested student leaders, but the other students returned to occupy the campus. The military then surrounded the campus and tear-gassed the crowds, and the Revolutionary Council declared martial law. Early the next morning, the military used dynamite to demolish the RUSU building, killing many students.

The following summer, the Revolutionary Council invited the newly formed Students' Rights Protection Committee to engage them in a process of dialogue that also would include members of various armed ethnic-minority rebel groups. But when these peace talks never materialized, the students organized a peaceful demonstration that was a quarter-million people strong. The Revolutionary Council closed the universities throughout the country and arrested large numbers of both student and nonstudent demonstrators.

By the mid-1970s, after a decade of rule under Ne Win's Burma Socialist Program Party (BSPP) and its isolationist economic policy known as the "Burmese way to socialism," Burma's citizens began to suffer economically as well. Burma, which had once been called the "rice bowl of Southeast Asia" and boasted the highest literacy rates and per capita levels of formal education in the region, was now suffering rice shortages and declining wages and standards of living. The state's repeated university closures were also posing a threat to the future of Burma's labor force. Students began joining labor strikes organized by railway, textile, and dock workers. Ne Win's troops opened fire on the protesters.

A good example of how the students' collective action preserves and activates the collective memory of the country's struggle for democracy and human rights, and provides a key resource for mobilizing other groups of supporters, is the "U Thant crisis." When former UN Secretary-General U Thant died in New York on November 25, 1974, his body and funeral became politicized as a struggle between the students of Burma and Ne Win's government. In New York, U Thant's body was laid in state. From UN headquarters his body was flown to Rangoon, but no guard of honor or high-ranking officials appeared at the airport to accept the coffin, except the deputy minister of education, who was consequently dismissed from office. Ne Win had ordered that U Thant be buried without any official involvement or ceremony. Ne Win was envious of U Thant's international stature and the respect that Burma's citizens accorded him for his tireless struggle on behalf of democracy, human rights, and international peace. He also resented U Thant's close ties to U Nu and his earlier years of service on behalf of U Nu's democratic government. The people of Burma expressed outrage at the state's desecration of U Thant's body and legacy, and the students once again led the charge.

On the day of U Thant's scheduled funeral, tens of thousands of people lined the streets of Rangoon to pay their respects. U Thant's coffin was displayed at a horse-racing course for several hours before the scheduled burial. Thousands of students attended. They voiced their dissatisfaction with the irreverent funeral arrangements and suggested that U Thant's body instead be buried at the site of the former RUSU that Ne Win's troops had demolished in 1962. Several of the students made off with the coffin, transported it to a temporary mausoleum that they had constructed in U Thant's honor at the former site of the RUSU on the campus of Rangoon University, and there, five days later, buried the coffin. But the following morning, soldiers stormed the campus. They killed several students who were guarding the makeshift mausoleum, arrested many other students and monks, and disinterred U Thant's coffin. The military reburied the coffin at the foot of Shwedagon Pagoda, which is the most sacred Buddhist pagoda for the Burmese—enshrining the relics of four past Buddhas—and dominates the Rangoon skyline.

The military's handling of the U Thant crisis spurred immediate rebellion throughout Rangoon that violently targeted government buildings and the offices of the BSPP. Ne Win declared martial law in Rangoon and the surrounding metropolitan areas. More students were killed. Many others, including monks, were arrested and sentenced from three to seven years in prison. The state once again shuttered the universities for the entire following semester.

A similar pattern of interaction between the students and the state continued over the next two years. The following winter, students and workers united to peacefully protest the military-backed BSPP. They marched from Rangoon University to Insein Prison, the most notorious of Burma's military-run prisons, which holds thousands of political prisoners. They chanted for the release of students who were arrested in the U Thant crisis and the workers' strike. They then returned to campus to set up a strike center, at which point the state closed all of the universities throughout the country. When the students moved their strike center to Shwedagon Pagoda, the police cracked down and arrested them.

After briefly opening the universities the following year, the BSPP government again shut them down nationwide on March 24, 1976. Students had requested permission to honor on the previous day the one hundredth birthday of Thakin Kodaw Hmaing, known in Burma as the "Father of Burmese Peace Activists" for his many years of trying to foster reconciliation between the successive Burmese governments and rebel groups. The BSPP government denied students permission. When students did so anyway, armed soldiers in full battle uniform blanketed downtown Rangoon and the cemetery of the revered peace activist. It was an intensified display of military force meant to intimidate the students and cow them into disbanding. Instead, the students framed the military's disproportionate response as indicative of a democracy deficit and a consequence of the state's stripping them of student unions to defend their rights. They collectively demanded democracy, permission to reestablish student unions, and the release of students arrested in past strikes. The military arrested the student leaders and sentenced them from five to fifteen years' imprisonment.

Democracy Summer

Burma's students also played a central role in what some historians have called "Democracy Summer" of 1988—one of the most critical periods of Burma's struggle for democracy. I offer a closer examination of its emergence, and the causes behind it, in chapter 2. Here, however, it is worth highlighting several key events that illustrate this critical turning point in how the student movement would hereafter understand Burma's broader struggle for democracy.

On March 12, 1988, several students from the Rangoon Institute of Technology (RIT) were hanging out together at a tea shop, where they eventually began quarrelling with a few local young men who were not students. A town and gown–type conflict broke out between them and the young men beat up the students. When the students informed the police, the police found and arrested the young men. However, the students discovered the following morning that the police had later released the young men because they were relatives of high-ranking local BSPP members.

Tensions between the students and the BSPP government were already high. Over the past year, while students were taking their national examinations, the BSPP had suddenly demonetized all twenty-five, thirty-five, and seventy-five Kyat banknotes without compensating the holders of these notes. The demonetization instantly created intense financial hardship for most students. The following day, the BSPP closed down all of the universities.

It is in this context that in March 1988, when news spread throughout the RIT community of the local BSPP's having turned a blind eye to the illegal actions of their relatives, students decided to protest. Riot police broke up the protest. They also shot and killed a chemical engineering student from RIT in the process. This event fueled further student protest.

But this time, the state's response was especially severe. Burma experts Martin Smith and Bertril Lintner, working from eyewitness accounts, describe the horrifying scene that to this day is called the White Bridge massacre.[42] Tanks in the streets were flanked by riot police who were shooting tear gas into the crowd. Approximately one hundred civilians were killed, including forty-one who suffocated in a prison van that was deliberately driven around the city for two hours before delivering them to Insein Prison. Dozens of detainees were beaten and tortured, and a number of female workers and students were raped. Police forced some students into Inya Lake, where they disappeared, presumably drowned.[43]

When the universities were reopened in early June, students at RIT and on Rangoon University's main campus wasted no time. They resumed their protests, demanding the release of their arrested colleagues, the reinstatement of the hundreds of students who had been expelled, and the restoration of their right to form a student union. The government again closed down all universities, banned all public gatherings, and imposed an evening curfew in Rangoon. However, by June 23, students managed temporarily to set up a strike center at Shwedagon Pagoda and, even after police cleared and cordoned off this holy shrine, large-scale demonstrations already were occurring in Mandalay and towns outside Rangoon.

One month later, these protests seemed, if only briefly, to be adding up to something of a significant force for revolutionary democratic change. On July 23, following an emergency congress of the BSPP, Ne Win resigned as chair, called for many of his senior colleagues to do the same, and, most surprising of all, proposed a national referendum to vote on the question of returning to a multiparty system of government. This revolutionary proposal, coming from a dictator who had ruled with violent force for more than a quarter century, was breathtaking.

Hindsight might temper the notion that Ne Win could ever have taken his own proposal seriously.[44] After all, the BSPP immediately voted down the proposal, and Ne Win, despite his reclusive habits, was not out of touch with his party.[45] But this moment also predated by only one year the democratic standoff between students and ruling party leaders at Tiananmen Square in Beijing, China, the fall of one-party states across Eastern Europe, and the toppling of Romania's Nicolae Ceauşescu and East Germany's Erich Honecker. It also postdated by two years the successful "people power" overthrow of the Philippines' Ferdinand Marcos. As the cold war was coming to an end, the people of Burma were no more out of touch with the movements for democratic change that were taking place around the world. Two weeks later, on August 8, 1988, Burma's civil society boldly sought to assert its democratic aspirations and reclaim from the military control over its own governance. But the military mounted its most violent response to date and brutally suppressed this nationwide display of people power. I devote chapter 2 to this fateful event.

In the wake of the military's crackdown on the pro-democracy movement, on September 18, 1988, the Burmese army assumed power from the BSPP government that it had formerly backed and formed a new government called the State Law and Order Restoration Council (SLORC).

This coup, or reconsolidation of the military's control of the state, was hardly discussed. The SLORC's troops immediately began arresting, detaining, and torturing thousands of students and other supporters who had participated in the pro-democracy demonstrations in August.

As a consequence of the SLORC's campaign to purge central Burma of its political opposition, at least ten thousand students and other pro-democracy activists from the cities (including doctors, lawyers, professors, monks, and even soldiers) fled to liberated zones controlled by rebel, nationalist, ethnic-minority armies. Most sought refuge in areas under the control of the National Democratic Front (NDF), a union of political parties and organizations from twelve ethnic-minority groups (Arakan, Chin, Kachin, Karen, Karenni, Kayan, Lahu, Mon, Pa-O, Palaung, Shan, and Wa) that was established in 1976.[46] The NDF is the first and most successful union of those ethnic groups that oppose the military regime and are working to develop a federal union.[47]

The military's violently repressive strategies unintentionally fostered new relations between the predominantly Burman students and the less privileged, nonstudent, non-Burman ethnic minority citizens. The students had largely discounted the significance of the ethnic nationality and minority groups to their own struggle for democracy and human rights. Yet ethnic conflict between the Burman and other ethnic groups was one of the key issues challenging the postcolonial state; even now, the restoration of democracy and human rights in Burma is intricately tied to the elusive resolution of conflict over the political rights of ethnic minorities who, favoring secession or not, have become caged within the modern state of Myanmar.

Until the 1990s, however, the killing of citizens and forced relocation of villages in Burma's border areas occurred without the knowledge of the (mostly Burman) people residing in the central regions of the country.[48] This, in part, explains why the students had largely discounted the significance of the ethnic nationality and minority groups to their own struggle for democracy and human rights. The students from the central regions who fled to the liberated areas in 1988 had been ignorant of the relevance of the ethnic nationality and minority groups to their own struggle for democracy and human rights. Yet by the time they had learned of the different struggles for democracy and human rights that ethnic groups of the border areas were experiencing, and formed the All Burma Students' Democratic Front (modeled on and in loose alliance

Figure 2. A forced migrant Karen woman shades herself and child from sun in Burma. The camp where they live is protected by the Karen National Union Army, which Myanmar authorities consider a rebel group. Photograph by author.

with the ethnic nationalities groups' National Democratic Front), the military's power over state and society had increased tremendously.[49]

The questions raised by the Panglong Agreement—of how to resolve the mosaic of political rights claims of ethnic nationalities and minorities in Burma—remains one of the central issues of contestation challenging Myanmar (and Burma) today. Formal political restoration of democracy cannot succeed for long without addressing the deep-rooted ethnic conflict in civil society. One of the hard lessons that democracy activists in Burma have learned is that, if Burma's struggle for democracy is ever to succeed, tripartite dialogue that includes the ethnic nationality and minority groups must be an integral part of the process.

In Part II of this book, we will see how Burma's civil society has continued to influence human rights outside of Burma. We will see how their creative transnational legal campaigns have produced new mechanisms for holding accountable corporations that collaborate with, and intentionally profit from, the Myanmar state's abusive human rights practices. We will also see that these mechanisms have created opportunities for transnational struggles around diverse issues in other parts of Asia,

Figure 3. Landmines of the Burmese military along with two victims in January 2001 at a village in Karen State, Burma. Photograph copyright 2001 D. Ngo/ZUMA Press.

Africa, Latin America, Europe, and North America. These examples should help us to see that Burma's civil society is not simply waiting for the international community to bring them democracy and human rights. Long before 1988, Burma struggled to bring democracy and human rights both to the institutions of its own communities, and to those of the broader international community.

Even the forces precipitating Democracy Summer of 1988 were not entirely internal to Burma. At that time, if Burma's democracy movement was intensely focused on changing the politics of the relationship between its own civil society, state, and military, its past and future were nevertheless linked to the politics of the region and to broader movements for democracy and human rights around the world. In this sense, Burma's struggle for power, self-determination, democracy, and human rights has always been a transnational one.

2

Locating Power in the Free Burma Movement

At 8:08 a.m. on August 8, 1988, nearly one hundred thousand people walked off their jobs and into the streets of cities all over Burma, calling for an end to military rule. In what has since become commonly referred to in Burma as *Shitlay Loan A-Yay A-Hkin*, or the "Four Eights Affair (8–8–88)," these citizens protested against the ruling military's then twenty-six years of economic mismanagement, political repression, indiscriminate violence, and monopolization of access to uncensored media and communication networks. They publicly denounced the military junta's practices that, under the "Burmese way to socialism," had dominated the state and economic activity from the time of General Ne Win's *coup d'état* in 1962. They chanted and displayed a mixture of pro-democratic slogans and reappropriated symbols of the country's nationalist independence struggle through which, by 1948, Burma had shed the yoke of both British colonization and post–World War II Japanese occupation and established a fledgling democratic state. They called for an undistorted account of the state's violent action over the previous months, including rape, torture, indiscriminate killings, and secret mass cremations.

These protesters wanted more than reform. They wanted a fundamental change in governance. They demanded the resignation of the military leaders, the establishment of a multiparty government and democratic elections, and the restoration of civil liberties. The military government violently and indiscriminately repressed the public protest, in ways more dramatic and bloody than the Chinese repression of protests in Tiananmen Square the following year.[1] Foreign embassies in Burma numbered the casualties as high as twelve thousand—three to four thousand of whom were shot dead, including monks, medical workers, and even elementary school students. Unlike the massacre in Beijing, however, the violent repression of Burma's statewide bid for democracy was not televised. The Myanmar military not only violently and indiscriminately repressed this people power uprising, but it also heavily restricted non-military access to communications and transportation infrastructure and effectively censored all civilian information flows.[2]

State repression, however, did not snuff out the movement. Instead, the state's indiscriminate violence fanned the movement's flames with more radical resolve. Although the military's leadership sensed sufficient control and an opportunity to secure international legitimacy by organizing "free and fair" elections in 1990, the majority of Burma's citizens foiled this plan. The main opposition party, the National League for Democracy (NLD), under the leadership of Aung San Suu Kyi, won more than 60 percent of the popular vote and 82 percent of the parliamentary seats.

The military exposed its rationale for holding democratic elections when it refused to honor the results and tightened its authoritarian grip. It outlawed opposition parties and systematically imprisoned or "disappeared"[3] members of the NLD. This time, however, no mass protest ensued.

Signs of organized, large-scale, nonviolent public protest reappeared briefly in the 1996 student demonstrations and again during the 1998 tenth-year anniversary of the "8-8-88" uprising. Yet the military quickly and easily repressed all of this collective action without significant casualties. Although pro-democracy activists have contested the legitimacy of the military's rule ever since,[4] the military has remained in power to this day.

The movement, if we think of it as occurring entirely within Burma, seems to have slipped into abeyance.[5] Indeed, most of the scholarship today describing the pro-democracy movement that first emerged in Burma in 1988 tells a story of its ultimate failure. Even some former leaders

Figure 4. In 1988, Burma's monks in Rangoon (then the capital city) led a statewide general strike that became known as the 8–8–88 affair, marking the date it began. Many of these monks were killed or imprisoned. The original panoramic print of this photograph hangs in the shrine of the Association for the Assistance of Political Prisoners in Mae Sot, Thailand. Photograph by author, 2009.

within the movement have gradually adopted variations of such a narrative.[6] Explanations of its contemporary insignificance range in their depictions from a failed "people power" movement[7] to a movement that has been hopelessly stalled by ineffective international foreign policy measures, an increasingly repressive military government, and divisive politics within the ranks of a resource-poor and organizationally outflanked domestic opposition.[8] The mass protests of the so-called Saffron Revolution in 2007 arguably do little to challenge this assessment, if measured in terms of their immediate impact on the political governance of Myanmar.

I challenge such representations of the movement by situating it in a transnational rather than purely domestic context. My account of the emergence of this movement shows how the dominant theoretical paradigm in social movement research fails to give sufficient attention to either the transnational or the symbolic dimensions of the political environment in which Burma's pro-democracy movement operates. Both dimensions are essential for understanding the history and future of this social movement. To appreciate the political effectiveness of pro-democracy activists within Burma, we must understand their political action within a transnational context. State-centered theoretical frameworks, which influence the political analysis of most Burma experts, prevent us from seeing important networks of relations linking pro-democracy activists across Burma's territorial boundaries. Aside from mass direct protest, pro-democracy activists have deployed a variety of less traditional forms of collective action. These include transnationally coordinated symbolic protests designed to evoke a state response that demonstrates to an international audience its willingness to use repressive measures that can be easily exploited by activists in transnational media campaigns throughout the world. They also include the transnational legal actions explored at length in chapters 3, 4, and 5.

As even Sidney Tarrow, one of the most influential proponents of the state-centered "political process theory," writes:

> If it was once sufficient to interpret or predict social movements around the shape of the national state, it is less and less possible to do so today. Because of multiple levels and sectors of *movement mobilization,* their changing shape in different phases of protest cycles, and their increasingly transnational links, national regularities in state structure must be seen as no more than the initial grid within which movements emerge and operate.[9]

I also argue that, both within and outside of Burma, symbolic politics have played a critical role in this movement's collective action. Whether we give attention to transnational networks in turn affects how we interpret the symbols constituted within or flowing through them, as well as the meaning of the collective action (and inaction) taking place within Burma. Only then can we understand the critical symbolic dimension of the politics sustaining this movement's power. As we will see, attention to the transnational context significantly enhances our understanding of even the initial emergence of Burma's statewide pro-democracy movement.

Emergence of a National Pro-Democracy Movement in Burma

The first set of questions to address concerns the emergence of the protest movement in the late 1980s. Aside from the role that the state's practices played in constituting the formation of this movement, how did activists coordinate such mass action, particularly given the state's severe restriction on civilian mobility and communication? And why did statewide collective protest finally emerge when it did? Finally, how did the initial movement plant the seeds for the increasingly trans-national movement that has been working for now more than forty years to secure democratic governance and human rights for the people of Burma? A great deal of social movement research has focused on the question of how to conceptualize the political environments in which movements operate. Political process approaches have dominated this effort, shaping the concepts, discourse, and research agenda of the social movement field. As critics Jeff Goodwin and James Jasper point out, political process theory "may be criticized, but it cannot be ignored."[10]

The political process thesis asserts that social movements emerge when people with shared grievances who are organized and perceive that they can successfully redress their concerns seize *expanding* "political oppor-tunities."[11] Concerned by criticism of the fungibility of the concept, some political process theorists have attempted to specify which variables would constitute a consensual list of political opportunities.[12] The effort has generated lively debates among political process theorists them-selves,[13] but it has also yielded a list of at least four variables that we can for now take as a starting point in evaluating the extent to which the political process thesis explains the *emergence* of Burma's pro-democracy movement: (1) increasing popular access to the political system; (2) un-stable elite alignments or competition; (3) presence of elite allies who encourage or facilitate protest; and (4) declining state repression against opponents.[14]

Before discussing the relevance of these variables to the emergence of the movement in Burma, it is worth noting that Bertil Lintner's *Out-rage: Burma's Struggle for Democracy* is widely recognized among Burma scholars as the most authoritative account of the Four Eights Affair. Lintner conceptualizes the movement as emerging with the "March Af-fairs," which occurred five months before the Four Eights Affair.[15]

Political process theorists, however, would be apt to conceptualize the boundaries of the movement's emergence more loosely than does Lint-ner as a "cycle of protest."[16] This would relegate the March Affairs to a triggering incident, but also would temporally extend the movement's

emergent period to include the statewide collective action that occurred five months later, in August 1988. How we temporally designate
the boundaries of the movement's emergence at the outset will affect
our evaluation of the explanatory utility of the political process thesis as
it pertains to this movement. We must then consider whether political
opportunities were "expanding" in light of both conceptions of emergence to show just how different our evaluations of the political process
thesis in general can be, even when applied to the very same movement.
Ultimately, I explain why this dominant paradigm for understanding the
emergence of social movements significantly fails to explain the emergence of Burma's pro-democracy movement.

If we begin with Lintner's specification of the movement's emergence—
that is, if we conceptualize the emergent period as ending with the initial events of the March Affairs—then three of the four variables from
our operational list of expanding political opportunities are irrelevant to
the movement's emergence. None of them (increasing popular access to
the political system; unstable elite alignments or competition; and the
presence of elite allies who encourage or facilitate protest) were present at the time of the March Affairs. Moreover, the one that, at least,
is relevant—"declining state repression against opponents"—is so for
exactly the opposite reason than the "expanding political opportunity"
thesis posits. The flip side (which is complementary, not opposite) to
the claim that declining state repression against opponents facilitates
movement emergence is that increasing state repression constrains movement emergence. However, Lintner's analysis offers no decisive support
for either claim.

Instead, his analysis suggests that, following the students' efforts to
have their grievances legally redressed by the People's Council, the state
responded by dismissing the grievances and by exercising increasing and
indiscriminate violence against the students and their ever widening
social base of sympathizers. This had the effect of facilitating the emergence of the movement. In short, increasing and indiscriminate violent
state repression (i.e., closing political opportunities, not expanding) contributed to the emergence of the movement.

This pattern finds ample support from state-centered analytical approaches to the question of how groups with a revolutionary agenda or
radical and high-risk strategic repertoire are able to attract broad popular

patronage.[17] Yet this pattern challenges the political process thesis. As Jeff Goodwin has pointed out, it suggests an alternative way in which state practices can play a role in constituting the formation of a radical social movement:

> Indiscriminate state violence against mobilized groups and oppositional figures is likely to reinforce the plausibility, justifiability, and (hence) diffusion of the idea that the state needs to be violently "smashed" and radically reorganized. . . . After all, a society in which aggrieved people are routinely denied an opportunity to redress perceived injustices, and even murdered on the mere suspicion of political disloyalty, is unlikely to be viewed as requiring a few minor reforms; those people are more likely to view such a society as in need of a fundamental reorganization.[18]

This state-centered explanation is not an insight that derives from political process theory. Rather, it reflects what Goodwin calls a "state constructionist" approach, which emphasizes not whether a state provides incentives or opportunities for preexisting networks of like-minded people to act, but instead how state action can "help to make cognitively plausible and morally justifiable certain sorts of collective grievances, emotions, identities, ideologies, and associational activities (but not others) in the first place."[19] In other words, Lintner's argument is that the state's indiscriminate, violent acts to repress the student's protest backfired, unintentionally fueling and further radicalizing the movement.[20]

When we extend the period of the pro-democracy movement's emergence to encompass the events of August 1988 (ending with, say, the formation of the SLORC and accompanying violent state repression of September),[21] then analysis of the state's role in constituting the radical orientation of the movement becomes more complex. Lintner argues that, during and after the Burmese Socialist Program Party's (BSPP) emergency congress in July, the political concessions offered by the state to pacify the public's growing dissatisfaction with the state's institutions and practices were perceived by movement supporters as "far too little, much too late."[22] Moreover, Ne Win, by suggesting a referendum on the issue of a one-party or multiparty system and then letting the congress overturn the proposal, not only made it possible for him to make a graceful exit from the scene and continue pulling the strings of power from behind it,[23] but also unintentionally provided a focus to the movement that it had not previously had.[24]

A political process theorist might interpret the political concessions following the emergency congress as a political opportunity, whereby increasing popular access to the political system facilitated (and thus accounts for) the subsequent movement mobilization. But Lintner's argument, once again, represents that of a state constructionist, not political process, approach. As Goodwin has argued, "A state that suddenly attempts to reform unpopular institutions *that it has long protected* may not be able to preempt thereby a revolutionary challenge; on the contrary, such reforms, or even attempted reforms, may be perceived as signs of the state's weakness and, accordingly, will simply serve to accelerate revolutionary mobilization."[25]

Not only does the state's role in constituting the movement become more complex when we elongate the emergent period of the movement, but another of the four variables—"presence of elite allies who encourage or facilitate protest"—then becomes important in Lintner's explanation of the emergence of the movement. The elite allies who emerged from within Burma following the statewide general strikes in August, as well as the presence of foreign elite allies, played a critical role before the Four Eights Affair. Indeed, as discussed later in this chapter, one foreign elite ally in particular, radio correspondent Christopher Gunness of the BBC, was unwittingly instrumental to the successful emergence of the statewide strikes.

Lintner argues that the appearance of former political leaders like Aung Gyi, U Nu, and Tin Oo, as well as new ones (particularly Aung San Suu Kyi), provided necessary focus, organization, coordination, and leadership for sustaining the movement. They did so by directly challenging the state for the first time with a proposal for institutionalizing their political inclusion by means of forming a "people's consultative committee," or interim government, until formal multiparty elections could be held to determine who should serve as the official political leaders of Burma. Lintner even argues that until the emergence of these elite allies, the statewide uprising had been "completely spontaneous" and had "lacked proper leadership."[26] Indeed, this seems to be an important refrain throughout his analysis.

Although Lintner and other analysts[27] have described the movement's emergence as "spontaneous," "unorganized," "having no clear focus," and "lacking in proper leadership and coordination,"[28] political process theorists would undoubtedly find ample evidence of organization within

Lintner's narrative of the events constituting the movement's emergence before the sudden appearance of these elite allies. For instance, Lintner tells us that "citizens committees," consisting of monks, community elders, and students, were formed as an alternative civil administration in every ward and township in Rangoon,[29] and "strike centers" were established in more than 200 of the 314 townships throughout Burma.[30] Local tea shops became the centers for their meetings and other antigovernment activities.[31] Students also built intricate networks among the four campuses of Rangoon University, the Institutes of Medicine, and even high schools, and sought out the advice of older former students who had participated in the antigovernment demonstrations of the mid-1970s.[32] They formed the All Burma Students' Union (ABSU), which not only had called for the first statewide general strike, but had already previously established an information department for producing leaflets and posters and conveying the student demands to the government; a social welfare department for collecting and distributing among students at campus rallies money, food, and water; an infirmary for administering first aid and stocking medicine (run by students who had gained experience with Burma's Red Cross); a protection department for collecting information on the movement of security forces and identifying government informers infiltrating their own ranks; and even a prison, inside one of the student hostels, where informers were interrogated and, in a few instances, judged guilty and killed.[33] The students also formed "underground cells" to organize antigovernment groups both inside and outside Rangoon.[34]

What Lintner seems to mean by claiming that the movement was spontaneous and lacking proper leadership, coordination, and organization up to this point is that there were no formal, hierarchical organizations driving it. Rather, the key to understanding this movement was to focus the analysis on the informal networks that coordinated the mobilization.

This is still true now, in 2010. Rather than mobilizing through formal organizations of civil society, many Burmese pro-democracy activists operate through informal social networks. These networks connect like-minded activists to one another through a complex web of personal relationships, small group interactions, meetings in private homes, and religious ritual. They are informal in the sense that they operate outside the juridical control of the state. As Quintan Wiktorowicz has pointed out:

The use of informal social networks in collective action is most often seen in less open political systems where overt protest and formal organizations risk harsh regime reprisals and activism is more subtle. Open and visible organizations represent public challenges to domination and are therefore targeted by political authorities and the state. Because formal organizations typically have a location, membership lists, and documents, they are vulnerable to repression. Under such circumstances, movements often instead mobilize through informal social networks, which are more impervious to state control because they embed collective action in everyday interactions.[35]

The democracy movement consisted of a large number of dispersed, locally and spontaneously formed protest groups before August 1988.[36] A state-centered approach that draws upon state-constructionist concepts rather than political-process concepts helps to account for ways in which the state's use of indiscriminate violence, as well as eventual concessions to students' demands, partially constituted the formation of the move-ment.[37] Yet we must rely on opportunities identifiable at a transnational level of analysis to account for the emergence of the next cycle of protest in which the movement coordinated a statewide general strike, which included the mobilization of Burma's Buddhist monks.

Movement activity is often shaped by networks of actors that stretch beyond the territorial boundaries of the state. If we focus solely on move-ment activity within the state's boundaries, or presume that the move-ment operates only within a state-delimited scope of action, then we will remain blinded to potentially crucial movement activity taking place outside the state that influences the activity under scrutiny and shapes interaction between the movement and the state.

Kurt Schock's political process analysis of Burma's pro-democracy movement serves as an instructive example of how this occurs. Schock compares the pro-democracy movements in Burma and the Philippines as "people power" movements, which he defines as "challenges to the policies or structures of authoritarian regimes that primarily incorporate methods of nonviolent action, such as protest demonstrations, acts of civil disobedience, and interventions."[38] In addition to exploring the dimensions of political opportunity (e.g., state repression, influential allies, divisions among the ruling elite, and freedom of the press and informa-tion flows) that facilitated the mobilization of people power in these states during the 1980s, Schock asks, "Why did the movement in the Philippines culminate in a regime change, while the movement in Burma did not?" By choosing to compare the movement in Burma with that in the Philippines, Schock is able to generate a common unit of analysis that distinguishes these movements as a type different from social movements in general—that is, as people power movements. As a result of this comparison, Schock finds that elite divisions and influential allies affect the mobilization and outcomes of these movements,[39] as predicted by the political opportunity framework of political process theory more generally.[40] This finding, suggests Schock, lends support for the political opportunity framework's capacity to account for the mobilization and outcomes of social movements in nondemocratic contexts.

Schock's sensitivity to this difference between the nondemocratic states he compares and the democratic states typically discussed in political process theory provides him a theoretical vantage point that allows him to detect a significant variable that research focused only on democratic states has largely taken for granted or treated as a constant condition: press freedoms and information flows. As Schock reports:

> This study suggests the important role that they [press freedoms and information flows] may have for social movement mobilization and outcomes. A freely operating press and the free flow of information are important mechanisms by which grievances become translated into action. Variations in these, like variations in the core dimensions of opportunity, should be related to the mobilization and outcomes of movements. The development of a substantial alternative press, the taking over of the state-run press, or the opening up of information flows should lower power discrepancies between challengers and the state and facilitate challenging movements.[41]

In Burma, Schock shows how the state's violent repression was mediated by bouts of information censorship. Using secondary historical accounts and a qualitative comparative method,[42] Schock, like Lintner, also finds evidence for the claim that the authoritarian military regime's violent state reaction in August 1988 initially facilitated the movement. Analyzed as a single variable, violent repression alone correlated with both the rise and decline of pro-democratic collective action. However, he also notes that the regime's renewed efforts at repression in mid-September of that year seem to correlate with a subsequent decline in the movement's collective action. Arguing for a "configurational analysis of political opportunities," Schock identifies a new variable of political opportunity structure that he asserts has particular importance for the analysis of nondemocratic states.

When Schock considered the mediating effect of press freedoms and information flows, he found that the period of decline in collective action occurred only when a heavy restriction on press freedoms and information flows combined with violent repression. He claims that the movement was in important ways facilitated by the temporary free flow of information made possible by the proliferation of local newspapers just before the emergence of the 8–8–88 Affair. He also shows a correlation between the subsequent state ban on such press freedoms and information flows beginning in September as part of the state's renewed campaign of repression and what he characterizes as the decline of an ultimately unsuccessful movement.

Shock's account, however, fails to account for the translocal coordination of the statewide 8–8–88 Affair, as well as the sustained transnational mobilization of the movement participants following this event. Even on his own terms, he does not account for the actions sustained by the movement in the wake of this repression, like the establishment of parallel institutions (e.g., strike centers and citizens' committees), including an illegal shadow government, which certainly may be characterized as qualities of a people power movement. Shock's analysis, by portraying the movement as a "people's power" movement, conflates one historical moment in the longer development of the movement with the life of the movement itself, leaving readers with the impression that the movement essentially came to an end in 1988, with the decline of domestic people power tactics.

Schock provides no acknowledgment suggesting that the pro-democracy movement survived this period. Yet the movement has continued both within and outside the state's territorial boundaries, albeit through the deployment of very different forms of collective action. In short, Shock's state-centered people power depiction of the pro-democracy movement that emerged in Burma in 1988 offers only limited insight for making sense of the sustained and subsequent transnational mobilization of movement participants following the Four Eights Affair. Appreciation for these dimensions of the movement's emergence begins with identifying opportunities that were created at a transnational level of analysis, through which the movement coordinated a statewide general strike that included the mobilization of the Buddhist monks in Burma.

Mobilizing the Monks among the Masses Translocally

On July 22, 1988, Christopher Gunness flew into Rangoon on a tourist visa.[43] Concealing his identity as a correspondent for the British Broadcasting Corporation's (BBC) Eastern (Radio) Service, he was sent to cover a reporting assignment on the Burma Program Socialist Party's (BSPP) emergency congress being held the next day. While many foreign audiences were pleasantly surprised by the outcome of the congress, local citizens understood clearly that the changes proposed by Ne Win were staged—another act in an overly long Burmese theater performance. Ne Win proposed both his resignation and a referendum for future multiparty democratic elections.[44] The party "permitted" Ne Win, the most powerful person in Burma, to step down, but overturned the proposal for multiparty elections. Appointed to the new post of president and chair of the BSPP was Sein Lwin, commander-in-chief of the dreaded *Lon Htein* (riot police) and most hated person in Burma. It was Sein Lwin who, in 1962 and again in March and June 1988, had ordered the shooting of student protestors. Ne Win had not resigned in any significant sense. He was reconsolidating power, pulling the strings of this military puppet show from above and behind the scenes.

Once again, state practices helped to constitute the formation of a radical movement. As a Western diplomat later explained:

> Up to then, the student movement and the sympathetic reaction of the masses was completely unfocused. It was in essence anti-government; protest against brutality, a frustrated reaction against the inane policies, the demonetization, the hopelessness of the students, the lack of any future. . . . Ne Win, unwittingly, provide[d] a focus by calling for a multiparty system, and from there on in, the student cry is for democracy.[45]

Gunness covered more than the emergency congress, however. And he too contributed—even more than he realized—to the focus and organization of the movement.

Through a string of local contacts, Gunness was secretly put in touch with the opposition. He recorded interviews with students who related their recent experiences from inside Insein Prison. Arrested for their participation in the protests of March and June, they were then tortured, beaten, and raped while in custody. Through another string of contacts, Gunness was able to interview an army officer who had just returned from the Karen front near the Thai border. Although the ethnic minority insurgent army officer reported of battle-torn morale and deprivation of rice and basic medicines, Gunness believed that his BBC Burmese transmissions were making a difference in morale. Burmese newspapers, television, and radio are completely state-controlled. Obtaining foreign publications at this time was almost impossible. The Burmese public relies largely on foreign radio broadcasts, especially the Burmese services of the BBC and, to a lesser extent, Voice of America and Radio Free Asia. All announcers for the BBC's service, however, were Burmese citizens by law, with families who might be put at risk were "controversial" domestic coverage to have been broadcast. Immediately popular, Gunness's reports were considered the only reliable source of news in the country:[46]

> Nothing of this was actually new to the Burmese. Everybody knew it. But to hear it over the radio, on the BBC, related by Burmese people themselves was an entirely different matter. For the first time, people spoke up in public. I think that had a tremendous impact on the morale of the Burmese people.[47]

One thing that most people, at least outside Rangoon, did not already know, however, was that the *ba ka tha*, the Burmese abbreviation for the underground All Burma Students' Union (ABSU), was trying to plan a statewide general strike. And one of Gunness's interviewees was farsighted enough to announce this, along with the launching date "8–8–88." The message spread to radio listeners throughout the country, and it was met with cheers and jubilation: "Let's rise against the government!"[48]

In Rangoon, this broadcast generated local mobilizing. The ABSU began distributing leaflets calling for a general strike and signed "Min Ko Naing"—a highly symbolic nom de guerre and term with a double meaning: "the Conqueror of Kings" as well as "I shall defeat you."[49] A cartoonist for a popular monthly magazine had also penned an image of the Statue of Liberty breaking a chain that resembled a series of four eights.[50]

But the date itself was of symbolic significance. First, as Lintner has observed, "there was widespread awareness that this [date] also marked the 50th anniversary of the mighty 1300 Movement of 1938, the beginning of the end of British rule in Burma."[51] Burmese activist in exile and scholar Mya Maung has provided a second popular association with

Figure 5. A wood and cardboard model (approximately 2 meters in diameter) of the interior of Insein Prison, which holds many political prisoners and is the most feared of Burma's prisons. Former political prisoners built the model from memory after their release from seven- to fourteen-year sentences. Photograph by author, 2009.

another date of historical significance. The year 888 of the Burmese Era (or A.D. 1526 on the Western calendar), "Three Eights," marked the beginning of the Second Ava Dynasty established by the ethnic minority Shan ruler, Tho Han Bwar: "The lyrical Burmese interpretation of the year 888, Mya Maung tells us, is 'Ga-ngel Thoan-gu Oat Shit-htu' signifying the dawning of an era of death and destruction."[52] Among the many atrocities committed by Tho Han Bwar over his next twenty-five years of rule, the one deemed most atrocious for its sacrilege, was the slaughtering of sacred Buddhist monks, whom he considered an imminent threat to his political throne. As Mya Maung explains:

> The date August 8, 1988 (8/8/88), "four eights," [by the Western calendar] . . . has a historical affinity to the year 888, "three eights" [by the Burmese calendar]—the beginning of an era of ruthless suppression, death, and destruction in the chronicles of the Burmese kings.[53]

On August 2, the first of Gunness's reports was broadcast on the BBC.[54] That same day, the monks joined the students outside Shwedagon Pagoda to call for a general strike.[55]

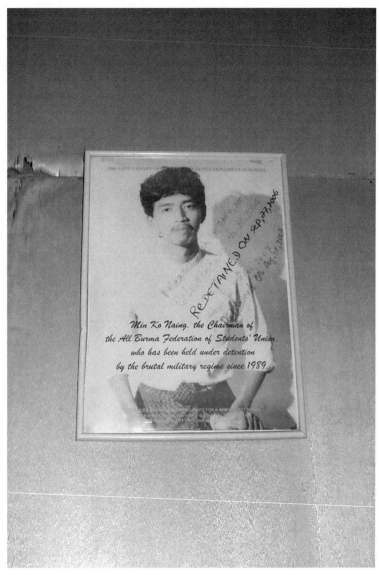

Figure 6. This framed poster of Min Ko Naing, student leader of the '88 generation, was printed to honor him on the tenth anniversary of the 1988 student movement in Burma. In different-colored markers, someone has handwritten across the poster the dates of the multiple times that the ruling military regime released and redetained him for his continued political activism. Photograph by author, 2009.

Alison Brysk argues that "under some conditions, symbolic politics becomes more than a framing device and produces a distinct logic and effects." Symbolic politics, she explains, "involves the maintenance or transformation of a power relationship through the communication of normative and affective representations," and "produces collective action through the narrative restructuring, interpretive resonance, and projection of affective information."[56] Thus, to explain how and when mobilization (as well as demobilization) occurs, we must be able to examine not just the strategy, but the cultural content and process by which it is interpreted, if we are to distinguish whether culture in the form of strategy, or culture in the form of symbols themselves, have made a difference.

This, of course, assumes that interests are culturally constructed and not fixed needs. Symbolic politics need not be reduced to a framing and signaling device for interests that coordinates and socializes interest-based mobilization, as some political process theorists have suggested.[57] Rather, interests are culturally mediated, for example, as deeply subsumed *stories* about needs, and actors mobilized by symbols can create new structures that reveal, deconstruct, and re-present narratives about interests and identities. As Alberto Melucci writes, "The solidarity [of movements in complex societies] is cultural in character and is located in the terrain of symbolic production in everyday life."[58]

Yet scholars of neither the political process nor transnational approaches have paid adequate analytical attention to how mobilizing networks are *created* by movement organizers and operate at multiple spatial levels. Rather, like political process theorists, scholars bringing a transnational approach to the study of social movements tend to view mobilizing networks as *preexisting*. They tend to identify preexisting mobilizing networks and then analyze how their members are activated or mobilized to participate in collective action. Rarely do they provide examples of how organizers create a mobilizing structure or network. The result has been, at least for political process theorists and those who look to their models of collective action for guidance in interpreting their own research, that mobilizing structures (preexisting or created) are presumed to be necessary to explain collective action.

Yet we cannot assume that personal networks are more apt to influence movement mobilization than culture. Nor should we think that we have to choose between networks and culture. Networks are always culturally constituted and amount to little (as tools for researchers) without the ideas and affective bonds that keep them together.[59] In fact, all social action in which we engage is embedded in networks, which are differentially enacted, simultaneously facilitating and constraining us in all that we do.

This, of course, is different from suggesting that all social action is embedded in *mobilizing* networks. Focusing on the role that symbolic politics or, more generally conceived, cultural persuasion, plays in mobilizing collective action provides a strategic dimension to our analysis that, unlike process theorists' framing devices, can be analytically distinguished from other aspects of culture. Combined with attention to how social networks also are culturally constituted, we can strengthen our analyses of how movements emerge.

For example, one might argue that the mobilization of the monks in Rangoon can be explained more parsimoniously, without resorting to an analysis of the symbolic politics encoded in the radio broadcast, by simply realizing that the monks were a part of the same movement of resistance as the students and others in Rangoon—a movement based on shared lived experience under the violent repression of the military and living in the same city where they undoubtedly networked with organized, mobilizing students. In short, the broadcast could as easily be seen as simply a signaling device activating preexisting, local mobilizing networks. Why bother analyzing the symbolic content of the frame? Is not the call to strike—aside from the symbol "8–8–88"—enough to explain the monks joining the movement?

Such an explanation, however, cannot account for why the monks in Rangoon joined the movement when they did. Most of Rangoon had already been mobilizing weeks before, not even knowing the date that the rumored strike was to take place. The radio broadcast, as a signaling device, may account for the timing of participants outside Rangoon who were for the first time receiving word of the plan for a statewide strike. But it does not account for why the monks in Rangoon waited until after the broadcast, and on the very day of the broadcast, to demonstrate their support.

The Buddhist monks were harder to mobilize than the other students and workers. In the 1960s, the *sangha* (monkhood) successfully resisted the state's efforts to register monks as a method of attaining control over the Buddhist monkhood.[60] Subsequent attempts by the Ne Win regime to exert control over the *sangha* had been relatively ineffective until May 1980, when the relationship between the state and the sangha was fundamentally altered. The state sponsored the First Congregation of the *Sasana*, which established rules for the registration of all monks and for the removal of monks who engaged in political activities.[61] This meeting, along with a second congregational meeting in 1985, led to much greater control over the Buddhist monkhood by its older and conservative leadership and by the state.[62]

Yet during the general strike of 8–8–88, columns of hundreds of Buddhist monks carried their alms bowls upside down, a symbol that the entire nation was on strike.[63] Approximately 80 percent of the 120,000 Buddhist monks supported the people power movement.[64] Nevertheless, Schock contends that

> while a significant segment of the *sangha* supported and participated in the people power movement, the state's control over the *sangha*, the leaderships' refusal to oppose the regime, and disapprobation of dissident monks, and the state's willingness to repress the dissident monks suggests that the *sangha* was not an influential ally to the people power movement in Burma.[65]

Nevertheless, the participation of the monks in the Four Eights Affair was crucial to its emergence. The monks' eventual participation added significant momentum to the movement. Despite the fact that they subsequently created important mobilizing structures of their own, existing studies of the movement have not explained how and when they were mobilized. The analysis of symbolic politics helps us to explain why they participated *when* they did and *without* forsaking their Buddhist allegiances. The story of the martyred monks, who at that time served as protectors of their community, and the subsequent reign of terror suffered by the community after the slaughter of the Buddhist monks, may well have transformed their conception of what they should do in response to the situation *as faithful Buddhist monks*.

What I have presented in terms of the ABSU's creatively transforming the presence of the BBC into an opportunity for broadcasting its symbolic politics is not a straightforward case of transnational *organizing* from below. Rather, in this case, local activists creatively seized temporary, informal access to a transnational information network that was introduced from above by transnational actors (i.e., a foreign correspondent serving as a local link embedded within the transnational communication network of the BBC) with intentions having little to do with spurring an uprising. In doing so, these local activists created their own temporary mobilizing network capable of linking multiple, but previously uncoordinated, local mobilizing structures throughout the state for the purpose of organizing a statewide and state-centered pro-democracy movement. Analysis of the role played by symbolic politics[66] and temporary access to a transnational radio communication network in mobilizing the Buddhist monks, as well as previously uncoordinated local mobilizing structures throughout Burma for the purpose of organizing a statewide and state-centered social movement, helps us to better understand the translocal coordination, and thus the emergence, of the 8–8–88 Affair. Yet at the same time, an unintended consequence of this state-centered strategic action was its transnational impact on a previous generation of Burmese in exile, who had been fleeing the country since the initial military coup of 1962. Information received by way of the transnational communication network about the state's recent brutally repressive actions helped to mobilize their support and inspired them to continue mobilizing outside of Burma in support of this pro-democracy movement.

The monks were simultaneously embedded in multiple networks, which were culturally constituted in different ways—some of which facilitated mobilization and others of which served a demobilizing function. Political process theorists, using the concept of *mobilizing structure*, have paid inadequate attention to the multiple embeddedness that characterizes almost everyone's life. They also have tended to ignore *how* certain mobilizing structures serve to *demobilize* people and virtually dismiss analysis of the nonstrategic cultural dimensions of such structures or networks.[67]

Significant to explaining the mobilization of the monks was not just the cultural dimension of the networks in which they were embedded, but the forms of culture flowing through these networks. When political process theorists attribute any importance to the role political symbols play in mobilization,[68] they treat the symbol primarily as a *signaling device*, drawn from cultural frames of meaning. Yet political process theorists' concept of cultural framing conflates strategy with other aspects of noninstrumental culture (such as symbols) in a way that makes it impossible to analytically distinguish the independent effects of either.[69] Thus, they cannot explain how or when the monks were mobilized.

Drawing upon an approach to the study of political symbols that allows for the analysis of symbols as more than a signaling device permits us to examine the ways in which symbols can exercise their own influence on the emergence of a movement and, in the case of the 8–8–88 Affair, demonstrates how one political symbol in particular had an independent effect on the mobilization of the monks. As Goodwin and Jasper (1997) have pointed out, certain types of movement mobilization may not require mobilizing structures: "Leafleting and television ads [or we might substitute, in light of the examples in Burma's pro-democracy movement, radio broadcasts] can, in some cases, replace organizational links and personal ties" not only to activate preexisting mobilizing structures, but also to create new ones, through the communication of normative and affective representations.[70]

Rethinking the Transnational Political Context

What is more germane to the *limits* of a state-centered understanding of the relationship between the pro-democracy movement in Burma and transnational networks is the way in which Schock's comparison gives meaning to the variables of political opportunity that he claims explain the movement's failure in the case of Burma. Elite divisions and international allies were not present in the case of Burma; rather, these were present only in the Philippines. Because Schock sees both of these movement phenomena as being cases of the same type, and because the people power movement in the Philippines successfully effected a change in the state regime, while the people power movement in Burma did not, he understands the absence of elite divisions and influential allies in Burma to be a *cause* of the pro-democracy movement's failure in Burma.

The conclusion that Schock draws from this tight comparison becomes problematic when we extend the time frame of Burma's pro-democracy movement beyond 1994. Burma's pro-democracy movement since then has forged many influential allies. At the least, its pro-democracy movement is embedded in many transnational networks whose goal is to transform the military state regime. Nevertheless, there has still been no regime change in the sense that Schock intends when defining movement success. The regime itself is still nondemocratic. But one would be hard-pressed from a transnational perspective to defend the claim that the movement today is operating in a nondemocratic context.

As Schock himself comments, based on his evidence from the case of the Philippines, where he identifies most of the influential allies to the movement as nongovernmental organizations:[71] "Given the closed nature of non-democratic regimes, influential allies to challenging movements are more likely to be transnational actors or foreign [democratic] states."[72]

Recent studies of transnational networks reveal how both nongovernmental organizations (nationally and internationally constituted) and international governmental organizations intervene on behalf of challenger movements seeking inclusion in the domestic polity.[73] States that are highly dependent politically and economically are particularly vulnerable to demands for greater institutional access when transnational networks secure the assistance of those external actors upon whom these states are most dependent. As such, the ability of transnational networks to manipulate various intersecting dependencies presents a potent form of political opportunity transcending territorial boundaries.

Schock is sympathetic to the charge that political process theory has given too little attention to how contexts beyond the state influence movements. "The political opportunity literature," he writes, "has ignored or under-theorized the international context of political opportunities."[74] Although he considers the role that transnational actors contribute to the divergent outcomes in these cases, there is still a state-centered bias, or what Ulrich Beck calls "methodological nationalism"[75]—operating within his analytical framework that foreshortens his exploration of their impact on Burma's pro-democracy movement. Schock measures the influence of these transnational actors primarily in terms of their geographical location in relation to the state's territorial boundaries—that is, whether such actors were physically situated within or outside the state. As an indicator of Burma's isolation and lack of transnational ties relative to the Philippines, he compares the number of social movement organizations listed in the Human Rights Index (1994). Schock reports that the index listed 28 human rights social movement organizations for Burma and 209 such organizations for the Philippines. He further notes that all of these organizations were located outside of Burma, whereas only 24 of those associating themselves with the Philippines movement were located outside the country.

Based on this finding, Schock concludes that transnational actors were isolated from the movement within Burma.[76]

However, the mere presence or absence of transnational actors within a state's boundaries is not a dependable indicator of their impact on a domestic movement. Even when researchers are attuned to the presence or absence of transnational actors and their impact on the movement, they may fail to examine the transnational *networks* impacting the context in which the movement is sustained or constrained. The point is that, by analytically confining the relational setting of the pro-democracy movement to the territorial boundaries of the state, and then examining that setting for the presence of actors that can be categorically ascribed a *transnational* identity based on their typical spatial organization of operations (e.g., Amnesty International), Schock precludes from his analysis the possibility of examining the presence of transnational *agency* that the pro-democracy movement may exercise as a result of being embedded in transnational networks linking them to actors situated physically outside the territorial boundaries of the state.

Thinking about the social structures connecting actors as networks allows us to avoid treating structures as black boxes and to disaggregate structures into their constituent elements of actors and relations. Of course, many of these actors, then, may be embedded in relations that link them to actors beyond the state's boundaries. Schock knows this. In fact, he writes, "non-governmental organizations promoting the pro-democracy movement in Burma subsequently emerged, but they were located outside of Burma, mostly in Thailand, the United States, and Europe, and their *links* to the movement within Burma were weak."[77] But he seems to assume that the strength of these transnational network ties would be strengthened by the institutional presence (i.e., presence within Burma) of these nongovernmental organizations (NGOs). Embedded in this assumption is the bias that proximity correlates with the strength of the network ties. Yet as urban sociologists have long taught us, one cannot measure the strength of a relationship between actors based on physical proximity per se.[78]

Today, in small villages of Thailand located along the Burmese border, there are many NGOs that serve Burmese refugees and receive regular visits from messengers smuggling information from Burmese rebel groups. The ties between these Thai NGOs and people living in Burma are strong. There are also NGOs located in the capital city of Rangoon

(Yangon) that are hardly known, much less visited, by people living in this city. In fact, although their institutional influence is highly circumscribed, the military government promotes their presence largely so that they may serve as a token show of democratic progress for foreign officials who may choose to engage Burmese officials on the matter.

Moreover, if there were a strong, positive relationship between NGOs and the pro-democracy movement (as I show in chapter 3 there has been), we cannot simply assume that such a relationship benefits the pro-democracy movement in Burma. Although some analysts assert that NGOs—particularly the subsets of NGOs we call international nongovernmental organizations (INGOs) and transnational social movement organizations (TSMOs)—are important new political actors who make significant contributions to political life and political change,[79] some observers disagree about the kind of impact that NGOs can have on governments. Whether focusing on the transformational impact of NGOs on political structures or processes,[80] or the ability of NGOs to influence legislation of public policy,[81] no consistent generalization has emerged. NGOs do not always successfully pressure local elites or local governments.[82] There is no reason to presume that NGOs located within the territorial jurisdiction controlled by Burma's military elite would be able to exert greater influence over the political process for democratic change than if they were located outside of it.

NGOs vary greatly in terms of their ideological agendas. As William Fisher writes, "There is no simple or consistent story of good NGOs confronting evil governments."[83] NGOs from liberal democratic states may serve to challenge the human rights practices of a state like Burma, but this does not mean that they will necessarily support an indigenous pro-democracy movement.[84] The policies that they promote are as likely to maintain the status quo as to change it.[85]

As seen from within Burma during its first two years, it is understandable that some observers would depict this pro-democracy movement as a *failed* people power movement, compared to the one that toppled Ferdinand Marcos's regime in the Philippines during the mid-1980s. Along similar lines, one might also compare the more recent people power movement in Serbia during September 2000, where dictator Slobodan Milošević's refusal to bow to democratic electoral defeat was countered by relatively peaceful mass public protest, resulting in his ouster and a new state regime.

However, it is one thing to assess the effectiveness of people power tactics in Burma's struggle to institutionalize democratic reform; it is quite another to reduce Burma's pro-democracy movement to the people power tactics that it deployed during the course of its emergence and then declare the movement itself a failure. In other words, one might argue that Schock's comparison was meant to apply only to a particular phase of the pro-democracy movement—one in which its collective action was channeled more by the kind of nonviolent, large-scale, mass protest that was exhibited in 1988, but which, at best, has reemerged only periodically on a much smaller scale. The pro-democracy movement may be no longer well characterized as a people power movement (the focus of Schock's concern), but then we should also re-identify this pro-democracy movement. It is not a failed people power movement. It is a pro-democracy movement still in progress for which people power tactics have been inadequate to depose the military regime.

In fact, we do not know if the people power tactics used in the Philippines would have been successful if the movement had not been embedded within the transnational networks that it was. Perhaps it is the agency of transnational networks in particular, rather than (national) people power in general, that might serve as a more fruitful unit of comparative analysis. If we were to use Schock's same indicator for measuring the impact of transnational networks on Burma's pro-democracy movement since 1994, we would continue to find a weak presence of transnational actors in Burma. What is needed is a different optic through which to identify the transnational agency operating within (and beyond) Burma.

Weaving a Transnational Free Burma Movement

Appreciation for this movement's viability begins with understanding that this initially nation-centered movement has been transformed significantly since 1988 to become a transnational movement. The movement's hope, and quite possibly its fate, has become woven into the transnational web of relations that its participants have been spinning for more than two decades. I point to three key developments that fostered the transnationalization of this movement: (1) transnational networks of solidarity; (2) increasing capacity to communicate with other activists within and outside Burma; and (3) transnationalist discourses deployed in transnational legal campaigns.

Since 1994, Burma's pro-democracy activists, many living in exile, have created transnational networks linking grassroots movements in both the East and West, between and within the global North and global South. These grassroots movements have organized transnational campaigns forged through alliances with local state and municipal governments in the United States and Australia, as well as nonstate actors, including regional governing bodies like the European Union, nongovernmental organizations (NGOs) throughout East and Southeast Asia, international governmental organizations (INGOs), and voluntary associations on every continent and in more than thirty countries across North and South America, Europe, Asia, Africa, and Oceania. Connections with preexisting transnational advocacy networks defending issues like human rights, women's rights, the natural environment, labor rights, indigenous peoples' rights, and socially responsible corporate investment have also sustained the movement.

Although Aung San Suu Kyi has been under virtual house arrest since the 1990 elections,[86] other leading NLD party officials elected in 1990 have formed a government in exile: the National Coalition Government of the Union of Burma (NCGUB), which has offices in Bangkok, Delhi, and Washington, D.C. Operating as an oppositional shadow government to the military's official party, the State Peace and Development Council (SPDC), the NCGUB passes alternative legislation and constitutional proposals and lobbies foreign states and INGOs to disregard the military's claims to legitimate state power. The NCGUB also garners and distributes philanthropic contributions from international sources to underground NGOs based in Southeast Asia that are promoting democracy in Burma. In the course of these activities, the NCGUB has come to serve as a major node in a transnational network of emergency information exchange on the military's attacks on ethnic minority villages and separatist groups located along Burma's frontier borders.[87]

We should not ignore the significance of the new communication networks, in particular the Internet. The Internet helped pro-democracy activists increase their capacity to communicate with other activists within and outside Burma and to create a worldwide audience to witness the pro-democracy movement's struggle. By 1995, these refugees began using the Internet to find fellow exiles from Burma and to organize an Internet-

Figure 7. Members of the National Coalition Government of the Union of Burma (a.k.a. Burma's government-in-exile) posing for a group photograph in front of an original slab of the Berlin Wall, located in Washington, DC. Photograph by Bonnie Jean Alford, 2003. Courtesy of U.S. Campaign for Burma.

based transnational information network called the Free Burma Coalition (FBC).[88] Using the Internet, the FBC built alliances with grassroots activists and transnational advocacy networks within and between more than two dozen countries throughout the world. The Myanmar military outlawed the civilian use of the Internet and nonlicensed computers (under penalty of prison sentences ranging from seven to fifteen years), and it banned foreign travelers from bringing laptops or software into the country. Nevertheless, pro-democracy activists established multiple tactics for clandestinely getting timely information to the borders, where NGOs (both registered and unregistered) immediately sent the information by Internet to the FBC's thousands of subscribers around the world. Although it no longer serves this function, the FBC, in the 1990s, became a loosely coordinated umbrella network for a wide variety of movement organizations promoting democracy and human rights in Burma.

Burmese refugees who joined the insurgents camped along the Thai border in 1988 initially relied upon communications networks that had been long established. To send messages in to and out of cities in central

Burma required up to two months and entailed transmitting messages via radio through a series of enemy encampments to the nearest ally, who would then organize the delivery by foot messenger to the intended destination.

By 1997, new and affordable communications technologies like FM wavelength walkie-talkies and shortwave radios, satellite imagery, and the transmission of news from around the world to the Thai border via the Internet (using Thailand's telephone system and computers and servers owned by various Thai-based NGOs) had not only shortened the time that it took to relay information, but also increased the volume and accuracy of that information. In addition, the new technology made the process of long-distance communication within Burma relatively less risky because foot messengers were used less frequently. The number of relay exchanges required to send the same message to a city in central Burma has been significantly reduced.

Of course, technology does not belong to the activists alone. The Myanmar government has also devoted significant resources since 1994 to develop its capacity to monitor activists *outside* of Burma and to contend with the transnational ties that have been forged by the country's pro-democracy and human rights activists. This reflects the Myanmar government's understanding and concern for the role that transnational networks of solidarity play in sustaining the movement that is challenging its rule. The Myanmar government has become increasingly suspicious of foreign activists who are working outside the country targeting the regime and who attempt to exchange information via all forms of communication and coordinate collective political action with citizens living inside Burma. The Myanmar government has taken significant action to monitor postal mail, all types of phone communication, fax machine correspondence, e-mail, Internet chat room discussion, Web sites, and face-to-face communication with Burmese citizens who are traveling to other countries or who are in exile.

From 1990 to 1994, something more significant, beyond the process of creating transnational solidarity and an enhanced capacity to communicate with activists inside and outside Burma, influenced the pro-democracy movement to alter its strategy and changed its character. It was during this period that the pro-democracy movement's leaders came to realize that the Myanmar state was not its only obstacle to domestic political change. Transnational corporations and foreign states' invest-

banks, the lifting of price controls on rice and other staples, and the privatization of its state-managed natural resources (teak, jade, and oil). Bertil Lintner derided the changes as the "Burmese way to capitalism." While foreign states remained more reticent to publicly ally themselves closely with the Myanmar state after 1988, many of them, including the United States, helped to sustain the very government that they denounced. The Myanmar military became the target of two different globalization discourses deployed by foreign actors. One of these discourses promoted free trade and the other proclaimed support for human rights. The resulting discursive contention yielded two polarized international foreign policy positions: (1) "constructive engagement," which (like the concept of *doux commerce*) prescribes international economic trade and development as the surest route to political stability and democratization; and (2) multilateral "economic sanctions" implemented through the coordinated action of individual nation-states against rogue-state challengers to the international community's new global order.

In 1997, the Association of Southeast Asian Nations (ASEAN) inducted Myanmar as a member of its economic regional trade association. But this was not an affirmation of Myanmar's domestic policies. Rather, it reflected a deliberate foreign policy choice that is based on the same political argument for international trade that the United States' constitutional framers embraced. The eighteenth-century concept of *doux commerce* (gentle commerce) was a phrase that the framers used to express the idea that nation-states engaged in trade with each other are more likely to smooth over their conflicting political differences.[89] The idea was based on the belief that (rational) economic interests could be used to tame or "counterpose" (irrational) political passions. While the general idea of counterposing passions and interests within and between individuals was common at this time, applying the idea to collective actors, particularly those as complex as nation-states, was novel. The neoliberal globalization discourse echoes this classical political argument for free trade, and it continues to influence foreign policy choices far beyond the confines of the United States. In short, ASEAN inducted Myanmar as a member of its economic regional trade association not simply to enhance its economic interests, but also in the belief that this international trade relationship would influence Myanmar's action in ways that would resolve the domestic conflict and transnational spillover effects that it had been producing over the previous decade.

Also in 1997, President Bill Clinton enacted an executive order that banned all new U.S. investment in Myanmar. This approach toward Myanmar would seem to be one that is in direct opposition to the one that ASEAN adopted. Yet these federal economic sanctions were enacted to trump much tougher sanctions (or selective purchasing laws) that local governments across the United States had legislated. Unlike the tougher local sanctions, the U.S. sanctions against Burma permitted U.S. corporations that already were partnering with the Myanmar state to continue their operations. This included one of the largest business partnerships with Myanmar at the time: the construction of a $1.2 billion Yadana natural gas pipeline project with Unocal Oil Corporation (now Chevron).

The transnational networks of actors supporting each of these foreign policies all proclaimed their support for human rights (and concern for Myanmar's human rights practices) while simultaneously jockeying for favorable economic partnerships and trade relations with the Myanmar military ruling the state. Moreover, these foreign policy discourses were mediated by a cultural structure of neoliberalism that channeled state power toward positions of discursive stalemate and toward practices that sustained the structures of military repression in Burma. That is, although these two foreign policies have become polarized as competing discourses at the international level, taken together they effectively channel discursive contention within a framework of conceptual distinctions that reinscribes the hegemonic power of the globalization discourse. In practice, however, neither of these international foreign policies curbed, nor were they intended to curb, transnational oil and gas corporations from seeking highly profitable new investment and development opportunities in Burma. For these corporations, Burma represented a crucial link to future natural gas markets in Southeast Asia and, most important, China.

Neoliberal Dimensions of the Globalization Discourse on Constructive Engagement

The constructive engagement discourse depicts a world of international relations in which the most effective way for foreign states to influence the internal political conduct of any "errant," "rogue," or "pariah" state is by postponing discussions of political reform while maintaining or pursuing economic relations in the present. It prescribes international economic trade and development as the surest route to political democratization and the institutionalization of human rights, while denouncing such state practices as economic isolation and political ostracizing as counterproductive and ultimately more harmful to the citizens than to the rulers of the states that they target. Note that at the root of this prescription is a neoliberal axiom: markets, when left to operate unhindered by states, will maximize economic efficiency and thus produce social order and political stability; but state intervention will distort the self-regulating mechanism of the market, which in turn will produce greater economic inefficiency and thus social disorder and political instability. Thus, the policy of constructive engagement combines discursive elements of human rights and free trade to produce a distinct globalization discourse of its own.

The constructive engagement discourse depicts the nation-state as having no role in the present unfolding process of globalization. It provides no conceptual room for the role that states play in shaping the global economic relations and actors that it foregrounds. In short, it implies that states do not shape, but rather are shaped by, globalization. Some variations of the constructive engagement position admittedly also project a future stage in the course of the international relationship, when increased economic interaction with Myanmar will foster opportunities for foreign states to strategically introduce benchmarks of political reform that the target state must meet to sustain gradually improving levels of international support. However, the supporters of constructive engagement have never raised formally the issue of benchmarks for reforming the Myanmar military's state practices.

The principal promoters of the constructive engagement policy toward Burma have been the member states of ASEAN, along with the additional support of China and Japan, as well as transnational corporations with operations in the East and West. In fact, the Myanmar military itself has publicly supported constructive engagement, explaining that the policy respects the distinction between economic trade and internal political affairs, and understands that Burma is still a poor developing nation that cannot yet afford such Western luxuries as human rights.

Neoliberal Dimensions of the Transnational Discourse on Economic Sanctions

In contrast, the economic sanctions discourse suggests a very different approach in the context of foreign policy toward Burma. It insists that any wealth generated within Burma through foreign investment will simply be appropriated by the Myanmar military state for its ongoing campaign to repress both rebel and reform movements within its borders. This discourse entertains a variety of potential ways in which one or more foreign nation-states might curtail its aid, investment, or trade with Burma. Yet it generally sees such action as a useful alternative to military action once all other diplomatic channels prove unable to alter the target state's practices to comply with certain norms—in this case, human rights—that the senders deem important.

The supporters of constructive engagement have observed that the main supporters of economic sanctions toward Myanmar are Western states. They have suggested that such a position reflects a neocolonialist disregard for the national sovereignty of Myanmar. But the economic sanctions discourse, in this context, denies that national sovereignty is relevant to this situation. It also denies that such an act represents a violation of Myanmar's national sovereignty. This last assertion rests on three points: (1) the military's egregious and ongoing human rights violations represent practices that fall within the jurisdiction of international law and, therefore, trump its defensive claims to state sovereignty; (2) the majority of the people in Burma have already expressed their national will through democratic elections, calling into question the military's legitimate claim to represent either the sovereign will of the people or the state; and (3) the elected party leaders, although denied access to their political seats by the military, have repeatedly expressed their support for the sanctions.

Notice that underlying this argument is a globalization discourse of human rights, which posits certain global norms that render powerless any contrary norms institutionalized within a single nation-state. The globalization discourse on human rights discourse, in other words, depicts state sovereignty as an institution that is increasingly weakened by, and secondary in authority to, normative practices of governance in a globalizing world.

Despite their discursive differences, each foreign policy has been culturally refracted through a common broader cultural structure of neoliberalism. This common cultural dimension shaping both foreign policies has facilitated the Myanmar military's efforts to build trade relations with transnational corporations and foreign states in Southeast Asia and has simultaneously constrained the efforts of foreign states in the West to effectively intervene in the formation of such trade relations.

Yet in emphasizing the diminishing capacity of states to regulate global flows of capital, information, and labor, the constructive engagement discourse precludes from discussion a host of other ways that states contribute to such global flows. It ignores, for example, how states are not mere regulators of markets but themselves also participate as economic entities within markets. It ignores how states confer legal rights of existence to certain transnational market participants through corporate charters. It ignores how states create transnational economic partnerships with existing corporations. States do a great deal to construct the kind of economic engagement that the policy of "constructive engagement" promotes, even though this policy is grounded in the neoliberal assumption that they do not.

The emphasis on human rights is not necessarily a neoliberal idea. Nevertheless, this globalization discourse on human rights embedded in the economic sanctions position has been effectively mediated by another (neoliberal) globalization discourse on free trade. Although this economic sanctions discourse posits, on the basis of international law, that human rights concerns trump concerns of the violating state's sovereignty, such sanctions are also portrayed as destined to fail if they are not organized "multilaterally." That is, if a single nation-state attempts to unilaterally invoke economic sanctions against another state in the name of international law, then, *particularly in a global economy*, the target state will likely be able to find alternative sources of support or trade within other foreign states. Thus, according to this discourse, the foreign "sending" state not only may fail to influence its "target" state through sanctions, but also may lose to other ready and willing state competitors a valuable economic opportunity as well.

The logic of such a decision is shaped by a cultural structure of neoliberalism. In short, states claiming to adhere to economic sanctions *in principal*, motivated by a concern for human rights, chose not to exercise sanctions *in practice*. The reasoning for not invoking sanctions was that a single nation-state does not have the power to hinder Myanmar's capacity to attract trade and investment and accumulate wealth in a market of freely trading market participants. This globalization discourse represents states that wish to impose sanctions in the name of human rights as having only two choices for responding to Myanmar: either by imposing morally principled, yet inevitably impotent, national sanctions or by competing with foreign states as market participants for favorable trade relations and thereby potentially creating conditions in which foreign states might effectively exert influence on the Myanmar state toward democratic reform. Thus, although supporters of the economic sanctions position publicly oppose the constructive engagement position that human rights will prevail in Burma as unrestricted trade with and economic investment in Myanmar increases, in practice they have chosen to sustain significant trade with and investment in Myanmar.

This foreign policy, in practice, suggests that it does not matter whether trade with Myanmar actually stems human rights abuses. What is important for foreign policy is that when this (neoliberal) idea—that trade with Myanmar stems human rights abuses—is shared by a significant number of states, then this idea represents a sound basis for trading with Myanmar. In this sense, neoliberalism shapes the very perception of what is practical and thus undermines the alternative foreign policy practices of states in situations where they may possess the power to challenge this idea. This reasoning prevented any state from initiating unilateral sanctions for nearly a decade. In practice, these two discourses became institutionalized as foreign policies that protected and legitimated trade relations with the Myanmar state. At the same time, neither foreign policy seriously pressured Myanmar's military toward democratic political reform. These foreign policies, therefore, have generated constraints for the pro-democracy movement while sustaining the structure of military repression in Burma.

The Free Burma movement has been developing a transnationalist discourse on corporate accountability that challenges these dominant foreign policies as well as the neoliberal logics informing them. It is a discourse that moves beyond holding accountable the Myanmar state for its human rights abuses, economic mismanagement, and political illegitimacy. It articulates an alternative understanding of the relationship between political process in Burma and global market dynamics and depicts a variety of ways in which actors outside of Burma help to sustain the Myanmar state's repression of democratic change. Exactly how the movement does this is the subject of the rest of this book.

Part II

Transnational Legal Action and Corporate Accountability in Three Types of Campaigns

3

Free Burma Laws:
Legislating Transnational Sanctions

The Massachusetts Burma law, passed in 1996, restricted the Commonwealth's own ability, including the ability of all of its agencies and authorities, to purchase goods or services from any individuals or corporations that were engaged in business with Burma.[1] The strategy behind this law was to use Massachusetts's purchasing power in a transnational marketplace, where it procures contracts amounting then to roughly $2 billion in goods and services annually,[2] to force domestic and foreign corporations to make a choice: *either* seek profitable contracts with the Commonwealth of Massachusetts *or* pursue contracts with the military state in Burma.

Massachusetts did not initiate these sanctions unilaterally. It took action as part of a broader selective purchasing law campaign that, in addition to this regional state, was successful at getting nearly thirty municipal governments across the United States to legislate and enact Free Burma laws. These laws successfully influenced corporations to abandon their business operations in Burma.

This case highlights legislative discursive contention over purchasing decisions by municipal governments and regional states over how they spend their money as market participants procuring contracts from transnational corporations. It illustrates how transnational legal space mediates the process through which global markets become embedded in politics.

The selective purchasing law campaign deploys a *transnational strategy* through which the Free Burma movement attempts to get at the purse strings and leverage the purchasing power of municipal governments and regional states across the United States to force any transnational corporation, not just those headquartered in the United States, to choose between doing business with the Myanmar government or lose valuable contracts with these municipal governments and regional states.

We should remember that at stake in this struggle is how, and by whom, state power can be legitimately used to reorganize transnational market relations with Burma. Neoliberal economic ideology asserts that markets, including global ones, function most efficiently and productively when states do not intervene in the natural process of their formation and operation. Yet it is clear that the state's legislative intervention plays a fundamental role in constructing markets. As the Burmese government opened its national market to global trade, we see how even the United States' legislative functions critically shaped the process of constructing the rules and regulations of market participant behavior and in no small way how the market can (and cannot) be organized. This case illustrates the political struggle over the legislative functions of the state to shape how (and how not) to regulate the way that corporations, as well as local governments acting to procure goods and services in a global marketplace, can legally both influence the formation of, and participate in, the market that was emerging in Burma.

Once these selective purchasing laws were enacted, however, the U.S. government passed its own economic sanctions legislation. Corporations immediately launched an effective legal countermovement to challenge the constitutionality of the selective purchasing laws. The case worked its way to the U.S. Supreme Court. Ultimately, the Court ruled the Massachusetts Burma law unconstitutional.

As we examine below the discursive contention regarding the constitutionality of the Massachusetts Burma law, I want to emphasize how the Commonwealth's attorneys skillfully deploy a series of transnationalist discourses that open a transnational legal space. As I explained in the Introduction, transnational legal space does not refer to a legal order or the institutions (e.g., the courts) within it. It is primarily a cultural structure that combines discourse and narrative to articulate a space of relations and practices whose legal meaning is unsettled, contested, and not yet institutionalized. Transnational legal space is constructed within and through the discourses and narratives that actors deploy in their effort to give particular legal meanings to these relations and practices. It is characterized by conflicts over the meanings of relations, practices, and rules that underpin the national and international legal order, as well as nonstate normative communities.[3] At least one way in which it emerges is when, amid legal discursive contention over the meaning of the relationship between states, markets, and social actors (individual or collective), at least one party to the contentious interaction invokes or deploys a transnationalist discourse. A transnationalist discourse not only challenges the binary distinction between globalization and the nation-state, but furthermore insists on the continuing significance of borders, state policies, and national identities even as transnational circuits and social practices often transgress them.

Transnationalist *legal* discourse is a form of symbolic action that represents, then, a kind of *place* claim—i.e., an effort to invest the space of transgression with legal meaning. It does this while also serving to identify the relations and practices within it in ways that resist interpreting them as already subject to existing national and international law. Additionally, it projects a representation of the relations between states, markets, and social actors in civil society, as well as an interpretation of the legal meanings of these relations that does not fit easily into the institutional distinction between domestic and international, national and foreign, or local and global.

There were noteworthy elements of the *transnationalist discourse*[4] that Free Burma activists produced within their legal struggle to defend the selective purchasing laws that they had created. For instance, they argued that if we take seriously the interpretation that it is unconstitutional for nonfederal entities to engage in the conduct of foreign affairs, then not only are many other local and regional governmental activities unconstitutional (e.g., sister-city programs), but so is the multitude of activities in which corporations directly influence foreign affairs (like establishing corporate codes of conduct). But the U.S. Supreme Court ultimately chose not to address this powerful transnationalist discourse regarding local states' transnational procurement as market participants. Nor did the Court address the contradictions that such a discourse posed for nonfederal activity that influences foreign policy.

Instead, the Court struck down Massachusetts's (nonfederal) Burma law on the specific grounds that it interfered with the *intentions* of the federal Burma law. Nevertheless, this campaign successfully forced the U.S. government to take more than symbolic measures toward addressing human rights abuses in Burma.

Why Selective Purchasing Legislation?

History of Massachusetts's Burma Law

The selective purchasing strategy was first conceived within a broader network of social activist discourse on corporate accountability. Its organizers sought to challenge the common claim of corporations (and many states) that they could both profit from doing business with a repressive regime and promote human rights. This was the cornerstone of the foreign policy of "constructive engagement" toward Burma that most corporations and the member states of the Association of Southeast Asian Nations (ASEAN) supported. The selective purchasing campaign simultaneously challenged corporate efforts to consolidate their own self-regulating regime of corporate social responsibility based on a host of voluntary and nonenforceable instruments.

It is important to note that this selective purchasing campaign targeting Burma was not an isolated initiative launched by the Commonwealth of Massachusetts, nor one sustained solely by Western activists. The campaign immediately garnered the public support of Burma's main opposition party, the National League for Democracy, as well as that of seven Nobel Peace Prize laureates, including Desmond Tutu, Nelson Mandela, and the Dalai Lama of Tibet, who attended the 1993 fact-finding mission to the border regions of Burma, but who were prevented by the military from visiting Burma's own Nobel Peace Prize laureate, Aung San Suu Kyi.[5] In Suu Kyi's words:

> In Burma today[,] our real malady is not economic but political. . . . Until we have a system that guarantees rule of law and basic democratic institutions, no amount of aid or investment will benefit our people. Profits from business enterprises will merely go towards enriching a small, already very privileged elite. Companies [that trade in Burma] only serve to prolong the agony of my country by encouraging the present military regime to persevere in its intransigence.[6]

Suu Kyi continued to express her support for this campaign even as corporations that continued to invest in Burma decried this legislation as a unilateralist and isolationist foreign policy that would ultimately serve only to hurt "the people" of Burma and fail to disempower, or alter the domestic policies of, Burma's military leaders. In the months preceding the U.S. Supreme Court hearing on the constitutionality of the Massachusetts Burma law, Suu Kyi issued a statement reemphasizing the NLD's position: "By investing now, business is supporting the military regime. The real benefits of investment now go to the military regime and its connections."[7]

Statements like these, coming as they did from the leader of Burma's democratically elected yet militarily repressed political party, flew in the face of the Burma law's opponents, who initially sought to depict its advocates' accompanying human rights discourse as a cultural tool of imperialist recolonization that brazenly threatened "Asian values." When ASEAN leaders like Malaysia's Mahatir Mohammed or Indonesia's Suharto denounced the Massachusetts Burma law by pitting human rights against Asian values and defending the latter in the name of state and regional sovereignty, it seemed more credible to westerners that they might be doing so only to protect the narrow, elite interests of an authoritarian and patriarchal network of power in Southeast Asia. When Western critics deployed the same Asian values counterargument, Burma law advocates could now more easily depict it as the political rhetoric of a racist imagination that could not understand how Asian culture was as capable as that of Western culture to embrace human rights. Thus, these statements from Burma's NLD party provided the Burma law campaign with an important resource in the cultural struggle to legitimate its moral voice and articulate its transnationalism even as the leaders of various nation states, within which the Burma law's advocates lived, denounced the campaign.

In the spring of 1994, Simon Billenness, a senior research analyst at Franklin Research and Development Corporation in Boston, then the largest money management firm in North America specializing solely in socially responsible investment,[8] worked with student activists at Harvard University to develop strategies for using market mechanisms to apply more than just symbolic pressure on large transnational corporations.[9] They successfully combined shareholder resolution activism and consumer boycotts to call for the corporate withdrawal of PepsiCo from Burma.[10] Their local activism raised enough student awareness of the issue to successfully pass student resolutions in the student government, which in turn affected Harvard University's investments in Burma.[11] The success of this student campaign began spreading rapidly to other campuses across the United States, and "Free Burma" student associations formed the early building blocks of the Free Burma Coalition.

Meanwhile, Billenness sought to link grassroots activism to the power of local state procurement. The Massachusetts Burma law was modeled on virtually identical legislation[12] adopted by twenty-five states and 164 local governments in an effective anti-apartheid campaign targeting business with South Africa in the 1980s.[13] Billenness approached Massachusetts state representative Byron Rushing, who had introduced selective purchasing legislation for the anti-apartheid campaign,[14] urging him to introduce state legislation on Burma. The Massachusetts Burma law required the secretary of administration and finance to maintain a "restricted purchase list" of all firms engaged in business with Burma.[15] Before a company was allowed to bid on a Massachusetts contract at all, it had to provide a sworn declaration disclosing any business that it was doing with Burma.[16]

Rushing did not secure support from the state legislature by the promise of economic gain. Massachusetts expected to lose valuable contracts as a consequence of passing this law. Nor did he gain legislature support by the promise of delivering votes. There was no significant constituency of Burmese migrants nor Burmese-American citizens working or residing within Massachusetts. Although the law did not include an explicit statement of purpose, representatives speaking on behalf of the law before the legislature, the court, and the media emphatically voiced their intention of improving human rights conditions in Burma.[17] Additional information regarding who was doing business in or with Burma was supplied by United Nations reports and private, nonprofit organizations like the Investor Responsibility Research Center and the Associates to Develop Democratic Burma. The list was updated every three months. The law applied to all new state contracts, as well as the renewal of expiring ones, but not to contracts that existed on its effective date in September 1996.[18]

In practice, the law meant that, in most cases, a company on the restricted purchase list could sell to Massachusetts only if the company's bid was 10 percent lower than any bid by a company that was not on the restricted purchase list. Thus, the law did not impose any *explicit* limits on the ability of private parties to engage in business in Burma or on the ability of private parties or local governments to purchase products from firms engaged in business in Burma. However, since the law effectively did force businesses to *choose* between doing business in Burma *or* Massachusetts, this legislation, in essence, was an economic boycott.[19]

Following Massachusetts's lead, twenty-three other municipal and county governments across the United States, including New York City and the cities of San Francisco and Los Angeles, enacted similar Burma laws. Four municipal governments in Australia, locally mobilized in the Marrickville Council by the Sydney-based Burma Support Group, the Australian Labor Party, and the No Aircraft Noise Party, enacted Burma laws as well (see Figure 8).[20]

The Moral Voice of Transnational Boycotts

In *The Art of Moral Protest,* James Jasper distinguishes between two types of boycotts—local (involving direct action) and national (involving indirect action)—to suggest that, while each type of boycott relies on different kinds of "companion tactics" (or accompanying, supportive forms of protest), generally, "boycotts need to provide mechanisms for collective moral voice."[21] Jasper does not discuss *transnational* boycotts. Nevertheless, transnational boycotts must also provide mechanisms for collective moral voice.

Jasper observes that it is because of these various companion tactics that "boycotts can attain their goals even without reducing consumer demand for the targeted product."[22] Companion tactics, as Jasper conceptualizes them, serve two functions: (1) "to maintain moral outrage and give it a voice," a function, he explains, that is crucial to moral protest movements; and (2) "to bring media attention and bad publicity to the targets," a function, he claims, that is sufficient for bureaucratic interest groups without memberships.[23] Jasper points out that it is the companion tactics, not the boycott per se, which can serve to embarrass corporate decision makers, influence their expectations of an economic impact, or foster in them a fear of even more restrictive government regulations.[24] And while "there are different audiences for the two kinds of actions . . . one [kind of action] or the other, if not both, is necessary for [local or national] boycotts to succeed."[25]

State actor	Date passed
Berkeley, California	February 28, 1995
Madison, Wisconsin	August 16, 1995
Santa Monica, California	November 28, 1995
Ann Arbor, Michigan	April 15, 1996
San Francisco, California	April 22, 1996
Oakland, California	April 23, 1996
State of Massachusetts	**June 25, 1996**
Carborro, North Carolina	October 8, 1996
Takoma Park, Maryland	October 28, 1996
Alameda County, California	December 10, 1996
Boulder, Colorado	December 17, 1996
Chapel Hill, North Carolina	January 13, 1997
New York, New York	May 14, 1997
Federal Burma Law	**May 20, 1997**
Santa Cruz, California	July 8, 1997
Quincy, Massachusetts	October 20, 1997
Palo Alto, California	October 20, 1997
Newton, Massachusetts	November 3, 1997
West Hollywood, California	November 3, 1997
Brookline, Massachusetts	November 5, 1997
Somerville, Massachusetts	February 12, 1998
Marrickville, New South Wales, Australia	March 17, 1998
Cambridge, Massachusetts	June 8, 1998
Portland, Oregon	July 8, 1998
Moreland, Victoria, Australia	November 14, 1998
Vincent, Western Australia, Australia	November 23, 1998
Los Angeles, California	December 15, 1998
Leichhardt, New South Wales, Australia	February 23, 1999

Figure 8. Dates of passage for local Free Burma laws, showing their chronological relationship to the enactment of the Massachusetts Burma Law and the Federal Burma Law. Key legislation that came into conflict in the story about the selective purchasing campaign was the Massachusetts Burma Law, at the heart of the lawsuit that went to the Supreme Court, and the U.S. federal sanctions enacted afterward as a way to trump the tougher sanctions represented by the Massachusetts Burma Law.

Not only the kinds of action, but also the scale of action affects the success of boycotts. The "voice," the "solidarity," and the "compliance" are not as strong in national boycotts as they are in the local boycotts.[26] Nonlocal boycotts operate differently than local boycotts, according to Jasper, because they "pos[e] *greater difficulties for organizing* the companion tactics needed to maintain and express moral outrage."[27] However, the primary companion tactic distinguishing nonlocal from "truly local" boycotts, he argues, is access to media coverage through which nonlocal boycotts can channel their political messages.[28]

Within Jasper's framework for distinguishing between these different types of boycotts, it would seem that he would treat the transnational Free Burma boycott similarly to the way that he treats national boycotts, in which voice, solidarity, and compliance are assumed to be more difficult to organize than in local boycotts. Yet in the selective purchasing strategy of local states exercising their purchasing power to target transnational corporations, the issue of relying on the goodwill of individual shoppers does not seriously pose an obstacle to the success of the boycott because the market participants that the boycott's organizers are mobilizing are collective rather than individual. That is, the market participants initially targeted for participation in the boycott are not individual shoppers but local governments whose purchasing power is exercised through the practice of contracting with corporations to provide their localities with goods and services. Once a local government has enacted selective purchasing legislation—at least in a system of representative democracy—it is voice, more than compliance and solidarity, which requires the most ongoing maintenance.

However, we should not assume that the construction of such a moral voice is necessarily more fragile or organizationally challenged, nor somehow less genuinely or truly grounded in *local* interests. A collective claim to community identity that locates its claim holders' interests within community boundaries that cross or extend beyond the boundaries of the nation-state does not necessarily represent a stretching (or thinning) of some more primary, or constant mass of, identity. We also should not assume that collective moral voice is weakened by the translocal heterogeneity of its claimants or, on the other hand, strengthened by the social homogeneity of its claimants. This is a question that should remain open to research. Crucial to this process is how the common interests of the boycott participants are socially constructed as shared *local* interests

Figure 9. Human rights activists protest against Unocal Corporation's partnership with the Burmese military regime at the annual Unocal shareholder meeting in Brea, California. Unocal's natural gas pipeline in Burma is alleged to have been built using forced laborers. Photograph copyright 2000 D. Ngo/ ZUMA Press.

(or even, *translocal* interests) vis-à-vis their target. Simultaneously, they must construct their target as nonlocal (or at least, less local). The local is a relative spatial orientation, and its particular meaning, identity, and boundaries are always created in relation to some other place.

In the Massachusetts boycott, it was their collective moral voice that enabled the network of advocates for the Massachusetts Burma law to achieve greater media attention for their political message than they had reasonably anticipated. Central to the success of this moral voice was the Burma law advocates' ability to articulate their claims, both as actors sharing a trans*local* identity that was manifesting itself in a pattern of selective purchasing legislation emerging in cities across the United States and as actors sharing a trans*national* identity as consumers who have come to understand how their own consumptive choices and practices are connected, or *linked*, to each other's through the practices of particular transnational corporations. Social theorist Ulrich Beck asserts that emerging from this conscious connectedness among consumers is a new counterpower of global civil society based on the figure of the *political consumer*:

What is fatal for the interests of capital is that there is no counter-strategy to confront the counter-power of consumers. . . . In the first place the consumer is globalized and as such is highly desirable to corporations. And in the second place, it is not possible to respond to consumer protests in one country by moving to other countries without going through considerable contortions. Moreover it is not possible to play consumers' national solidarity off against one another. The nature of consumer protests is that they are transnational. . . . This is what makes their counter-power such a threat to the power of capital—and so far they have hardly begun to exploit it.[29]

The campaign was not simply a *local* boycott, nor even a *national* boycott. It was a *transnational* boycott. Not only was the strategy of this boycott transnational, but also its organization was transnational. This boycott linked grassroots activists in local cities and states throughout the United States and pro-democracy activists in cities and villages throughout Burma, where the NLD maintained local offices. The principal targets were transnational networks linking transnational corporations and Burma's military state. Even the discourse that the organizers of this boycott deployed to explain the meaning of their action was transnationalist.

The initial results of this transnational strategy were impressive. Not only did many companies based in the United States (e.g., Compaq, Hewlett-Packard, Apple, Disney, Pepsi, Federal Express, Canon, Kodak, Motorola, Levi-Strauss, Macy's, Eddie Bauer, Liz Claiborne, Chanel, Procter and Gamble, and Caterpillar) withdraw their operations and investments from Burma, so did many companies based in other nation-states (e.g., Guinness, Evian, Toyota, British Airways, Fuji, Sony, and Siemens). All cited the Massachusetts Burma law or the fear of the negative publicity that it channeled toward corporations as the reason for pulling out.[30] More impressive was that electronics manufacturer Phillips and oil producers Texaco and Amoco terminated their dealings with the Myanmar military's state-owned company, Myanmar Oil and Gas Enterprise (MOGE). That is, even corporations with products that depend much less on brand-name distinctions for their competitive profitability margin, and thus which typically remain less vulnerable to negative publicity campaigns, nevertheless felt the economic teeth of this boycott. The key to their success was not only in their ability to provide a means of expressing their moral outrage over the violation of human rights in Burma and to amplify their moral voice to audiences beyond their immediate communities through skillful media access and manipulation; rather, their success also derived from their ability to translate these violations of transnational human rights norms into a credible threat of material losses.

Pro-democracy activists inside Burma helped to monitor the practices of corporations that publicly chose to continue doing business with the military, like Unocal, with its $1.2 billion pipeline investment in Burma, as well as the ones that claimed to have withdrawn their operations, by relaying information through personal social networks established with NGOs in Thailand. It was during the first year of mobilizing this campaign that the Free Burma Coalition (FBC) was founded, in September 1995.[31]

Legislative Countermovement

As this transnational legal campaign built momentum, voice, purchasing power, and results, the U.S. government enacted its own Burma law. Corporations headquartered both outside and within the United States also responded with their own legal countermovement. They challenged both the morality and the legality of this campaign, attacking its injurious imposition of "unfair trade barriers" and "unilateral economic sanctions," as well as its unconstitutional interference in foreign affairs.

Federal Sanctions

Three months after Massachusetts enacted its Burma law, the U.S. Congress authorized the Omnibus Consolidated Appropriations Act of 1997 (hereafter, "federal Burma law"). The law imposed conditional sanctions on Burma "until such time as the President determines and certifies to Congress that Burma has made measurable and substantial progress in improving human rights practices and implementing democratic government."[32] This federal Burma law directed the president to develop a "multilateral strategy"—calling for cooperation with members of ASEAN and Burma's other major trading and investment partners—"to bring democracy to and improve human rights practices and the quality of life in Burma, including the development of a dialogue between the ruling State Law and Order Restoration Council (SLORC)[33] and the democratic opposition groups with Burma."[34]

It is important to understand that this federal Burma law was a much weaker form of sanctions than the local Burma laws that Massachusetts and other local governments had legislated. This statute prohibited all but humanitarian assistance to the Myanmar government; directed the executive branch to vote against assistance to Myanmar in international financial institutions; and barred Myanmar officials from entering the United States.[35] The federal Burma law also prohibited U.S. "persons," including both individual and corporate entities, from new investment in Myanmar, provided that the president later determine and certify to Congress whether "the Government of [Myanmar] has physically harmed, rearrested for political acts, or exiled Daw Aung San Suu Kyi or has committed large-scale repression of or violence against the Democratic opposition."[36] Yet Congress specifically authorized the president to restrict only new investment in development of resources in Myanmar and chose not to restrict contracts for goods, services, and technology. Thus, preexisting investment in the development of resources, like Unocal's oil pipeline project with Burma, were not affected by the federal Burma law. Importantly, this restriction on investment applied *only* to U.S. companies and their foreign branches, *not* to foreign companies or to their U.S. subsidiaries.

In May 1997, President Clinton issued an executive order, as called for in the federal Burma law, which certified that "the Government of [Myanmar] has committed large-scale repression of the democratic opposition in Burma . . . [and that] the actions and policies of the Government of [Myanmar] constitute an unusual and extraordinary threat to the national security and foreign policy of the United States."[37] This executive order left intact the original exemptions regarding new investment that Congress had stipulated in the federal Burma law. Worth noting as well is that neither Congress nor the president explicitly preempted the Massachusetts Burma law, nor the twelve other local governmental sanctions that had been enacted before the federal Burma law (see Figure 8).[38]

Corporate Backlash

It was Massachusetts's Burma law, rather than the federal sanctions against Burma, that attracted the most criticism from transnational corporations, including those headquartered both domestically and abroad.

For corporations, the most threatening aspect of the dissemination of selective purchasing laws was not simply their power to mobilize transnational grassroots support for human rights in Burma. Most threatening to corporations was the power of local selective purchasing legislation as a more general model for mobilizing such support around a wide variety of foreign relations issues and in ways that potentially undermined the agendas and diplomatic strategies of both transnational corporations and nation states. These corporations, while expressing their consensus with Massachusetts and supporters of the Burma law on the need to improve human rights conditions in Burma, challenged the grassroots Burma law campaign's discourse on corporate accountability.

As Massachusetts's blacklist was growing,[39] a network of transnational corporations was fomenting corporate backlash that can best be understood as a three-pronged, "elite-driven counter-movement."[40] In the following subsections, I examine each prong.

The WTO Agreement on Government Procurement and "Unfair Trade Barriers"

In January 1997, six months after Massachusetts had enacted its Burma law, transnational corporations chartered within France and Japan deployed regional and nationalist identities, respectively, to persuade the European Commission (EC) and Japan to file a formal complaint with the World Trade Organization (WTO). The EC and Japan did so, alleging that the Massachusetts Burma law constituted an "unfair trade barrier" for European and Japanese corporations, thus violating the WTO Agreement on Government Procurement that these governments had negotiated with the United States in 1994.[41]

The Agreement on Government Procurement bars public entities from using noneconomic criteria, such as human rights or environmental considerations, in public procurement. The term "noneconomic criteria" refers to discriminating on grounds other than price and performance when purchasing goods and services.[42] The operative principle guiding this discourse on unfair trade barriers in the context of public procurement echoes the one underlying Chapter 11 of the North American Free Trade Agreement (NAFTA), which was adopted in 1993. In each agreement, a new system of private arbitration has been established for foreign investors to bring injury claims against governments.[43] Foreign investors in nation states that have established formal free-trade agreements through the WTO (as is the case for foreign investors in the United States, Canada, or Mexico under NAFTA) may demand compensation if the profit-making potential of their ventures has been injured by a nation-state's public policy decisions, including "preferential bidding" practices. In short, these transnational corporations, by invoking a discourse on "unfair trade barriers," sought to transform the meaning of the Commonwealth of Massachusetts's legislation. Instead of holding corporations accountable, this discourse asserted, the Massachusetts Burma law should be conceptualized as an injurious form of state expropriation against which foreign-based companies have a right to be protected.[44]

The Massachusetts congressional delegation responded to the charges with a letter to EC president Jacques Santer expressing their strong objections to the EC's protest:

> We do not believe it is appropriate for the European Union to involve itself in the internal affairs of Massachusetts. If the EC chooses to place dollars ahead of human rights, it has that sovereign right, but the EC should not attempt to intimidate Massachusetts into changing the standards it has established for doing business with the state government.[45]

President Bill Clinton's administration responded to these WTO complaints by claiming that the Commonwealth of Massachusetts, under the U.S. Constitution, holds state sovereignty in the area of procurement.[46] In a media conference addressing the issue, U.S. trade representative Charlene Barshefsky said that the U.S. government is "not about to negotiate away the constitutional prerogatives of state and local authorities."

However, it was the Clinton administration that was expressing—although not loudly—the more contradictory position. The following month, U.S. commerce secretary William Daley, in a speech sponsored by the European Institute,[47] revealed that the Clinton administration had been trying to persuade "U.S. industry" to pressure Massachusetts to repeal or amend its Burma law.[48] In other words, the Clinton administration was openly supporting the Commonwealth of Massachusetts's Burma law in the WTO conflict at an international level, while simultaneously working in the shadows of the media's public scrutiny at a national level to undermine the same law.

USA*Engage and the NFTC: Unilateral Sanctions and Local Foreign Policy

If one wished to speak to "U.S. industry," one need not look much further than the National Foreign Trade Council (NFTC). The NFTC is a Washington, D.C.–based lobby association representing about three hundred top U.S. manufacturing corporations and financial institutions. At the time the NFTC filed suit against Massachusetts, it represented roughly 680 such members.[49] The companies comprising the council's membership not only included the largest manufacturing companies and most of the fifty largest banks in the United States, but also accounted for at least 70 percent of all U.S. nonagricultural exports and 70 percent of U.S. private foreign investment.[50] Of the fifty-seven member companies serving on the NFTC's board of directors, ten were on Massachusetts's Restricted Burma Purchase List when the formal WTO complaint was filed to challenge Massachusetts's Burma law, and thirty-four companies among the association's membership overall were listed at the time the NFTC filed suit.[51]

The NFTC deals exclusively with U.S. public policy affecting international trade and investment and opposes the use of foreign policy sanctions. Founded in 1914 under President Woodrow Wilson's administration, the NFTC is the oldest and largest U.S. association of businesses. Since then, it has been an outspoken lobbyist on behalf of an open international trade and investment regime embodied in international agreements and institutions like the General Agreement on Tariffs and Trade (GATT) and the WTO. According to its Web site at the time that it had filed suit, "the fundamental goal of the Council is to develop policies reflecting the interests and consensus of Council members, designed to expand exports, protect U.S. foreign investment, enhance the competitiveness of U.S. industry and promote and maintain a fair and equitable trading system."[52]

The second and third prongs in the corporate countermovement against the Burma law campaign both involved these domestically headquartered transnational corporations in the United States spearheaded by the NFTC. One of the first decisions that these corporations had to make was how best to represent their own identities in relation to the U.S. and Myanmar governments, as well as the Commonwealth of Massachusetts. WTO agreements extend to foreign-based companies certain rights to compensation when states that are parties in those agreements act in ways that curb their profitability. Corporations headquartered within member states of the EC and in Japan had rights under the terms of their WTO agreement to claim compensation from the United States. Yet such compensation rights are not extended to the domestic businesses operating within the state that violates the agreement. In other words, U.S.-headquartered companies cannot claim compensation for profits lost in Myanmar if it is the U.S. government that has violated the terms of the WTO agreement. Therefore, these U.S.-headquartered transnational corporations adopted a different strategy, turning not to the WTO but to the U.S. Courts. They represented themselves primarily in terms of their linkages to local corporate subsidiaries in the United States rather than in terms of their transnational linkages to their state-owned business partners in Myanmar. They deployed a national identity rooted in specifically "American" business interests and challenged the Massachusetts Burma law with an eye toward protecting their foreign capital investments in Burma. Of course, when Massachusetts had originally accused these companies of financially sustaining human rights abuses in Burma through their transnational business partnerships with the Myanmar government, the companies defended their transnational identity, but argued that they were not responsible for the abuses in Myanmar. Still, they explained, they are beholden to the laws of the state in which they operate and from which they derive their profits.

Instead of invoking the discourse on unfair trade barriers, these corporations deployed two different ones. The first discourse asserted that the Massachusetts legislation represented "unilateral economic sanctions" that "undermine American leadership and competitiveness" because they "almost always fail to achieve their intended foreign policy goals, disrupt relations with our allies, hand markets (frequently the fastest growing markets) to our competitors, and hurt American companies, farmers, and workers."[53] The second discourse emphasized the American citizenship of these transnational corporate entities, legitimating their effort to mount a challenge to the "constitutionality" of the Massachusetts Burma law. This discourse asserted that the Massachusetts Burma law represented "local [government] foreign policy," which unconstitutionally intrudes on the federal government's exclusive power to conduct U.S. foreign affairs.

Both discourses expressed concern for the alarming proliferation of such legislation, particularly its enactment by local governments across the

United States. As attorneys for the NFTC argued, perhaps intentionally invoking Maoist imagery of the cold war and the attendant binary
paired-categories (un-American-Communist/American-Capitalist) produced during that period in the United States: "Allowing a thousand, or
ten thousand, different foreign policies to bloom would be a detriment
to the nation and contravene the constitutional plan."[54]

Initially, the NFTC sought to shift the dialogue about who is for and
who is against human rights in Burma to one about the best *means* of
improving human rights conditions in Burma. From the outset, the
NFTC unequivocally proclaimed its support for human rights in Burma.
The NFTC's attorneys maintained the same position in court:

> There is no disagreement between the parties as to the need for reform
> in the Union of Myanmar. The current authoritarian regime, the State
> Peace and Development Council, has reportedly committed egregious
> human rights violations and has refused to recognize the results of the
> democratic election held in that country in 1990.[55]

Although the NFTC was unwilling to challenge the internationally proliferating media depictions of the Myanmar military regime as
a "pariah state," it would not go as far as the campaign activists had in
denouncing the legitimacy of the military's rule in Burma. The NFTC
refrained from using the name "Burma" to refer to the country, choosing
instead the new name, "Myanmar," that the military adopted in 1990,
thus carefully lending affirmation to the Myanmar military's claim to be
the legitimate, sovereign state authority in the country. In doing so, the
NFTC also was working to defend the legitimacy of its member corporations' existing (and potential) partnerships with the Myanmar military. Thus, in challenging the campaign activists' discourse on corporate
accountability, the NFTC invoked a discourse that carefully affirmed
the goal of improving human rights while distinguishing from this goal
the notion that corporate withdrawal is a viable means for achieving
it. Instead of defending its own practices in the name of "constructive
engagement," however, the NFTC attacked its challengers' selective purchasing legislation. It attacked this legislation through various channels
of public opinion, using the media, policy think tanks, academic publications, professional conferences, and congressional lobbying, and later,
through the U.S. judicial system.

In April 1997, the NFTC founded a separate lobbying organization
called USA*Engage. Within its first three years, USA*Engage grew

from 440 to 674 member corporations, although the vast majority were already members of the NFTC.[56] In contrast to the NFTC's unshakeable image as a longtime Congressional lobbying strong arm for "big business," the NFTC used USA*Engage to carefully craft an identity as a grassroots coalition of businesses (small and large, and from a full spectrum of industry sectors) and "American" workers whose jobs, these lobbyists asserted, would be inevitable casualties of unilateral sanctions.

The home page of the USA*Engage Web site nicely captured the purpose of this organization. It displayed a cartoon of Uncle Sam standing in the middle of a world map, with his feet planted firmly within the territorial outline of the United States, his arm cocked and a boomerang in his hand. The boomerang apparently symbolizes U.S. unilateral economic sanctions and their effect on U.S. foreign policy: "Unilateral sanctions are counterproductive and almost always ineffective—disrupting relations with our allies and providing ammunition to our opponents."[57] The organization's purpose has been to lobby the U.S. Congress to legislate a Sanctions Reform Act that adopts a standard of ongoing accountability to evaluate unilateral foreign policy sanctions.[58]

USA*Engage depicted the Massachusetts Burma law in particular as being representative of a new and even more dangerous trend in unilateral foreign policy, namely "secondary boycotts." USA*Engage's Web site representations, news releases, research papers, congressional testimony, congressional "report cards," and conference brochures all emphasized how the Massachusetts Burma law posed a threat to the federal government's capacity to conduct foreign policy "with one voice."

By invoking the image of secondary boycotts as an analogue for the local Burma laws, USA*Engage was comparing the governmental practice of selective purchasing to the kind of activity through which Teamsters effectively transformed San Francisco's Port Strike of 1933 into a general strike. They organized unionized workers to target not only their immediate employers, but also any other business that tried to use the port, including the railroads. The Taft-Hartley Act later declared such secondary boycotts to be illegal and a threat to national security.

Furthermore, in cases where secondary boycotts have not posed a national security threat, the Supreme Court more recently has declared them illegal if they threaten even indirectly the interests of neutral parties. In *International Longshoremen's Association, AFL-CIO v. Allied International, Inc.* (1982), the Supreme Court held unlawful, under the

National Labor Relations Act, a union's refusal to handle cargo arriving from or destined for the Soviet Union to protest the invasion of Afghanistan.[59] The court rejected the union's argument that the secondary boycott simply "freed members from the morally repugnant duty of handling Russian goods."[60] Rather, it held that such secondary boycotts threaten neutral parties on whom they impose a heavy burden.

The implication of the analogy offered by USA*Engage was that the Commonwealth of Massachusetts was unfairly (and harmfully) punishing "neutral" American businesses in its effort to punish Burma for its human rights abuses. However, the Commonwealth of Massachusetts came to understand during this process that its discourse on corporate accountability, through which it had thus far effectively channeled a collective moral voice, was facing an opponent that intended to draw upon more resources than public opinion for empowering its own collective moral voice. The NFTC was mounting a challenge to the Massachusetts Burma law on the basis of the U.S. Constitution.

This contention over the Massachusetts Burma law that had been taking place outside the courts up to this point focused largely on questions of the legislation's justice. For example, the NFTC had argued that the Massachusetts Burma law unjustly harmed "neutral market participants" and killed jobs for American and Burmese workers. Massachusetts argued that it should not have to do business with a regime that violates human rights, nor even with corporations that directly help to financially sustain such abusive practices through their business partnerships with that regime.

But now the NFTC was prepared to test its moral reasoning against that of Burma activists and the Commonwealth of Massachusetts in a federal court battle over the legality—the constitutional legitimacy—of this kind of local legislation. These litigants were now bringing the politics of their *legislative* contention before the institutionalized morality of the U.S. judiciary.

Challenging the Constitutionality of the Massachusetts Burma Law

In November 1998, the NFTC brought a suit against two officials of the Commonwealth of Massachusetts, alleging that the Massachusetts Burma law was invalid for three reasons: (1) it intrudes on the federal government's exclusive power to regulate foreign affairs; (2) it discriminates against and burdens international trade in violation of the Constitution's foreign commerce clause; and (3) it is preempted by a federal statute and an executive order imposing sanctions on Myanmar (Burma). Below, I examine this court case and the statutes that are at the heart of the conflict. To illuminate the transnational legal space that emerges in this conflict, I focus on three sets of competing discourses and accompanying narratives. Before doing so, I should clarify what I mean by these terms.

The Meaning of Discourse and Narrative

Anne Kane fruitfully theorizes the interplay between these two kinds of cultural structures: discourse and narrative.[61] Reflecting a contemporary trend in cultural sociology, particularly in the United States, she begins her analysis with the assumption that meaning is embodied in the specific arrangement of symbols in cultural structures.[62] However, she reminds us that interpretation and action—i.e., cultural *practice*—is as important as cultural *structure* in studying how meaning is constructed. Kane observes that narrative and discourse, when functioning either independently or combined as elements of a single cultural structure, are also "modes of symbolic action."[63] In other words, narrative and discourse function as both cultural practice and cultural structure.

Structurally, Kane conceptualizes discourse as "organized sets of symbolic meaning and codes representing a pattern of opposition and distinction."[64] And, drawing upon Marc Steinberg's insight that discourse involves dialogue situated in particular social contexts, she also conceptualizes discourse as "the symbolic practice through which people create and reproduce their cultural codes for making sense of the world."[65] Thus, as a cultural structure, "discourse intertwines particular symbolic codes with social relationships and conditions, thereby articulating meaning and understanding of specific issues and problems," and, as cultural practice, "a discourse asserts a particular argument in dialogue with others."[66]

Narratives, structurally speaking, are "stories that embody symbolic codes" and "configurations of meaning through which an individual and/or community comes to understand itself."[67] As cultural practice, narratives "afford a vehicle of communication and interaction between social actors."[68]

As a vehicle of visual/written or aural/spoken *communication*, narrative relies upon plot. A narrative plot, or storyline, maps or orchestrates for its readers or listeners a pattern or an arrangement of particular events, actors, institutions, and social structures. The cultural practice of constructing a plot and the constellation of relationships or "conceptual networks" is what Margaret Somers and Gloria Gibson refer to as "emplotment."[69] It is emplotment that empowers narrative to perform some of the most crucial functions of interpretation, as well as of *representation*.[70] Among these functions is the capacity to explain experience, to evoke emotion, to normatively evaluate courses of action, and to engage participation. All of these functions are crucial to the art of persuasion and the mobilization of collective action.

As a vehicle of *interaction*, narratives depend heavily on engagement as well because narrative practice achieves meaning through interaction with an audience. Symbols are inherently ambiguous and possess multiple meanings. Narratives give symbols meaning in the process of arranging (i.e., structuring) them. That is, a narrative's meaning derives not simply from its author's intentions but from its audience's interpretation of it. Narratives do not speak for themselves; they do not tell their own story. They require interpretation to give them meaning, and an audience may derive multiple meanings from the same narrative. A storyteller does not interpret but rather (re)presents a particular relationship of actors, events, institutions, and social structures to an audience. Of course, for an actor to perform the function of a storyteller, the actor must first perform the function of an audience and interpret the relations from which it constructs a narrative; but it is the actor-as-audience that interprets the narrative.

Actors, when asserting a discourse, may invoke a narrative that authorizes a particular emplotment in an effort to construct meaning, yet this is not sufficient to "channel" the audience's understanding of the relations emplotted in the narrative. The meaning that the actor-as-storyteller intended to communicate (or even intentionally miscommunicate) remains open to contestation and to alternative representations to the extent that the actor-as-audience interprets these relations in significantly different ways. Thus, we must examine how the narrative engages the audience and keep our examination open to the possibility that the representations of the relations and events authorized by the storyteller's narrative may also serve as interpretive resources for the audience's own construction of alternative representations, narratives, and discourses. In the example I examine below, it is in how the local state as an actor is differently situated in relation to other actors within competing narratives that we see very different meanings of local state action emerge. The narrative engagement that ensues, in turn, channels the unfolding process of discursive contention over the meaning of foreign affairs. It is the competing transnationalist discourses that each party to the conflict invokes that transfers the typically national/international conceptual space of *foreign affairs* into a transnational legal space.

The Authority to Conduct Foreign Affairs: Federal vs. Nonfederal Entities

Massachusetts initially contested the NFTC's legal standing to sue, asserting that the NFTC's members had not been injured by the Massachusetts Burma law. The NFTC, however, convinced the court that it had standing, claiming that more than thirty NFTC members were presently on the "restricted purchasing list"; that some NFTC members had severed their business connections with Myanmar, thereby affecting their competitive edge in the global market; that at least one member, who previously had contracts with Massachusetts, did not bid on new contracts because of the statute; and, finally, that at least one member on the "restricted purchasing list" had lost a contract before joining the NFTC because its bid was not 10 percent lower than the winning bid.[71]

A discursive repositioning was taking place in which the Commonwealth of Massachusetts was denying the economic impact of the Free Burma law on these corporations, contrary to what their earlier discourse on corporate accountability had rather victoriously proclaimed. The NFTC was now not only conceding, but also providing evidence to support, the point that advocates of the Massachusetts Burma law had proclaimed all along: namely, that this boycott had teeth capable of affecting corporations' bottom lines.

The deployment of these new discourses represented a strategic choice on the part of each actor. The Commonwealth of Massachusetts abandoned (within the courts) its discourse on corporate accountability in an effort to skillfully redefine the meaning of its action in relation to these corporations to defend the constitutionality of its Burma law. Instead, it represented its selective purchasing legislation as having only an indirect effect on corporations. The primary purpose of the legislation, it argued, was not to regulate the conduct of corporations, but rather to exercise its Tenth Amendment rights as a market participant, and in doing so to exercise its First Amendment rights to choose with whom it wished to conduct business. Based on its respect for human rights,

Massachusetts argued, it was choosing not to conduct business with the Myanmar military.

Therefore, while the NFTC effectively constructed itself in court as an injured plaintiff, it also strategically avoided reinforcing this representation of the relationship between the Massachusetts Burma law and the NFTC, which the discourse on corporate accountability had promoted. Instead, the NFTC sought to depict Massachusetts as a powerful and overreaching local state regulating the conduct, and recklessly destroying the economic opportunities, of American business in the name of a liberal policy that, despite its noble concerns for human rights, unwittingly promoted ineffectual and possibly even self-defeating means.

Massachusetts, however, was deploying a new discourse through which it represented the meaning of its own action in relation to corporations. No longer was it asserting how local government might hold corporations accountable for the injurious consequences of their economic partnerships and the practices through which corporations deliberately sought to externalize the costs of these consequences. Instead, to justify the constitutionality of its Burma law, Massachusetts represented itself as an economic entity, a local procurer of goods and services participating in a transnational marketplace along with other economic entities, like corporations, regional trading blocs, and other actors that choose to enter into economic contracts. From the perspective of this new discourse on transnational procurement, any of these "other" foreign corporations cited by the NFTC that, as a result of "American" corporate withdrawal, might choose to do business with Burma would be equally subject to Massachusetts's restrictive purchasing list. The Massachusetts Burma law applied equally to *all* of its corporate contractees, regardless of the corporation's national affiliation or national identity. Thus, Massachusetts could interpret its legislation to be neither creating a competitive *disadvantage* for any corporation choosing *not* to conduct business with Burma, nor, for that matter, creating a competitive *advantage* for any corporation that *did* choose to conduct business with Burma.

After it had become evident that the U.S. Courts were willing to extend legal standing to the NFTC on the matter, Japan, ASEAN, and the EU announced their decision to "indefinitely withdraw" their WTO complaints.[72] Yet the EU, before doing so, had written an amicus brief supporting the NFTC that the District Court cited as evidence of the Burma law's disruptive impact on foreign relations. In this brief, the EU claimed that Massachusetts's Burma law (1) interferes with the normal conduct of EU–U.S. relations; (2) raises questions about the ability of the United States to honor international commitments it has entered in the framework of the WTO; and (3) poses a great risk to the proliferation of similar state sanction laws, which in turn would aggravate international tensions. "Contrary to Massachusetts' claims," the District Court asserted, "their Burma Law has more than an indirect or incidental effect in foreign countries, and a great potential for disruption or embarrassment." The NFTC, in one of its key arguments, cited the complaint filed with the WTO against the Burma law as proof that Massachusetts had unconstitutionally infringed upon the federal government's foreign affairs powers. The federal district court, agreeing with the NFTC's representation of the law as "local foreign policy," ruled that the Burma law violated the foreign affairs clause of the Constitution:

> The Massachusetts Burma Law was designed with the purpose of changing Burma's domestic policy. This is an unconstitutional infringement on the foreign affairs powers of the federal government. State interests, no matter how noble, do not trump the federal government's exclusive foreign affairs power.[73]

In opposition to Massachusetts's discourse on the constitutionality of its Burma law, the NFTC invoked USA*Engage's earlier discourse on secondary boycotts:

> There is nothing *local* about either the objectives of the Burma Law or its effects. The Burma Law was designed to, and does, conduct Massachusetts' own little version of foreign policy with the identifiable goal of "free democratic elections in Burma"; indeed, Massachusetts concedes that its goal is "to promote human rights in Burma." It directly affects companies doing business in Myanmar *and has evoked protests by foreign nations*. This Court has itself recognized that secondary boycotts are not mere disassociative actions, but are heavily coercive.... Thus, the Burma Law, in both design and effect, sanctions private companies that do business with Myanmar. This is a typical *foreign*-policy measure.[74]

Insisting that Massachusetts had altered substantially its own representation of the history and objectives of its legislation, the NFTC attempted to depict Massachusetts as instrumentally and disingenuously characterizing the objectives and effects of their Burma law as local rather than foreign policy. The NFTC's argument was that any local (meaning in this context, nonfederal) policy affecting foreign affairs directly is unconstitutional, and that even if the legislation's effects are indirect, they nevertheless constitute illegal secondary sanctions that have direct effects on the "neutral" corporate members of the NFTC conducting business with Burma.

The U.S. Court of Appeals for the First Circuit affirmed the lower court's ruling, adding that the Massachusetts Burma law also unconstitutionally violated the foreign commerce clause as well as the supremacy clause.[75] The Massachusetts attorney general petitioned the U.S. Supreme Court, criticizing the lower courts for their reliance on the WTO complaint as evidence of the state's interference in foreign affairs: "The court's reliance on trade complaints—inevitable rows in an era of global procurement—grants to foreign countries and firms a 'heckler's veto' against state laws."[76] On November 29, 1999, the U.S. Supreme Court agreed to hear the case.[77]

By the time the case was argued before the Supreme Court on March 22, 2000, ten members of Congress, the European Communities and their member states, the Chamber of Commerce of the USA, the Organization for International Investment, the National Association of Manufacturers, the U.S. Council for International Business, the American Insurance Association, the American Petroleum Institute, the American Farm Bureau Federation, the Washington Legal Foundation, the American Legislative Exchange Council, the Associated Industries of Massachusetts, the Retailers Association of Massachusetts, and a handful of retired public officials who had served in previous administrations and who were charged with responsibility for conducting U.S. foreign relations (including George Schultz and Alexander Haig) filed amicus curiae briefs in support of the NFTC's position.[78]

Still, neither Congress nor President Clinton had exercised explicitly their power to preempt the Massachusetts Burma law before the Supreme Court's ruling on June 20, 2000. Despite the support expressed by the ten members of Congress who wrote amicus briefs supporting the NFTC, another seventy-eight members of Congress also wrote amicus briefs on behalf of Massachusetts. In effect, the legislative and executive branches chose to leave to the Supreme Court the task of interpreting their inexplicit intentions behind enacting the federal Burma law.

In the end, the Supreme Court upheld the decision of the lower courts, and Massachusetts was forced to repeal its Burma law. This ruling was far from predictable. Supreme Court watchers were genuinely puzzled as to which way it would rule in this case because the bench consisted of justices who had established a fairly reliable pattern of support for both states' rights *and* minimal state regulation of foreign commerce. This issue, however, seemed to force the Supreme Court to choose between these two positions.

What is more interesting than the fact that the Supreme Court's ruling in this case ultimately favored corporate interests, however, is the accompanying reasoning supporting the Supreme Court's ruling. The Supreme Court had at its disposal a number of possible discourses from which to represent the Massachusetts Burma law as unconstitutional. Yet the Supreme Court founded its decision only on the supremacy clause of the Constitution, claiming that the Massachusetts Burma law "undermined the intended purpose of, and was preempted by" the federal Burma law. Although the District Court, during the previous year, had found the Massachusetts Burma law unconstitutional with respect to the foreign affairs clause, it had *rejected* the NFTC's claim that the Massachusetts Burma law violated the supremacy clause. Moreover, the Supreme Court chose *not* to base its ruling on the one issue that both the district court and the U.S. Court of Appeals for the First Circuit had agreed: namely, that the Massachusetts Burma law violated the foreign affairs clause. Thus, even though the courts at every level of the judicial system agreed that the Massachusetts Burma law was unconstitutional, they did not agree on *how* to discursively construct this law as such.

Since it is the Supreme Court's ruling that ultimately struck down the Massachusetts Burma law, I will now examine how the Supreme Court constructed this law as unconstitutional and how the Court used this discourse to negotiate the competing claims of the transnationalist discourse asserted by the Commonwealth of Massachusetts. Let me be clear: I am not attempting to identify the contradictions, inconsistencies, or conflicting claims of the various courts that ruled on the Burma law's unconstitutionality. Rather, my inquiry will focus on how and to what effect the Supreme Court considered certain concepts (and not others) to be a reasonable basis for its ruling.

Courts, particularly the Supreme Court, typically deliver their rulings, or "truth claims," through some form of discursive reasoning. As is the case with all kinds of meaning, truth claims are "always transmitted to us via some kind of cultural schema," and "they gain their legitimacy, at least to some extent through the cultural expressions by which they are articulated."[79] Moreover, a discourse asserts a particular argument in dialogue with and therefore must negotiate the competing claims of the other discourses it confronts in the process. With this process in mind, I will depict the Supreme Court's ruling as an "argument," and do so with an eye toward showing how and with what effect, in dialogue with prior discourses, it gives meaning to signs and thus puts them into action. I am insisting, then, that courts' discursive practices do not merely clarify preexisting meanings; they produce meanings in every case that they adjudicate in order to construct their interpretation, and official representation, of what the case under scrutiny is a case of. I will therefore examine how the U.S. Supreme Court constructed this suit, *Stephen P. Crosby, Secretary of Administration and Finance of Massachusetts, et al., v. National Foreign Trade Council*, as a case of a violation of the Constitution's supremacy clause.

Appreciation for the U.S. Supreme Court's discourse on how the Massachusetts Burma law violated the supremacy clause of the Constitution begins with understanding the discursive contention generated in the lower courts by the NFTC and the Commonwealth of Massachusetts over the meaning of the foreign affairs clause and the competing narratives invoked during this unfolding process. I argue that, in the discursive contention over the meaning of the foreign affairs clause, both the NFTC and the Commonwealth of Massachusetts invoked narrative interpretations of the original framers' intention in providing this clause, and that the Supreme Court found aspects of each narrative culturally salient. However, instead of legitimating the foreign affairs discourse associated with either narrative, the Supreme Court creatively engaged aspects of both narratives to deploy a discourse on federal preemption that favored, although for different reasons, the NFTC's general claim that the Massachusetts Burma law was unconstitutional. The Supreme Court's discourse on federal preemption was distinct from those offered by not only the contesting parties but also the lower courts.

Although the Supreme Court struck down existing local selective purchasing legislation regarding Burma, the scope of the Supreme Court's reasoning was sufficiently narrow to permit future nonfederal influence on the conduct of foreign policy, including not only that in which local states engage but also corporations. As I explain below, the transnationalist discourse deployed by the Commonwealth of Massachusetts significantly influenced the Supreme Court's reasoning.

In the following subsections, I first introduce the concept of *narrative engagement* and its importance to my analysis of discursive contention. I illustrate this concept by describing the NFTC's discourse and narrative on why and how the federal state holds exclusive power to conduct U.S. foreign affairs. Next, I examine Massachusetts's transnationalist discourse on the power to conduct foreign affairs and explain how it posits a significantly different conceptual network of actors, events, and institutional practices, as well as a different understanding of space, time, and emplotment. Finally, I explain how and with what effect the Supreme Court constructed the Massachusetts Burma law as unconstitutional and assess to what extent the transnationalist discourse in particular, and the Burma law campaign more generally, contributed to the pro-democracy movement.

The Foreign Affairs Clause: States as Regulators vs. States as Market Participants

The NFTC's discourse on foreign affairs asserted that the federal government has exclusive power to conduct foreign affairs and, therefore, that local state legislation, which attempts to influence foreign affairs, encroaches upon and diminishes the federal government's power:

> Under our Constitution, the conduct of foreign affairs is the responsibility of the federal government, and only the federal government. . . . The holding that Massachusetts seeks would effectively remit our Nation's foreign policy to the same confused state of affairs that existed under the Articles of Confederation. . . . Virtually all prior cases in the lower courts have invalidated state laws intruding into the field of foreign affairs.[80]

The NFTC's discourse on foreign affairs invoked a historical narrative in an effort to portray its argument as consistent with the meaning of the foreign affairs clause originally intended by the eighteenth-century framers of the Constitution. Margaret Somers has pointed out that "at the heart of every narrative is a crisis or flash point that cries out for a solution."[81] By identifying such a crisis within a narrative, she instructs, we can gain access to the internal logic of that narrative. The crisis presented in the NFTC's narrative was an incoherent American foreign policy stemming from the intractable differences in local state policies that existed before the Constitutional Convention during the period between 1783 and 1789.

Significantly, this distinction provides no conceptual room for the role that corporations play in influencing foreign affairs. This discourse depicts states and the foreign affairs they conduct as regulating corporations; but corporations are depicted only as market participants and as neutral, apolitical actors in relation to the conduct of foreign affairs. In short, the NFTC's discourse implies that corporations are shaped by, but are not themselves shapers of, foreign policy.

By creating a national government, the U.S. Constitution fundamentally altered the relationship among the individual states. In short, the claim is that it was the framers' intention of placing complete and exclusive control of foreign affairs in the hands of a single national government, rather than multiple local governments. "If each state were to enact its own foreign policy," the NFTC warned, "then—as was true under the Articles of Confederation—all of the other states would be forced to live with the consequences."[82] Distinguishing between local and national foreign policy, the NFTC postulated several specific consequences that inevitably result from the former—that is, from allowing local states to conduct their own foreign policy.

First, the NFTC postulated that "fifty different foreign trade policies would create significantly higher barriers to trade generally, and could risk maneuvering by each of the states to gain a position more favorable than that held by its neighbors." In addition to these economic consequences, military and security-related consequences would result, the NFTC reasoned, because "the ability of any single state to establish effective international security on its own behalf is much less significant than the ability of the federal government to provide security for the fifty states collectively." According to the NFTC, local foreign policy vis-à-vis foreign nation-states not only weakened the influence of the United States in foreign affairs, but also created the potential for conflicting state-sanctions legislation, with one state favoring trade with a particular foreign country and other states opposing such trade. Such problems, the NFTC claimed, would be further exacerbated by potentially hundreds of municipalities adopting their own foreign policy.

A narrative requires a sense of space and place. We see this illustrated in the NFTC's narrative as well, which relies on a conceptual distinction between "federal states" and "local states." A narrative also posits a sense of time: establishing causality through the temporal sequence of events that it describes. Something that comes before something else, in the narrative schema, causes it. This is not chronological time but epistemological time. A narrative endows cause and effect.[83] But a narrative also recombines the spatial with the temporal elements to depict a meaningful sense of place. The NFTC's historical narrative of the conduct of U.S. foreign policy depicts a sphere of action confined only to state actors. The NFTC has embedded this historical narrative within a broader discourse that asserts that foreign affairs are effective only when mobilized around a national identity.

However, the Commonwealth of Massachusetts presented a transnationalist discourse that constrained the Supreme Court from establishing its ruling on the basis of the NFTC's understanding of the federal state's exclusive power to conduct foreign affairs. Amid these competing discourses on foreign affairs, the Supreme Court constructed a more narrowly circumscribed discourse on the federal Burma law's "multilateral strategy" and "calibration of force" through which it depicted the federal and state Burma laws to have been designed with conflicting purposes. It was on the basis of these conflicting purposes that the Supreme Court was able to ground its ruling that the Massachusetts Burma law violated the supremacy clause of the Constitution.

Within the U.S. Court system, the Burma law campaign activists chose *not* to deploy the discourse on corporate accountability through which they had thus far explained the meaning and purpose of their legislation. To defend the constitutionality of the Massachusetts Burma law, attorneys for the Commonwealth of Massachusetts represented the identity of the local state during the trial not as a *regulator*, holding accountable the transnational practices of corporations, but rather as a *participant*, exercising its choice as a consumer in a transnational market.

The Commonwealth of Massachusetts argued that the Supreme Court traditionally invokes the "dormant" commerce clause of the Tenth Amendment to limit its judicial power to policing the coercive forms of state power, regulation, and taxation, and that the Court traditionally stops short of policing the exercise of state purchasing power, whereby states act more as market participants than as market regulators. Moreover, the Commonwealth of Massachusetts invoked the First Amendment to argue that, like corporations (and other market participants), states acting as market participants have the right to choose with whom they wish to purchase goods and services. Finally, the Commonwealth of Massachusetts extended this metaphor of states acting as market participants to their reading of what Constitutional scholars call the "foreign affairs clause," and in doing so, generated an unprecedented interpretation of its meaning. Despite losing this case in the U.S. Supreme Court, however, one of the most significant outcomes of the Burma law campaign was the discursive contention that it generated in the context of foreign policy and foreign commerce over the meaning of the relationship between transnational corporations and states operating at multiple spatial scales. This is a transnationalist discourse because it recognizes the persistent influence of nation-states in shaping foreign policy, and yet simultaneously asserts that subfederal entities, including corporations, also interact regularly as participants in a global marketplace with foreign states to shape foreign policy and commerce. Thus, this transnationalist discourse, contrary to the globalization discourse, suggests that global markets are embedded in politics and, moreover, that they are embedded in politics that intersect with and transcend politics between nation-states.

It is also a transnationalist legal discourse that attempts to invest this space with transnational relations and practices with legal meaning. But it does so in ways that resist interpreting these relations and practices as already settled by or subject to national and international law. We see this in the example of Massachusetts's spin on the federal versus local government distinction. Its alternative "federal versus nonfederal entities" distinction recodes Massachusetts as a nonfederal entity rather than as a local state. This creates a space for Massachusetts's assertion that it is acting as a market participant, like the member corporations of the NFTC, rather than as a state regulator. This, in turn, creates a discursive space for Massachusetts's argument that nonfederal entities (i.e., both Massachusetts and the member corporations of the NFTC) shape foreign affairs all the time. It also brings corporations back into the discourse, forcing them to position their own practices in relation to the conduct of foreign affairs. Thus, in dialogue with the NFTC and the U.S. courts, Massachusetts deployed this transnationalist legal discourse to skillfully open a transnational legal space that potentially transforms our legal understanding of relations and practices constituting foreign affairs, and that has the power to legitimately conduct foreign relations or affect foreign affairs.

Attorneys for Massachusetts offered the district court a very different history lesson on the meaning of the foreign affairs clause and its implications for the Massachusetts Burma law. Their historical narrative depicted the foreign relations of the United States as having never been, nor ever understood by the framers to have been, so wholly insulated from the individual states as the NFTC's historical narrative would suggest. They pointed out that, in fact, the Constitution never uses the terms "foreign relations," "foreign affairs," or "foreign policy." And regardless, the issue at hand is not about federal power to *conduct* foreign relations, but rather about state power to *affect* foreign affairs:

> The NFTC labors to establish that the federal government has "exclusive authority" to "conduct foreign relations." This case, however, does not implicate the federal power to conduct foreign relations, but rather state power to affect foreign affairs. . . . In the governance of their affairs, states have variously and inevitably impinged on United States foreign relations. They regulate and tax commerce with foreign nations. They regulate the rights of foreign nations resident or present in their territory. The exercise of these powers by the States reflects the allocation of powers made by the Framers. The Constitution does not expressly grant *exclusive* power to conduct foreign policy to the federal government or deny *general* power to affect foreign affairs to the States. Indeed, the Constitution does not even use the term "foreign relations," "foreign policy," or "foreign affairs."[84]

Massachusetts hoped to persuade the court that "the Constitution permits state actions that *indirectly* affect foreign affairs, even where such actions are intended to influence the conduct of a foreign government."[85]

That is, Massachusetts depicted the framers of the Constitution as having understood that local state action inevitably impinges indirectly upon the United States' foreign relations. The framers, they argued, intentionally allocated state power across the boundaries of authority that separate the federal from the local so as to grant *certain* powers to the federal government and deny *certain* powers to the states. Massachusetts's strategy was, first of all, to persuasively distinguish between "federal power to [directly] *conduct* foreign policy" and "[local] state power to [indirectly] *affect* foreign affairs"; second, it hoped to demonstrate that the Burma law does not *interfere* with the conduct of American foreign relations toward the government of Myanmar and that its effects on foreign affairs are indirect because they address the local state's business with corporations, not with the government of Myanmar.

Massachusetts argued that, even if the federal government does have exclusive *authority* to conduct foreign affairs as the NFTC asserts, then it is obvious that the federal government has not in this case, does not in general, and, as a practical matter, could not *exercise* exclusive authority to conduct foreign relations. On the last and boldest point, they explained that this is clear from the numerous transnational actions of state governments and private companies that "affect" foreign affairs. Under increasing conditions of globalization, it is "inevitable":

> The terms "foreign affairs" and "foreign relations" now describe many more topics than at the end of the 18th century; improvements in communication and transportation have inevitably married the States with foreign nations, for better or worse. Countless state and local laws affect foreign business people, traders, investors and tourists. The Commonwealth of Massachusetts maintains twenty-three "sister-state" and other bilateral agreements with sub-national foreign governments and trade promotion organizations. The Commonwealth also routinely helps companies "increase their business in international markets" by *maintaining overseas* trade offices and introducing businesses to officials of foreign governments. Massachusetts has organized foreign trade missions attended by Digital Corp. and Gillette Co., two members of the Board of Directors of the NFTC.[86]

The Commonwealth of Massachusetts argued before the U.S. District Court that the companies comprising the membership of the NFTC are, in practice, ambivalent about leaving to the federal government the power to conduct foreign affairs and reflect not their concern for constitutionality of the Burma law, but rather the politics of constructing and participating in contemporary global markets:

> These companies are pleased to benefit from actions by Massachusetts that "affect" or "seek to influence" foreign governments or commerce when the actions increase profits. However, when state action might decrease profits, the same companies through the NFTC want the judiciary to preempt the State even where Congress has not. These inconsistent positions show that the Burma Law does not usurp federal power but rather applies a traditional state power—procurement—to a changing world in which the lines between national and state and foreign and domestic concerns are much less clear than in 1787.[87]

The foreign activities of private companies underscore the same point. Members of the NFTC conduct their own selective purchasing through voluntary codes of conduct that govern their purchases from contractors and subcontractors in foreign countries. Some of the codes specifically refer to laws imposed on employers by host countries and punish suppliers who violate these laws. These punishments are private boycotts that present at least the same risk of "more than an indirect effect or incidental effect in foreign countries" as that presented by state and local laws. While the Constitution may not proscribe these private boycotts, the actions of NFTC members around the world show that in the modern era the federal government has no monopoly on action with foreign resonances and that Congress has tolerated a wide range of *nonfederal* activities that generally affect foreign affairs or are intended specifically to end human rights abuses by foreign governments or firms.[88]

Massachusetts's transnationalist discourse attempted to give new meaning to the relationship between states and corporations. This discourse also invokes a narrative of the framers' original understanding of the foreign affairs power, but it suggests how the transnationalization of local state procurement and corporate regulation has unavoidably had an influence on foreign affairs. The narrative presented by the Commonwealth of Massachusetts also persuasively influences the ruling of the Supreme Court to the extent that it shows how the framers may not have given exclusive control of all foreign affairs practices to the federal government.

The Role of Political Contingency

The Supreme Court reasoned that the federal Burma law gives the president full discretion in deciding when to apply or terminate economic sanctions in Burma, depending on what national security requires, but the Massachusetts Burma law applies sanctions that are immediate and perpetual, with no termination provision. In this case, the Court explained, it is the fact that Congress has delegated full discretion to the president that controls the issue of preemption:

> The President has been given this authority not merely to make a
> political statement but to achieve a political result, and the fullness
> of his authority shows the importance in the congressional mind of
> reaching that result. It is simply implausible that Congress would
> have gone to such lengths to empower the President if it had been
> willing to compromise his effectiveness by deference to every position
> of state statute or local ordinance that might, if enforced, blunt the
> consequences of discretionary Presidential action.[89]

Invoking the metaphor of the bargaining chip to describe the president's control of funds valuable to a hostile country, the Supreme Court represented the Massachusetts Burma law as "reduc[ing] the value of the chips created by the federal statute,"[90] and, thus, as an obstacle to the

full purposes and objectives of Congress. The state act does so, according to the Court,

> by imposing a different, state system of economic pressure against the
> Burmese political regime . . . , making it impossible for [the president]
> to restrain fully the coercive power of the national economy when
> he may choose to take the discretionary action open to him, whether
> he believes that the national interest requires sanctions to be lifted, or
> believes that the promise of lifting sanctions would move the Burmese
> regime in the democratic direction.[91]

In short, as long as the Massachusetts Burma law is in effect, the president has less to offer Burma as an economic incentive for changing its
domestic policies and therefore less diplomatic leverage.

Although the Court acknowledged that the state and federal Burma
legislation shared the same goals (to promote improved human rights
conditions in Burma), it was more concerned by the two policies' conflicting means. The Court saw clearly the difference in not only the
scale, but also the scope and reach of the state and federal sanctions
strategies:

> While the state Act differs from the federal in relying on indirect
> economic leverage through third parties with Burmese connections, it
> otherwise stands in clear contrast to the congressional scheme in the
> scope of subject matter addressed.[92]

It noted that the Massachusetts Burma law penalizes companies
with preexisting affiliates or investments, "all of which lie beyond the
reach of the federal act's restrictions on 'new investment' in Burmese
economic development."[93] Moreover, it pointed out that the state act
imposes restrictions on foreign companies as well as domestic, whereas
the federal act limits its reach to U.S. persons.[94] "Sanctions," the Court
wrote, "are drawn not only to bar what they prohibit but to allow what
they permit, and the inconsistency of sanctions here undermines the
congressional calibration of force."[95] Unlike Massachusetts's Burma law,
the Court explained, "Congress's calibrated Burma policy is a deliberate
effort to steer a middle path."[96]

The final point in the Supreme Court's reasoning was to explain precisely how the federal and state sanctions held conflicting purposes. In
doing so, however, the Court did not merely address how the Massachusetts Burma law unconstitutionally violated the supremacy clause; it
also indirectly challenged the reasoning of the lower court rulings that

had suggested how this state act unconstitutionally violated the foreign affairs clause. The Supreme Court wrote:

> The State Act is at odds with the President's intended authority to speak for the United States among the world's nations in developing a "comprehensive, multilateral strategy to bring democracy to and improve human rights practices and the quality of life in Burma." Congress called for Presidential cooperation with members of ASEAN and other countries in developing such a strategy, directed the President to encourage a dialogue between the government of Burma and the democratic opposition, and required him to report to the Congress on the progress of his diplomatic efforts.[97]

As the Court explained, this explicit congressional command to the president to take the initiative for the United States among the international community invested him with the maximum authority of the national government. The Court concluded: "This clear mandate and invocation of exclusively national power belies any suggestion that Congress intended the president's effective voice to be obscured by state or local action."[98]

We are now in a position to understand the full meaning of the Court's point that the fact in this case controlling the preemption issue is that "Congress has delegated full discretion to the President" (cited above). In other words, the Massachusetts Burma law is unconstitutional not because the U.S. Constitution has given exclusive authority to the federal government to conduct foreign affairs, but because the U.S. Congress explicitly delegated to the executive (i.e., the president of the United States) its measure of authority—giving full authority to the executive. As the Court's argument unfolded, the congressional delegation of "full discretion" came to mean the "maximum authority of the national government." Moreover, the Court's argument asserts that, because this maximum authority of the national government has been delegated to the president in particular, Congress meant to give exclusive power to the national government (and not the local states) in conducting foreign affairs with Burma. Thus, this is an issue that is controlled by the supremacy clause, not the foreign affairs clause.

What the Court's reasoning here also suggests, but which it did not draw attention to, is that the federal Burma law's purpose reflected that of the "constructive engagement" approach (as opposed to "economic sanctions") that had been debated among nation-states since 1988, in the context of the international foreign policy on Burma. But had the federal government's position been different, then the result would have been different. That Massachusetts lost the court case was not a product of a losing transnational strategy, but of being on the wrong side of a political debate about how the United States should balance its mix of carrots and sticks in its effort to influence regime change in Burma.

The Court struck down Massachusetts's (nonfederal) Free Burma law on the specific grounds that it interfered with the intentions of the federal Burma law. The Court interpreted the federal Burma law as legislation that was intended not simply to impose "blunt" sanctions, but rather to exert a "finely calibrated" amount of pressure on the Myanmar government in combination with economic incentives—akin to those offered under the existing policy of constructive engagement that the federal government had publicly denounced as "soft on human rights abuse" when enacting its federal Burma law. In contrast, the Court explained, the selective purchasing legislation enacted by Massachusetts represents an extreme form of economic sanctions by comparison and offers the president too little room for diplomatic maneuvering in its effort to coax the Myanmar government toward democratic reform.

Ironically, in personal interviews with original organizers of the selective purchasing law campaign, I discovered that they had considered it an achievement when President Clinton enacted the federal Burma law. Initially, they assumed that this federal act would serve to reinforce their local Burma laws and lend immediate and significant symbolic gravitas to their broader movement for democracy and human rights in Burma. They had not anticipated that the federal Burma law, which they had actively supported in the beginning, might be interpreted as a significantly different policy toward Burma, much less one that would be used to undermine their own Burma laws.

In principle, this ruling has not affected the legality of selective purchasing legislation more generally. It does not, for example, affect the use of selective purchasing legislation to hold Swiss banks accountable to Holocaust survivors and their relatives for the money that they stole from them during World War II. Nor does it call into question the constitutionality of the selective purchasing legislation that was used to influence corporations to sever their ties with South Africa's apartheid regime in the 1980s. Nor, for that matter, does it affect the Free

Burma legislation enacted by several municipal townships throughout Australia. Rather, it affects only the Free Burma legislation enacted by local and regional governments throughout the United States. Therefore, the transnationalist legal discourse that the Free Burma movement deployed in this campaign may still be used in the future by other actors to challenge neoliberal foreign policy monopolized by nation-states to influence the process through which global markets are embedded in politics. The transnational legal space provided by selective purchasing legislation remains an open terrain for future political struggle.

Conclusion

Selective purchasing legislation was a successful form of economic sanctioning. The federal Burma law and subsequent sanctions,[99] by comparison, have been far less effective. Moreover, due to their allowing existing investment, like Unocal's $1.2 billion Yadana gas pipeline construction project that I will examine in more detail in the Conclusion, the federal Burma law, in practice, operates much more like a policy of constructive engagement.

Ironically, this point has been lost on U.S. foreign policy makers today, who are rethinking their approach to Burma. U.S. Senator Jim Webb (D–VA), after initiating an independent visit to meet with Myanmar officials in August 2009 (and orchestrating the release of U.S. citizen John Yettaw, who had been sentenced to seven years in prison for swimming uninvited to the lakeside home of Aung San Suu Kyi), began arguing publicly and vociferously that the U.S. policy of economic sanctions against Burma has failed, and that it is time to offer Burma more carrots in the form of foreign investment.[100] In other words, he was suggesting that the United States needs to replace its sanctions policy with a constructive engagement policy toward Burma. What proposals like this one fail to acknowledge is that the U.S. policy toward Burma has been, in practice, more akin to a constructive engagement policy that for symbolic purposes has been called a sanctions policy. The Supreme Court rescinded the United States' real sanctions policy toward Burma a decade ago, despite the fact that it was working very effectively. The current policy calls for a constructive engagement policy amount not to a new policy toward Burma, but rather more of the same. In this sense,

4

Corporate "Death Penalty": Executing Charter Revocation

We are not just focusing on one company's violations of laws to protect American citizens. We are saying that we, the people of the United States acting in our several states, chartered the U.S.-based transnational corporations that now range across the world—Unocal was chartered in 1890—and we assert our moral responsibility for, and therefore our democratic control over, offenses against people which our corporations commit or in which they become complicit anywhere and everywhere in the world.

—Ronnie Dugger, "Foreword," in Robert Benson, *Challenging Corporate Rule: A Petition to Revoke Unocal's Charter as a Guide to Citizen Action*

For the Free Burma movement, the legislative struggle of the selective purchasing law campaign raised an important question: under political conditions in which the federal government seems unwilling to challenge existing relations between U.S.-chartered corporations and the Myanmar government, what, if any, existing legal powers then are fundamentally vested in local and regional states that they can exercise to influence the conduct of transnational corporations operating in Burma? They found one answer in the transnational legal space provided by corporate charters.

The selective purchasing law campaign had successfully persuaded all but one U.S.-based corporation (and many foreign corporations as well) to quit doing business with Burma. The lone holdout was Unocal Oil Corporation. Unocal was the only remaining California-chartered corporation still doing business in Burma. From the outset of the selective purchasing law campaign, it had been also the largest U.S.-based corporate investor in Burma. The next campaign targeted Unocal specifically, seeking to revoke its corporate charter on the basis of newly emerging evidence provided by NGOs that had documented Unocal's reliance on forced labor in constructing its natural gas pipeline through Burma, severely undermining the corporation's claim that its investment in Burma was providing jobs for the Burmese people and that, in turn, its "constructive engagement" with the Myanmar government would likely promote greater protection of human rights and democratic political change.

In 1992, Unocal Oil Corporation made a deal with the authoritarian government of Myanmar (Burma)[1] to build the Yadana Project, a natural gas pipeline. As Free Burma activists continued to focus on alternative means of sanctioning transnational corporations that continued to engage in business with the Myanmar regime, the reformative influence of Unocal's economic partnership with that regime was, by 1999, called significantly into question as INGOs began to publicize well-documented evidence of the pipeline project's forcibly conscripting local villagers as laborers for its construction. As part of pipeline construction partnership, the military junta that runs Myanmar forced local villagers to work for Unocal under some of the most deplorable conditions imaginable. The junta forced the peasants from their homes and made them work literally at gunpoint. Soldiers from Myanmar's army raped, tortured and, in some cases, murdered the forced laborers.[2] They also used the workers as human shields and munitions porters against other peasants, often from their own villages, whom the government had branded as rebels. The peasants working for Unocal on the Yadana Project were essentially slaves, joining the ranks of the approximately 12.3 million people in the world today who are subjected to modern forms of forced labor.[3]

On the basis of this evidence, Free Burma activists helped to organize two subsequent transnational campaigns that more directly focused on Unocal. In doing so, they helped to create two new transnationalist discourses on corporate accountability.

This chapter describes the first of these two campaigns targeting Unocal. This campaign was an effort to mobilize Californians to petition their state attorney general and governor to revoke Unocal's corporate charter, effectively stripping the corporation of its rights and power to exist. In chapter 5, "Alien Tort Claims: Adjudicating Human Rights Abuses Abroad," I describe the second of these campaigns, which activists initiated before the charter revocation campaign but which continued years afterward, in an effort to hold Unocal liable, within the jurisdiction of the U.S. court system, for variously alleged human rights abuses (but especially the use of forced labor) that their business partners committed for the purpose of completing (and profiting from) their gas pipeline project in Burma.

Like the selective purchasing law campaign, these two subsequent campaigns each deployed transnationalist discourses on corporate governance and targeted the relationship between states and corporations. Yet unlike the particular discourse on corporate governance deployed in the previous selective purchasing law campaign, which stressed that market participants were the enforcer of the human rights norms that corporations were transgressing, the discourses on corporate accountability deployed in these subsequent campaigns both stress that states (as regulators, not market participants) are the enforcers of human rights norms against corporate misconduct. Both of these campaigns deploy existing U.S. law that states used to regulate corporations before the mid-nineteenth century. The particular laws that each campaign deploys survived the century-and-a-half-long aggressive, liberal transformation of corporate law. Yet in light of the state's cultural structures of neoliberalism, their

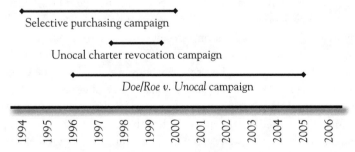

Figure 10. Time line of the three Free Burma legal campaigns, illustrating the extent of their overlap.

current reappropriation renders them at once obscure and radical. Re-tooling these dusty statutes within a transnationalist discursive context to meet the challenges posed by contemporary corporate visions of eco-nomic expansion beyond national boundaries, Free Burma activists and their diverse movement allies have used them effectively to wrestle from the state new opportunities and resources for changing the ways in which we think about and govern our relationships to corporations, to states, and to each other.

The International Labor Organization, Amnesty International, and Human Rights Watch Asia presented new evidence of human rights offenses committed in the furtherance of Unocal's gas pipeline project in Burma. But the Free Burma activists who participated in this cam-paign forged a new set of alliances with mostly California-based affili-ates of national, nonprofit, public interest organizations. Deploying a more local identity as "citizens of California," they combined elements of three discourses that were new to the Free Burma movement: (1) the state's power to revoke corporate charters, (2) the corporation as a state-constituted, nonhuman entity, and (3) the recidivist offender as deserv-ing of exclusion from the community. In doing so, they elaborated the transnationalist discourse that had emerged in the course of the NFTC's constitutional challenge to the state of Massachusetts's power to con-duct foreign policy.[4]

Why Revoke Unocal's Corporate Charter?

On September 10, 1998, a coalition of thirty public interest organiza-tions,[5] including the Free Burma Coalition, organized three simultane-ous news conferences in Sacramento, San Francisco, and Los Angeles, at which they denounced Unocal as a corporate criminal and demanded that Unocal—as a corporation—receive the "death penalty." These corporate reform activists presented ten counts of criminal action that Unocal allegedly committed over the previous two decades in the United States, Canada, Afghanistan, and Burma. These allegations included environmental destruction in California and elsewhere; unfair treatment of workers; hundreds of occupational health and safety law violations; usurpation of political power; deception of the courts, shareholders, and the public; and complicity in gross human rights violations abroad against women, homosexuals, workers, villagers, and indigenous peoples.

With regard to Burma in particular, these activists made a host of public allegations. First, they alleged that Unocal's business partner, the SLORC's Myanmar Oil and Gas Enterprise (MOGE), was guilty of using forced and slave labor to clear the land for Unocal's pipeline route, build related infrastructure in the area, and provide security for the pipeline.[6] Additionally, they charged Unocal's business partner with having committed widespread killings, torture, and rapes in the process of providing security for the pipeline, and that Unocal continued to work with MOGE on the project, despite having been aware of their partner's actions.[7] Moreover, they alleged that Unocal had "knowingly profited from the large-scale forcible relocation of Burmese villages and villagers without compensation."[8]

Building on an argument that the state of Massachusetts had made in the Supreme Court relating to how nonfederal state entities (not only local and regional states, but also corporations) intentionally and regularly influence foreign policy, these activists also accused Unocal of having usurped political power "that it cannot, by its corporate nature, exercise," and having aggressively undermined democratic processes at home and abroad. In specific terms, they claimed that Unocal, "acting in hostile opposition to the democratically elected government, has worked to subvert the Burmese people's right to self-determination." Reappropriating the language that the NFTC had used in challenging the constitutionality of the State of Massachusetts's power to conduct foreign policy, these activists depicted Unocal as deciding to become "a global economic and political force unto itself," deploying diplomats as if they were the State Department itself and "working to thwart U.S. foreign policy."[9]

The "Unocal Petition"

The simultaneous news conferences were more than an exercise in First Amendment rights to free speech. They were meant to draw attention to a 129-page formal petition demanding attorney general of California Dan Lungren to revoke the corporate charter of Union Oil Company (Unocal) and thus strip the corporation of its rights to exist. Also, the petition demanded that, under a judge's order, the corporation would be forced to sell its assets to law-abiding corporations. Three copies of the petition were delivered during the news conferences: one to the attorney general's office in Sacramento and one each to his representatives' offices in Los Angeles and San Francisco.

Selective Purchasing Laws

- 78 members of Congress
- 9 States
- 12 municipalities
- AFL-CIO
- Consumer's Choice Council
- American Lands Alliance
- Preamble Center
- Institute for Agricultural and Trade Policy
- Friends of the Earth
- Humane Society of the United States
- Defenders of Wildlife
- Rainforest Relief
- Center for Constitutional Rights
- Citizens for Participation in Political Action
- International Labor Rights Fund
- New England Burma Roundtable
- Unitarian Universalist Service Committee
- EarthRights International

Unocal Charter Revocation

- Action Resource Center
- Alliance for Democracy of USA
- Alliance for Democracy of Austin, TX
- Alliance for Democracy of San Fernando Valley, CA
- Amazon Watch
- Asian/Pacific Gays and Friends
- Burma Forum Los Angeles
- Democracy Unlimited of Humboldt County, CA
- Earth Island Institute
- Feminist Majority Foundation
- Free Burma Coalition
- Free Burma – No Petro Dollars for SLORC
- Global Exchange
- National Lawyers Guild USA
- National Lawyers Guild of Los Angeles, San Diego, Santa Clara Valley, and San Francisco
- National Organization for Women
- National Organization for Women, California
- Program on Corporations, Law & Democracy (POCLAD)
- Project Maje
- Project Underground

Figure 11. Organizations supporting the three Free Burma legal campaigns.

Unocal Charter Revocation
(continued)

- Rainforest Action Network
- Surfer's Environmental Alliance
- Transnational Resource and Action Center

Doe/Roe v. Unocal

Twenty-seven attorneys and law professors representing the following organizations:
- Center for International Environmental law
- Global Exchange
- Rainforest Action Network
- Sierra Club
- Center for Constitutional Rights
- EarthRights International
- International Labor Rights Fund
- Center for Human Rights and Constitutional Law
- Howrey & Simon (Los Angeles, CA)
- Munger, Tolles & Olson (San Francisco, CA)
- Munger, Tolles & Olson (Los Angeles, CA)
- Hadsell & Stormer, INC (Pasadena, CA)
- Schonbrun, De Simone, Seplow, Harris & Hoffman, LLP (Venice, CA)
- Krafchak & Associates (Los Angeles, CA)
- Kohn, Swift, & Graf, P.C. (Philadelphia, PA)
- Fulbright & Jaworski (Los Angeles, CA)
- Law Offices of Cristobal Bonifaz (Amherst, MA)
- Boston College of Law (Newton Centre, MA)
- Seattle University Law School (Seattle, WA)

Figure 11. Organizations supporting the three Free Burma legal campaigns *(continued)*.

It is important to emphasize that this petition was distinct from a lawsuit. Nor was it a petition in the sense of a list of signatures that one gathers on a clipboard in front of the supermarket. It was a lengthy legal brief filed with the attorney general and asking him to go to court on behalf of the public to revoke a corporation's charter. A version of this petition, which was subsequently published under the title *Challenging Corporate Rule: The Petition to Revoke Unocal's Charter as a Guide to Citizen Action* (1999), explains the nature of this petition and, in part, why these activists, organized largely by lawyers, chose this form of collective action instead of pursuing a lawsuit:

> We titled the Unocal document "Complaint Lodged with the Attorney General," because the California statute says the attorney general may take action "upon the complaint of a private party." But we decided to refer publicly to our document as the "Unocal Petition," because we are petitioning the attorney general to act.... Whatever it is called, the legal mechanism of filing a document with the attorney general is more attractive than a lawsuit because it avoids litigation costs and invokes the political process.[10]

There was more to this strategic choice than saving money. The process of revoking a corporation's charter—of having the attorney general go to court on behalf of citizens to dissolve a corporation for malfeasance and selling its assets to others who operate in the public interest—provides a form of corporate sanction that targets the corporate actor itself, not simply the corporation's wrongful actions, one toxic spill at a time, one layoff at a time, one human rights violation at a time. Ultimately, however, these activists did not base their strategic choice on arguments regarding the efficiency of this form of corporate sanction. Rather, these activists filed this petition on the basis of both long-term and short-term goals that they perceived to be more likely achievable. In the long term, these activists filed this petition to change the legal and political culture. As the author of the petition explained:

> We are not politically naïve. We don't think that this is going to get so far along the road that Unocal will actually be broken up anytime soon, although it should be. Our fundamental goal here is to change the public discourse and the media perception of the power of corporations versus people, to float the idea that people are sovereign over corporations.[11]

In the short term, the campaign strategy was to make elected officials politically accountable by challenging their frequent refrain that they have no power to control the actions of giant corporations. It reminds people that these state actors have made a choice to give such corporations the power that they exercise.

The Corporation's State-derived Right to Exist

Regardless of our opinions on sentencing individual criminals to death, we understand what it means. What is intriguing about the idea of delivering a death penalty sentence to corporations that have committed criminal acts—that is, of having a state withdraw its permission for a corporation to exist—is that so few of us understand that a corporation depends upon the state's permission to exist. One of the key aims shared by many of the organizations participating in this campaign is to educate the public on this aspect of the relationship between states and corporations to generate more public debate in favor of (human) citizens playing a greater role in governing corporate behavior rather than allowing corporations to regulate their own conduct.

Thus, this case highlights administrative discursive contention over the enforcement of an existing but long-forgotten law in California that emphasizes corporations as legal entities that owe their existence to the regional state that created them. The law also specifies conditions under which corporations may be stripped of the charters that grant their right to exist. It provides a legal procedure allowing the people of California, acting through their attorney general, to initiate the charter revocation of any of its corporations that have violated existing law. Similar laws regarding the revocation of corporate charters still exist, yet remain unenforced, in most regions throughout the United States. This case study illustrates how corporations are embedded in law. But it also illustrates how transnational legal action, and the discursive space that it produces, can mediate the process through which global markets continue to become embedded in *law*. The campaign to revoke Unocal's corporate charter deploys a transnational strategy through which the Free Burma movement attempts to get the California state attorney general to bring a lawsuit on behalf of the people of California that would decharter Unocal on the basis of "crimes against humanity," "environmental devastation," and other violations of international law that it has committed not only in California, but also in Burma and other foreign states.

Networking Corporate Charter Revocation

A quick comparison of the organizations formally supporting this Unocal charter revocation campaign with those that had formally supported the selective purchasing law campaign would suggest that there is no continuity between them; that is, that no organization formally supported both campaigns. (See Figures 12 and 13.) Also included among the thirty organizations supporting this campaign were the Free Burma Coalition (FBC), Burma Forum Los Angeles, and Free Burma—No Petro-Dollars for SLORC.

Selective Purchasing	Unocal Charter Revocation	Doe/Roe v. Unocal
Center for Constitutional Rights		Center for Constitutional Rights
International Labor Rights Fund		International Labor Rights Fund
Earth Rights International		Earth Rights International
	Global Exchange	Global Exchange
	Rainforest Action Network	Rainforest Action Network

Figure 12. Organizations participating in more than one of the three Free Burma legal campaigns. No single organization formally supported all three campaigns, but there are several links between campaigns, and some organizations formally supported two of the three campaigns.

The FBC, at the time, was a loosely coordinated umbrella network for a variety of movement organizations promoting democracy and human rights in Burma. It was one of several projects formally housed under the Institute for Community and Institutional Development (ICID). Zarni, who had played an important role as the Burmese face and voice of the selective purchasing law campaign, founded and served as the executive director and as a board member of the ICID. By mid-2003, the FBC no longer served this function. New organizations created in the wake of infighting within the network absorbed its key roles. Most of the leadership, excluding Zarni, helped to form what is now known as the U.S. Campaign for Burma. The FBC has become little more than a Web site maintained by Zarni, who since has personally renounced sanctions against Burma in favor of engagement.

Nevertheless, during the selective purchasing law campaign, the Free Burma Coalition had worked behind the scenes to mobilize, organize, and coordinate other participating actors and flows of information. The FBC also had an affiliate organization known as the New England Burma Roundtable (which was then coordinated by Simon Billenness, a key organizer of the selective purchasing law campaign), through which it expressed its interests directly in an amicus brief that it filed in support of the state of Massachusetts. In the Unocal charter revocation campaign,

Selective Purchasing	Unocal Charter Revocation	Doe/Roe v. Unocal
New England Burma Roundtable	Free Burma Coalition	14 Karen peasants from Burma (Plaintiffs in Doe/Roe v. Unocal)
	Burma Forum Los Angeles	
	Free Burma – No Petro Dollars for SLORC	

Figure 13. Organizations closely linked to the Free Burma Coalition. The fourteen peasants from Burma were closely connected to one of their village members who escaped a SLORC forced labor camp and eventually found employment with EarthRights International (ERI). ERI worked closely with the Free Burma Coalition to prepare the plaintiffs' travel to and accommodations in the United States.

the Free Burma Coalition played a more visible role as a signatory of the Unocal petition, as did another of its affiliate organizations known as Burma Forum Los Angeles.

After the Supreme Court struck down the Massachusetts Burma law, Burma Forum Los Angeles, anticipating that Los Angeles's Free Burma Law also might be rescinded, campaigned successfully to get the Los Angeles City Council to vote in support of selling all stock in the city's pension funds from companies that invest in Burma.[12] Burma Forum Los Angeles has also been a key organizer in campaigns to pressure the University of California regents to divest more than $50 million from companies that were continuing to invest in Burma. Because most of the members of Burma Forum Los Angeles resided in the same city where Unocal was headquartered, they were also able to play a leading role in organizing direct protest action against the corporation during its annual shareholder meetings. Another of their notable campaigns targeted the International Olympic Committee (IOC). Upon discovering that the Olympic torchbearers' uniforms were produced in Burma by a coerced labor force, Burma Forum Los Angeles organized a campaign to halt the IOC's support of slavery in Burma.[13]

Another of the key organizations driving the campaign to revoke Unocal's charter was the Free Burma—No Petro-Dollars for SLORC. It was not an affiliate organization of the Free Burma Coalition, but rather a loosely networked project in its own right that was coordinated by International Rivers (IR)—then called "International Rivers Network—a nonprofit all-volunteer organization of activists experienced in challenging economically, environmentally, and socially unsound river intervention projects."[14] At the time, the IR had a core staff of about twenty activists trained in economics, biology, engineering, hydrology, anthropology, and environmental sciences. From its main office in Berkeley, California, it organized a network of supporters, funding sources, advisers, interns, and volunteers spanning North America, Latin America, South and Southeast Asia, Africa, and China. Its primary aim is to halt and reverse the degradation of river systems by combining campaigning on specific key projects around the world while working to change global policies that negatively impact directly related issues of environmental integrity, social justice, and human rights. International Rivers also monitors and critiques the policies of financial institutions, including the World Bank, and provides analysis and recommendations for reforming their practices; mobilizes international support from their network of activists and experts; assists in fundraising for campaigns at the local level; and generates publicity through industry, alternative, and mainstream media.

The Free Burma—No Petro-Dollars for SLORC campaign was initiated by a request for support from ethnic minorities (the Karen, Mon, and Tavoy) living in the Tenasserim area of Burma where Unocal was constructing its gas pipeline. According to the campaign's independent Web site, its objective was "to escalate public attention and pressure on these oil companies [working on the gas pipeline in Burma] so that they withdraw their operations and investments from Burma until a genuine democratic government is in place."[15]

As in the selective purchasing law campaign, social movement organizations supporting the Unocal charter revocation campaign represented a variety of issues, including civil and human rights, environmental rights, indigenous peoples' rights, women's rights, and gay and lesbian rights. Despite the fact that the petition condemned Unocal's alleged use of forced labor, there were no organizations participating in the campaign that explicitly represented themselves as working on labor rights. However, several organizations represented themselves as working to promote corporate accountability and economic justice. Spearheading this campaign was Robert Benson, corporate reform activist, law professor, and lead attorney for the National Lawyers Guild's (NLG) charter revocation project. The National Lawyers Guild is a nationwide membership organization that styles itself as an alternative bar association of progressive attorneys, law students, legal workers, and jailhouse lawyers. The International Law Project for Human, Economic, and Environmental Defense (HEED), affiliated with the NLG's Los Angeles chapter, spearheaded the charter revocation project and hosted the Unocal Corporate Charter Revocation Action Center. In addition to providing information and news on the charter revocation project, HEED sold copies of its book version of the Unocal petition and a twenty-four-minute documentary videotape that they produced, *How Many Strikes Do Big Corporations Get?* The video traces the development of HEED's campaign as well as live footage of its news conference/protest in Los Angeles in 1998, when it filed its petition.

The general aim of HEED's charter revocation project was to reinstate the kind of social contract through which human citizens in the United States (as opposed to corporate citizens) previously exercised substantial control over the power and objectives of corporations. The more specific Unocal Corporate Charter Revocation Campaign represents a strategic first step toward that end. As Benson writes in the published edition of the Unocal petition:

> To redefine the corporation will be a daunting task, given the power of big business and given the last 100 years of special privileges granted to corporations by legislatures and courts. But the people of California, acting through you, our attorney general, do have one straightforward remedy already on the books that can accomplish much: The power to revoke a corporation's charter, that is to dissolve the company and have its assets sold to others who will carry on a business more appropriately. *We ask you to start with Unocal.*[16]

It is important to understand that the scope of this campaign is transnational. Certainly, because regional states within the United States are responsible for the revocation of a corporation's charter, there is a sense in which the campaign targets states as enforcers of corporate governance at a "local" level. We have also seen how the campaign's participating organizations are linked throughout, yet primarily within the territorial boundaries of, the United States. In other words, most of the campaign's mobilization effort seems to be exerted within a national scope. Nevertheless, as in the case of the selective purchasing law campaign, there is an important sense in which the meaning of this campaign has been shaped by a transnationalist discourse on corporate governance. The following articulation by Ronnie Dugger, another key organizer of the Unocal Corporate Charter Revocation Campaign, and cochair of the Alliance for Democracy, represents an eloquent distillation of this discourse:

> We are not just focusing on one company's violations of laws to protect American citizens. We are saying that we, the people of the United States acting in our several states, chartered the U.S.-based transnational corporations that now range across the world—Unocal was chartered in 1890—and we assert our moral responsibility for, and therefore our democratic control over, offenses against people which our corporations commit or in which they become complicit anywhere and everywhere in the world.[17]

In both the selective purchasing law campaign and the corporate dechartering campaign, we find actors identifying ways in which they locally empower corporations and thus facilitate (as well as potentially constrain) their action, wherever that corporate action takes place. In this campaign to revoke Unocal's corporate charter, these activists are asserting that, in many countries but particularly in the United States, corporate entities *qua* "persons" have gradually obtained for themselves entitlement to both civil and human rights. Indeed, over the past century and a half, most U.S. human citizens have become so accustomed to thinking of powerful corporate "persons" as citizens of equal (if not greater) status in law that they have largely forgotten that there ever existed a time when human citizens very much dominated corporate citizens and the very terms of their business operations.

Although today's transnational corporations often depict markets as natural and operating most efficiently in the absence of state regulation, and so cavalierly proclaim themselves to be the engines of contemporary globalization, the power of *corporations* as market participants fundamentally derives from states. U.S.-based transnational corporations owe their very creation and ongoing existence to the state's protection of their rights of personhood.

"By What Authority?" Reconstituting Corporate Citizenship

Appreciation for the power of this petition begins with understanding that it is not a request to change existing laws regulating the malfeasance of corporations. In the previous chapter, we saw that the U.S. Supreme Court has chosen to refrain from answering at this time the historio-judicial question of how much foreign policy the Constitutional framers had intended to authorize local and regional states to exercise, particularly with regard to those states' efforts to shape the conduct of corporations with whom they do business. However, the Constitution clearly did vest in the individual states the power to grant existence to corporations (as a legal entity), whereby each state was responsible for controlling activity within its own domain.[18]

For the first century of the United States' existence, forming a corporation required permission from the state in the form of a corporate charter.[19] Initially, these states granted charters to corporations to build public works and conveniences. These were not-for-profit corporations. Although the states at that time also chartered some private corporations for profit-making enterprises, and even granted special privileges to promote their economic viability, businesses at the time typically involved small numbers of people operating as partners, sharing the risks of the business. Each partner retained individual responsibility for all the actions of the partnership.[20] Entrepreneurs required a special act of the legislature granting a charter of incorporation; private initiative alone was insufficient.[21] The U.S. legislators, until the last half of the nineteenth century, required individuals who wished to form corporations to obtain such permission because they conceived of corporate charters as conveying privileges, such as limited liability, that could not be acquired by means of ordinary contracts.[22] As is still true today, the process of incorporation provided individuals who might otherwise carry out business in their own names to obtain for their business relationship a distinct legal identity that was separate from the people who ran it. This identity as a "corporation" enabled those individuals who actually ran the business to shield themselves from responsibility for their actions.[23] In other words, a corporation was constructed as an entity in its own right—in short, as a "person."

Yet, because legislators conceived of the corporate person as a creature of the state, they assumed that it was subject to whatever limitations or regulatory burdens that might emerge from the political process.[24] Moreover, legislators perceived no contradictions in conceiving of the corporation as having a legal status that was different from "natural" (that is, individual, human) persons. For example, as Naomi Lamoreaux

has documented in her work exploring how nineteenth-century corporations in the United States acquired legal personhood, legislators generally believed that

> unlike a natural person, a corporation could not "be deemed a moral
> agent, subject to moral obligation." Nor could it "be subject to personal
> suffering." Nor could it generally participate, like an ordinary citizen, "in
> the civil government of the country."[25]

While the United States' first politicians viewed commerce as innoc-
uous, they did not, as modern politicians are so prone to do, easily associate corporations with "free trade." In practice, the majority of people
during this period expressed widespread opposition to and distrust for
the economic and political power of corporations through citizen vigi-
lance and activism, and, as a result, these early legislators granted few
charters. Significantly, they denied charters when communities voiced
their opposition to the plans of prospective incorporators.[26] Legislators
also imposed statutory limits on corporate size, wealth, and longevity.[27]
Citizens themselves played a role in governing corporations by specify-
ing rules and operating conditions laid out in corporate charters, and
thus narrowing the definition of a given corporation's purpose.[28] The
state deemed any corporation that acted in violation of its corporative
purpose to be acting *ultra vires*, that is, beyond the legal power or authority of the corporation. In effect, citizens acting through their legislatures
banned incorporated businesses from taking any action that they did not
specifically allow.

The penalty for abuse or misuse of corporate charters was revocation
of the charter and dissolution of the corporation. Although corporate
charter revocation is not a new legal mechanism, its use has been so
limited over the past century and a half, particularly as U.S. courts increasingly recognized corporations' multiplying claims to rights of personhood, that most citizens today are unfamiliar with it. The authors of
the Unocal petition attribute their inspiration for the campaign to the
(1993) treatise, "Taking Care of Business: Citizenship and the Charter
of Incorporation," coauthored by Richard Grossman and Frank Adams.
In this treatise, Grossman and Adams trace the corporate charter revocation practices of regional states within the United States during
the nineteenth century. They observe, for example, that Pennsylvania
included revocation clauses in their charters as early as 1784, and even

included such clauses in the charters of insurance companies by 1809 and in banking charters by 1814. In 1825, Pennsylvania's legislators went even further by adopting broad powers to revoke, alter, or annul corporate charters whenever they thought proper; and by 1857 amended their constitution to instruct legislators to alter, revoke, or annul any of the subsequent corporate charters that they granted whenever they deemed these charters to be posing a risk of injury to the community's citizens.

During the 1840s and 1850s, Grossman and Adams point out, states revoked charters routinely. Not only Pennsylvania, but also Ohio and Mississippi revoked banking charters for engaging in practices that the states deemed likely to leave the corporations in a financially unsound condition. During that same period, the states of Massachusetts and New York revoked the corporations responsible for maintaining the turnpikes when they were found guilty of not keeping the roads in repair.

By the late 1800s, however, states had relinquished their monopoly over the process of incorporation, in the name of democratizing it, by enacting "general incorporation laws," allowing any company to register itself as a corporation within the state in which it operates, and to do so without any preestablished expiration date.[29] The institutionalization of general incorporation laws was part of a more gradual process of liberalization initiated in response to the Jacksonian criticism that corrupt politicians were abusing their power by granting corporate privileges to a favored few. These general incorporation laws were preceded by laws making it easier to obtain special charters, and later, altered by subsequent legislatures in favor of further liberalization by adding provisions to the state constitutions that forbid altogether the chartering of corporations by special legislative act.[30]

Lamoreaux has convincingly documented the dramatic increase in the number of charters resulting from this process of liberalization; yet she concludes that, "as their numbers increased, corporations inevitably lost their public character."[31] To be sure, in many states, corporations gradually lost much of their public character; yet it is not clear that this outcome was the inevitable result of the state's permitting an increasing number of charters to be registered with the state apart from any special legislative act per se.

First of all, such a conclusion represents somewhat of an overgeneralization. Even at the end of the nineteenth century, Grossman and Adams find that nineteen states had amended their constitutions to make corporate charters subject to alteration or revocation by legislatures. The states of New York, Ohio, Michigan, and Nebraska successfully revoked the charters of oil, match, sugar, and whiskey trusts. In the case of New York, for example, the Central Labor Union of New York City, citing a pattern of abuses, successfully petitioned the state attorney general, in 1894, to request the state Supreme Court to revoke the charter of the Standard Oil Trust of New York. It would seem that one lesson we might take from the history of the institutionalization and deinstitutionalization of regional states' charter revocation practices is that the states' deregulation of corporations is a process that has developed unevenly across the United States, and that has simultaneously been marked by legislative acts of corporate charter revocation.

Second, although the liberalization of the existing process of incorporation in the nineteenth-century United States did not *inevitably* lead to the loss of the public character of corporations, it did significantly change the relationship between the state and the corporation. The legislature, in effect, gradually delegated to the courts what would become the increasingly greatest proportion of the responsibility for regulating corporations and discrepancies between their actions and contractually specified corporative objectives. The shift to general incorporation laws retained a role for the state in the incorporation process and thus represented a continuation of the state's traditional constitutive role.

Lamoreaux is correct to emphasize how the ready availability of corporate status and substantially minimized state involvement made the state's role in the creation of the business corporation seem distinctly secondary to the creative energy of the entrepreneurs who were responsible for launching the venture. However, this shift alone does not explain why corporate law was not used to address traditional concerns about economic concentration by using extant regulatory techniques, such as the limits on capitalization and restrictions on combinations. Indeed, part of the explanation lies in the new generation of economic theorists who argued that economic concentration was inevitable. Rethinking the work of traditional theorists, who embraced Adam Smith's assumption that increasing size eventually yields economic inefficiency (and by extension, that corporations can succeed only through unfair monopolistic advantages), these new economic theorists perceived an emerging and efficient form of large-scale, bureaucratized, industrial capitalism that could be the result of natural, impersonal market forces. Moreover, this new organizational form seemed to require only a minimal role for the state. This logic, asserting the inevitability of its assertions, contributed to a tendency to "naturalize" the workings of the market; and this same tendency began to have an impact on the way that legal thinkers depicted the corporation as an entity.

In *The Transformation of American Law, 1870–1960: The Crisis of Legal Orthodoxy*, Morton Horwitz argues that the idea that corporations were both natural persons and citizens, and therefore deserving of the same protections that the U.S. Constitution provides American (human) persons, began to dominate legal reasoning by the early twentieth century.[32] This natural-entity theory of the corporation, Horwitz argues, facilitated the formation and increasing domination of large-scale corporations within (and ultimately beyond) the territorial borders of the United States. Moreover, contends Horwitz, this natural-entity theory of the corporation provided judges, as well as other proponents seeking to legitimate and safeguard such large-scale corporate enterprises, clear conceptual advantages over the two main competing theories of the corporation at the time.

The first of these competing theories of the corporation was the artificial-entity theory, which conceptualized corporations as "(mere) creatures of the state." The disadvantage that this theory posed for proponents of large-scale corporations was that it understood corporations to possess only those attributes of personhood (i.e., rights) that the state chose to grant them. By contrast, natural-entity theory, because it constructed corporations as natural persons, made it much harder for state actors to single out corporations for special regulatory treatment.

The second of these competing theories of the corporation was the aggregate theory, which conceptualized the corporation not as an entity at all, but rather as merely one of a number of possible contractual arrangements that businesspeople could use to organize their enterprises. According to this theory, corporations do not have rights of their own per se; rather they benefit from constitutional protections only to the extent that the individuals comprising them possess rights as citizens.

A good deal of legal scholarship has persuasively argued that Horwitz's historical narrative of the evolution of corporate theory is overly unilinear, sequentially monolithic within its periodization of U.S.

corporate legal discourse, and ultimately fails to recognize the conceptual confusion among these discourses that existed not only in the U.S. courts of the nineteenth century, but also that persists today.[33] Nevertheless, these same critics generally concede that legal scholars, judges, and treatise writers in the United States, by the early twentieth century, increasingly tended to discuss corporations in terms of natural-entity theory. This tendency to think about the corporation as a natural outgrowth of private initiative rather than state action also seems to have encouraged a broader rethinking of the state's traditional regulatory authority, which had been justified by the state's constitutive role in corporate formation.[34] State legislatures, in turn, began introducing further changes in general incorporation statutes that eliminated some key restrictions during the last years of the nineteenth century. For example, the states scrapped traditional prohibitions on corporate ownership of stock in other corporations, facilitating the creation of gigantic holding companies; abolished capitalization limits; and replaced limited-term grants of incorporation with presumptions of eternal life for corporations.[35] Following the removal of these restrictions, states began competing with one another to attract corporations and their tax revenues by removing all but the most basic restrictions.[36]

Over the course of the twentieth century, corporations fought for and obtained through the courts the kind of substantive due process that individual citizens receive, including First Amendment rights to free commercial and political speech, Fourth Amendment rights against searches, and certain Fifth Amendment rights protecting criminal defendants, property, and liberty interests like reputation.[37] These gains have been largely built on the notion that corporations are natural persons.

To challenge this natural-entity discourse on the corporation, the activists in the Unocal Charter Revocation Campaign have deployed an artificial-entity discourse on the nature of corporations to offer a historical narrative similar to that of Horwitz, namely, of how courts over the past century and a half have "naturalized" the concept of the corporation to construct them as being not only "entities," but as having the attributes (and thus rights) of personhood. Their artificial-entity discourse, reappropriated from the mid-nineteenth century, emphasizes that corporations are fundamentally constructed by states and can be fundamentally reconstructed by them as well. Again, it is worth quoting at length, for illustrative purposes, the words of Ronnie Dugger:

By giving our rights to what should have remained our subordinate creations, the judges of the Supreme Court, across time, have stolen our country from us. In consequence, the corporations are Superpersons, and we are their subpersons. And the corporations we created as servants of our public interest have broken free of our democratic control and metamorphosed into the international creatures of greed and rapacity that now dominate the world. . . . We the people have the right to control the shape and terms of our economic life, as well as our political life. What—God help us—we should have learned by now from the long history of civilization is that if the people don't control economic life, the inevitably gathering economic oligarchy, the plutocracy, will strangle democracy. That is what has been happening, again, in the United States since the defeat of the populists at the end of the last century.[38]

To the extent that we today conceptualize corporations and markets as primarily naturally occurring phenomena and *inevitably* driven by existing forces, we risk not only blinding ourselves to the historical contingency and significance of the choices that we make about the ways in which we regulate our economic and political relations, we may unwittingly play an instrumental role in sustaining those very forces that we wish to change.

There is a third reason that we should be cautious in assuming that the liberalization of the incorporation process led *inevitably* to the corporation's loss of public character. States never relinquished their power to revoke such charters when corporations break the law. Even today, all fifty states and the District of Columbia have statutes providing for revocation of corporate charters.[39] It is precisely upon these statutes that the leaders of the Unocal charter revocation campaign have based their authority to demand the attorney general to act. Indeed, what these campaign activists hope to demonstrate as much as anything else is that the first step toward rebuilding the public character of corporations comes not necessarily with changing the laws, but with better understanding the existing laws that allow both states and human citizens to regulate (and even terminate) corporations.

According to the legal analysis that these campaign activists provided in their petition, these statutes codify the English common law writ of quo warranto (meaning "by what authority"), which allows the attorney general to demand that the corporation show by what authority it continues to exist.[40] Not only have courts consistently held that certain acts of wrongdoing clearly warrant charter revocation, but also that a single act of wrongdoing is enough.[41] Most state courts, including those within the state of California, agree that an attorney general may be compelled by a writ of mandamus ("by command") to file a quo warranto action in a proper case where evidence can be presented that demonstrates a private grievance or public harm. Under California law, the attorney general has a mandatory duty to bring a quo warranto action whenever he has reason to believe that a violation has occurred or when he is directed to do so by the governor.[42]

Perhaps the most interesting observation that this petition offers regarding these quo warranto statutes is that attorneys general employ them frequently to challenge the right of public officials to hold office or municipal governments' right to annex land, yet they so rarely use it against corporate violators.[43] Focusing on the pattern in California, the petition's author sarcastically notes:

> In California, the *quo warranto* statute, *Code of Civil Procedure* § 803, has been litigated dozens of times, and the Attorney General's office has written scores of official legal opinions on it, the majority in cases not involving corporations. The California attorney general has a deputy attorney assigned to specialize in all cases under this statute, as well as several pages on the official web site devoted solely to *quo warranto*. So the attorney general knows the statute well, and uses it, but inexplicably fails to use it against corporate violators.[44]

Unocal is not, however, the only corporation in recent times to face the challenges posed by the quo warranto statute. There has been one case in which the quo warranto statute has been used in California to revoke a corporate charter. In 1976, California attorney general Evelle Younger went to court to force the forfeiture of the franchise of a company that was supplying allegedly impure water to customers in Alameda County.[45]

Additionally, individuals acting independently of this charter revocation campaign have filed two more separate cases, which are still pending. In 1998, the New York state attorney general filed a petition with the Supreme Court of New York to dissolve two nonprofit corporations that he alleged had illegally served the causes of the tobacco industry while fraudulently posing as scientific research organizations. His petition to the court asserts that the corporations must be dissolved because they obtained their charters by fraudulently representing their purposes to be scientific and objective, they persisted for years in this deception of the public, and this activity exceeded the authority conferred upon them by law.[46]

During the same year, Alabama circuit judge William Wynn, acting as a private citizen under an Alabama statute that allows any individual without the permission of the attorney general to initiate quo warranto proceedings, sued several major tobacco companies themselves (including Philip Morris, Brown & Williamson, R. J. Reynolds, the Liggett Group, and the Lorillard Corporation), asking state courts to revoke their charters to do business in Alabama on the ground that they are causing minors to consume and become addicted to "lethal" tobacco products.[47] The state's most influential newspaper, the *Birmingham News*, not only ran a news story about the lawsuit, but published a long opinion piece by Richard Grossman, titled "Slaying Big Tobacco." Mainstream readers were thus exposed to the characteristically radical style of Grossman, arguing that Judge Wynn is "on solid ground when he demands the state of Alabama provide its sovereign people with a proper remedy to end the corporate usurpation of the people's authority."[48]

Dehumanizing Corporate Behavior: Corporate Persons as Repeat Criminal Offenders

The subversive spin on the discourse of corporate citizenship that this campaign introduced—one that emphasized not only the corporate citizen's obligations to the community vis-à-vis its rights of personhood, but also the "death penalty" as a particular solution to repeat corporate offenders—was not just the product of abstract theorizing. Their discourse on "corporate punishment" drew upon existing local political debates over how to deter the recidivist criminal action of individuals and upon controversies regarding the human rights of citizens who have so thoroughly and intentionally offended the community's norms as to raise the issue of whether the state should continue to respect their right to exist, at least, as a citizen within the community.

Attorney General Lungren, who was running for governor of California at the time, had made capital punishment and tougher crime laws a central component of his election campaign platform. Along with Governor Pete Wilson, Lungren's name had become quickly associated with California's controversial "three strikes" law (a name designed to allude to a popularly understood rule of America's national pastime of baseball). This law prescribed a compulsory life-imprisonment sentence for third-time felony offenders. The petitioners seeking the revocation of Unocal's corporate charter seized upon this new slogan of community exclusion ("three strikes and you're out") that is directed at individual citizens of California who repeatedly break the law, as well as the new "get tougher on crime" meaning that it signified, and creatively extended it to encompass recidivist *corporate* persons as well.

The activists' appropriation of this discourse did not reflect their support of the "three strikes" law. This law deployed a dehumanizing discourse to legitimate nullifying a person's rights under conditions in which those persons willfully betrayed norms that the state deemed foundational to the maintenance of human communities. These activists strategically deployed this same discourse on how to deal with lawbreaking human persons and extended it as a metaphor to challenge what it saw as the state's double standard in dealing with corporations. On the one hand, when it benefits corporations, the state treats corporations as persons, extending to them all of the rights that it extends to its human citizens; on the other hand, it does not hold these corporate persons to the same tough standards that it holds human persons when they violate the law.

The charge of hypocrisy against Governor Pete Wilson's administration was only thinly veiled: if our elected politicians are serious about stemming crime and other violations of our community's rules and standards by forcibly removing perpetrators from the community, then they should start with those corporate "persons" whose criminal actions they have not only ignored but rewarded with an expanding bill of rights. As Benson writes in the introduction to the published version of the petition:

> Charter revocation is a particularly apt legal mechanism to deal with corporate repeat offenders. When large corporate violators, as contrasted with small businesses, pay fines, what they pay is often insignificant in relation to assets, and is flicked off the corporate suit merely as a cost of doing business rather than as a serious warning to change unlawful, anti-social corporate behavior. Unlike individuals who face tough "three strikes, you're-out" prosecutors, big corporations typically run decades-long rap sheets of criminal and civil violations. They are incorrigible recidivists. Yet they are rarely put out of business. . . . Our attorneys general and governors have been soft on crime.[49]

Attorney General Lungren quickly dismissed the petition. However, this did not put an end to the campaign. Indeed, the campaign outlived the terms of the attorney general and governor. Within six months, this coalition had quadrupled in size to more than 130 organizations and individuals. On April 19, 1999, they refiled the legal petition and brief with the newly elected attorney general Bill Lockyer, along with a letter addressed to the newly elected governor Gray Davis, urging them, unlike their predecessors, to undertake a serious review of the petition and asking them for a meeting. The letter was addressed to Davis as well as Lockyer because under California law the governor has the power to direct the attorney general to act on such petitions. Benson's letter notes that, "in the [election] campaign, you both vowed to be tough on crime. We assume that you did not mean to carve out an exception for corporate crime. And we assume that when you backed the 'three strikes' law you meant to apply the 'three strikes' policy to powerful corporations as well as to pizza thieves."

Lockyer, like his predecessor, dismissed the petition immediately without explanation. However, the following year, when he confronted a group of protesters (many of whom were from the same organizations that had signed the petition) in front of Loyola Law School in Los Angeles where he was scheduled to give a speech, Lockyer explained that he had no intention of going after Unocal because his office has no capacity to investigate the foreign human rights offenses of which the company has been accused. Furthermore, he told the demonstrators, he has no "client" in the matter because he is the attorney for state agency clients. To this, one protester in the crowd loudly retorted, "We're your clients—the people of the state of California!"

Conclusion

Ironically, although we have seen how the Free Burma activists in this campaign have attempted to pressure the state of California to revoke the rights and powers of Unocal's corporate personhood for the human rights abuses that this corporation allegedly has committed, it is worth noting as well that it is this very same concept of corporate personhood that has made it possible for another collection of Free Burma activists to charge Unocal in both federal and state (of California) court with being an overseer in slave trading and to seek liability for the victims of

Figure 14. Human rights activists confront California Attorney General Bill Lockyer in front of Loyola Law School in Los Angeles. Lockyer rejected the petition to revoke the corporate charter of Unocal Corporation. The activists accuse Unocal of abusing the environment, labor, and human rights in California and abroad. Photograph copyright 2000 D. Ngo/ZUMA Press.

this human rights abuse. One might argue that by suing Unocal in court for liability, the plaintiffs are reinscribing the power of the natural-entity theory of corporate personhood in the court, and possibly working at cross-purposes with the campaign to revoke Unocal's corporate charter. Benson does not seem to see it this way, however, for he argues that,

> in the final analysis, the charter revocation mechanism works through making elected officials politically accountable. There may be litigation or other formal legal proceedings pending against the company. Charter revocation opens an additional front, offering a new way to attract support for your struggle.[50]

Rather, he seems to suggest that both types of campaigns are compatible, although not necessarily precoordinated, and that charter revocation, unlike a lawsuit targeting a corporation, allows activists to bring to center stage elected officials who otherwise might hope to remain unassociated with the conflict or the alleged misdeeds of the corporation.

The activists leading this Unocal corporate charter campaign have reappropriated an artificial-entity discourse to denaturalize contemporary understandings of corporate personhood and to challenge the rights claims of corporations like Unocal, which seek to evade responsibility for the social consequences of their actions. However, the artificial-entity discourse on the nature of corporations does not confront the primary discourse that is deployed by corporations when they become challenged on the grounds that they are acting in socially irresponsible ways. Although business corporations tend to deploy some version of the natural-entity discourse when pursuing their rights, they tend to deploy discursive variations of the aggregate-theory of the corporation when they attempt to avoid responsibility for their malfeasance, arguing that corporations are nothing more than a "nexus of contracts" and thus cannot be held responsible for their actions. They argue that only individuals within the corporate relationship who violate, in a given instance, the contractual terms of the corporation can be held responsible. Unocal, as we will see in the following chapter, has deployed just such a discourse in U.S. courts in an effort to evade responsibility for alleged human rights violations that a group of Burmese citizens suffered as a result of Unocal's gas pipeline project.

The Free Burma movement's effort to petition the California state attorneys General Lundgren and Lockyer, respectively, to bring a lawsuit against Unocal that would revoke its corporate charter had mixed results. Neither attorney general was persuaded to bring such a lawsuit against Unocal. But then again, this campaign's organizers never really expected that they would. The primary goal of this campaign strategy was to challenge the apologetic claim of California's regional state actors that they had no power to regulate the conduct—however morally questionable—of corporations choosing to do business with the Myanmar government in Burma. The problem, these politicians frequently suggested, is that the conduct of corporations in Burma falls within the administrative jurisdiction of the Myanmar government, and the Myanmar government has greeted these corporations and their conduct with open arms, despite their domestic citizenry's outcry to the international community for economic sanctions.

This campaign sought to educate the public about the legal power that regional states in the United States have to challenge the misconduct of the corporations that they charter, regardless of where in the world those corporations conduct their business. It sought to show that Unocal's violations of human rights in Burma could be stopped by California's legal administrators—if they had the political and moral will to do so—because the state of California had chartered Unocal and California's legal administrators have the legal grounds and power to revoke Unocal's charter.

The transnationalist discourse on corporate governance that emerged in this campaign then extends the one produced in the selective purchasing law campaign. In the selective purchasing law campaign, the Free Burma movement challenged the claim that only the federal government has the power to conduct foreign affairs. It did so by expanding the category "nonfederal entities" that the courts had used to distinguish and marginalize the foreign affairs power of municipal governments and regional states in its interpretation of the Constitution's foreign affairs clause. When the courts created this variable, they assumed that they were creating dichotomous categories that would be applied only to states. They failed to consider that nonstate actors also influence foreign policy. However, the Free Burma movement introduced a transnationalist discourse that compared the foreign policy activity of municipal governments and regional states with that of corporations—all of which, they pointed out, constituted nonfederal entities influencing the conduct of foreign affairs.

In the campaign to revoke Unocal's corporate charter, however, the transnationalist discourse is extended further to suggest that the very existence of these nonfederal entities called "corporations" is dependent upon the nonfederal (governmental) entities called "regional states," and thus could not exercise the influence that they do on foreign affairs without their ultimate nonfederal governmental authority. This transnationalist discourse that the Free Burma movement deployed in this campaign is, like that produced in the selective purchasing campaign, still serviceable as a potent tool for challenging, on a broadly coordinated scale in regional states throughout the United States, the political and moral choices of state actors who have the administrative power to enforce existing laws (and human rights norms) that directly affect the conduct, indeed the existence, of transnational corporations within the global market. The transnational legal space provided by corporate charters also remains an open terrain for future legal struggle.

It is worth considering the recent 2010 decision of the U.S. Supreme Court in *Citizens United v. Federal Election Commission*.[51] In this ruling, the Supreme Court determined that corporations, including financial firms, are indeed legal persons with First Amendment rights, and that they can contribute unlimited amounts of money to political campaigns.

There also has been a push among some corporations to press beyond the notion of corporate civil rights to test the U.S. Court's willingness to extend to corporations human rights. For example, in July 2009, the U.S. microchip manufacturer Intel Corporation appealed the $1.45 billion fine leveled against it by the European Union for engaging in anticompetitive behavior, claiming that the proceedings had violated its human right to due process. Several European companies are also testing the tactic to fend off Europe's aggressive antitrust regulator. They argue that in antitrust cases, the European Commission unfairly plays the role of prosecutor, judge, and jury—hindering their ability to mount an effective defense. They argue that they should instead be entitled to the due process rights that European human rights law grants in criminal cases to ensure that the accused—usually powerless individuals—are not steamrollered by the overwhelming power of the state.[52]

It is clear that a more transnationalist discourse will be necessary to challenge the efforts of transnational corporations to use the law to acquire not only the civil rights of personhood that humans have, but also to acquire the human rights that humans have.

5

Alien Tort Claims:
Adjudicating Human Rights Abuses Abroad

Free Burma activists' transnational legal strategies were not limited to partnering with sympathetic local lawmakers to create new legislation, nor to pressuring politically unwilling state executives to simply enforce existing law to rein in corporate partners sustaining the Myanmar government's abusive regime. They also developed a transnational legal strategy that centered squarely on suing such corporate partners that would force the U.S. federal courts to voice their opinion on the morality of these corporations' conduct in Burma.

In 1996, a dozen ethnic-minority peasants from Burma sued the Unocal Corporation in a U.S. court in a case titled *Doe v. Unocal*.[1] They alleged that Unocal had been complicit in human rights abuses against them and demanded that Unocal stop the human rights abuses and pay money damages. For eight years, this case wound its way through the courts. Then suddenly, in December 2004, Unocal announced that it had reached a settlement with the plaintiffs.[2] The settlement was a victory for the peasants.

What makes this transnational legal action significant is that, had the court been left to decide the case, and had it ruled in favor of the peasants (an outcome that Unocal seems to have understood as likely), it would have been the first time that foreigners had won a case against

Figure 15. The people of Meela Po Hta Internally Displaced People's camp are mainly of the Karen ethnic minority. They escaped direct persecution by the Burmese army and fled to this camp near the Thailand border. Photograph copyright 2000 D. Ngo/ZUMA Press.

a transnational corporation in a U.S. court for an injury that took place in another country. The peasants filed the suit under the U.S. Alien Tort Claims Act (ATCA).[3] Since *Doe v. Unocal*, more than a dozen similar suits have been filed against other corporations on the model of the transnational legal strategy used in the Unocal case.

The judicial struggle of the *Doe v. Unocal* case in itself represents a stunning achievement for the Free Burma Movement. This long-shot of a transnational legal strategy soon became a landmark suit. The publicity from the suit brought stories of Burma's struggle for democracy into living rooms across the United States. But the negative publicity that this case generated is not ultimately what threatened Unocal's corporate conduct. Rather, this case threatened Unocal's "bottom line" of profitability by forcing it to build into its calculus the costs of litigation and liability for violating the human rights of foreign nationals in foreign countries in which it conducted business. It also sent a clear message to other corporations: that if activists can win a case like this, corporations must consider these costs in deciding whether to partner with rogue states. This could provide an important tool for weakening the

Figure 16. Maung Nyunt Than protests against Unocal Corporation's partner-ship with the Burmese military regime on May 21, 2001, at the annual Unocal shareholder meeting in Brea, California. Unocal's natural gas pipeline in Burma is alleged to have been built using forced laborers. Photograph copyright 2001 D. Ngo/ZUMA Press.

authoritarian grip of Burma's ruling junta and others like it that depend upon foreign corporate investment.

Standards of Liability as a Moral Issue

On March 28, 2000, just months before the Federal District Court in Los Angeles was expected to decide the outcome of the *Doe v. Unocal* case, the American Broadcasting Corporation (ABC)'s *Nightline* introduced to American audiences the silhouettes and voices of the *Doe*-plaintiffs re-sponding through a translator. In a special report, *The Peasants vs. Unocal*, ABC framed the precedent-setting case within the provocative yet famil-iar story line of an improbable but virtuous band of rural, "dirt poor" challengers from "an ugly corner of the [Third] world" against the power-ful Western captains of industry:

> The defendant, a huge U.S. energy company building a pipeline in a
> country known for its brutal dictatorship. . . . The plaintiffs, a dozen
> peasants who say they were brutalized by the troops guarding that

pipeline. . . . Tonight, the Peasants versus Unocal, right and wrong in an ugly corner of the world.[4]

The report depicts the *Doe*-plaintiffs as the victims and underdogs throughout its representation of the pending court case. Their status as the protagonists in *Nightline*'s narrative is never questioned. However, as *Nightline*'s narrative unfolds, Unocal's role as the antagonist is, first, vaguely redefined as a business partnership with an irredeemably evil dictatorial state, and then called into question as a morally ambiguous actor (yet one that is hardly comparable to its clearly evil state partner):

> Does doing business with the Burmese government mean Unocal is in some way legally responsible for the government's evil acts from forced relocations to the allegations of slave labor to torture and rapes? Or might it be that Unocal is trying to do good in a bad place, providing jobs to hundreds, thousands of people who are dirt poor? Does American participation give legitimacy to a ruthless government? Or does its presence restrain that government from behaving even more ruthlessly?[5]

Thus, an "American" Unocal, initially serving as the principal antagonist to our heroic peasants from an underdeveloped and lawless society, is gradually superceded by whom we are led to believe is the "real" antagonist: the dictatorial (and thus "un-American") Myanmar military. Although *Nightline*'s correspondent makes explicitly clear that it is the peasant plaintiffs with whom we should sympathize, the result is less of what the special report's title suggests (*The Peasants vs. Unocal*) and more of a struggle between competing "third world" (i.e., socially distant, or "other"-worldly) actors. In the end, *Nightline* encourages us to wonder if the target of the peasants' pursuit of justice is not somehow misplaced.

The business partnership linking Unocal to Myanmar's military is skillfully dissolved through ABC's representation. It is nicely captured in the sound bite they present from Unocal's then President John Imle:

> We—we cannot—I cannot, personally, take responsibility for the conduct of the government of Burma, any more than I can take responsibility for the conduct of the—of the Los Angeles Police Department.[6]

Rather than examining the conduct of the business partnership between Unocal and Myanmar's military, which was hired to provide security for the pipeline's construction, *Nightline* emphasized Unocal's poor judgment in "doing business" with a distinctly separate actor with a poor human-rights record.

This is not to suggest that *Nightline* did not present the plaintiffs' perspective. Jennifer Green of the Center for Constitutional Rights (CCR), one of several nonprofit organizations helping the *Doe* plaintiffs file and argue their case, countered Unocal's Imle with a sound bite of her own:

> And you, my business partner, you're going to take responsibility for making sure that the military barracks are built, that the helipad is built, that—that enough soldiers are in the area to guard this pipeline. And you can do whatever you want. But I'm not responsible because it's— it's this other person. And U.S. law is particularly designed to say you can't have two people in the same business operation, one of them being clean and the other one playing dirty... without them both being held responsible.[7]

Ultimately, however, *Nightline* placed greater emphasis on Unocal's morally questionable choice of partners rather than on the legal liability of the joint venture's human rights' violations. The moral of *The Peasants vs. Unocal*, as *Nightline* reports to us from Burma, is that, "By choosing Burma, one of the world's most notoriously repressive military dictatorships, as a *place* to do big business, Unocal has brought on itself big trouble" (emphasis mine). *Nightline* was less interested in conveying the alternative moral implied by CCR's Green that, by choosing to rely on abusive human rights *practices* to do big business, Unocal has helped to constitute the kind of repressive place where the Karen villagers live. One might shrug off Unocal's impact on their local community as just another chapter in the long book on the globalization of capitalism. Yet it is worth noting that Unocal is profiting from a precapitalist form of labor: not wage labor, but coerced labor or slavery, albeit in a modern, and today illegal, form.[8] Indeed, in this context, "free trade" has become a euphemism for "free labor." Even further obscured by *Nightline*'s framing of the issue was the key legal question that the Ninth Circuit Court of Appeals remanded to the Federal District Court: Is Unocal individually liable for directly and actively "aiding and abetting" the Myanmar military's use of forced labor, murder, and rape in its effort to construct their joint venture gas pipeline project?

My critique of *Nightline*'s report is not meant to suggest that the moral issues relating to Unocal's choice to do business with the Myanmar government are somehow less significant than the legal issues of their liability for doing so. Rather, I mean to show that this distinction both downplays the legal dimensions and obscures the moral dimensions of Unocal's liability. It downplays the notion that Unocal should be held legally liable for its moral choice to do business with the Myanmar government. At the same time, it obscures how the issue of liability (and various standards of liability) speaks to a moral relationship between two or more parties whereby one of the parties has taken wrongful action that causes harm to another of the parties or to the relationship itself.

Using the Alien Tort Claims Act to Sue Corporations

The *Doe v. Unocal* suit, filed under the Alien Tort Claims Act (ATCA), deploys a transnational strategy through which the Free Burma movement attempts to use the statute *for the first time* to hold liable in a U.S. court *transnational corporations*, not just state actors or private individuals, for their complicity in human rights abuses committed outside the United States in furthering their transnational joint ventures with states like Burma. The original legislators of this statute had never, nor could have, imagined using it for this purpose. Yet movement activists, deploying a transnationalist discourse, creatively appropriated this statute to address relations among states, citizens, corporations, and human rights that had significantly changed over the two centuries since ATCA's adoption. This suit illustrates how movement activists created a transnational legal space to shape the meaning and application of the ATCA for reining in the power of transnational corporations that violate human rights. This transnationalist discourse also challenges the idea that corporations are, unlike most governments, not required to respect universal human rights principles if the states in which they operate do not.

An appreciation for how the *Doe v. Unocal* suit brought under the ATCA provides an example of a transnational legal space begins with understanding the historical development of the act itself, and how the peasants and their lawyers reappropriated it in a new way. In 1789, the First Congress of the United States adopted the ATCA. It remained largely unused for the next two centuries. The text of the act is short. It reads simply, "The district courts shall have original jurisdiction of any civil action by an alien [non-U.S. citizen] for a tort only, committed in violation of the law of nations or a treaty of the United States."[9] The Alien Tort Claims Act is not a human rights law per se, but it allows for civil suits for violations of the law of nations. The law of nations is the law of international relations, embracing not only nations but also individuals, such as those who invoke their human rights or commit war crimes.[10]

The members of the United States' First Congress were obviously cognizant of the law of nations as they crafted their nascent nation's Constitution. Yet they could not have anticipated, in 1789, the extent to which the law of nations would develop over the course of the following two centuries. Nor, for that matter, could they have imagined the radical development of two other legal concepts that have significantly transformed the context within which contemporary actors have begun to interpret the ATCA: "human rights" and "the corporate rights of personhood."

The Law of Nations

Although litigation under the ATCA remained dormant for two centuries following its passage, lawyers in the United States appropriated it during the past two decades to challenge the abuses of foreign state agents, and even nonstate actors, that were committed in foreign states between non-U.S. citizens. While some have cheered these ATCA cases as a progressive step forward in the development of international norms, others have decried the very same cases as a creeping American imperialism that threatens to export the legal standards of the United States to other nations, raising the question of whether these ATCA cases represent an erosion of state sovereignty in sheep's clothing.

In 1980, lawyers at the Center for Constitutional Rights rediscovered ATCA and put it to modern use in the landmark case of *Filartiga v. Pena-Irala*.[11] The decision in that case interpreted the ATCA to provide jurisdiction for U.S. courts in cases where the perpetrator (even though not a U.S. citizen) is properly served within the United States' borders, but it left open whether the ATCA applies only to state actors or also to nonstate actors. In addition, this decision drew attention, amid increasing international concern with human rights issues, to a new legal tool that human rights advocates might find workable in a variety of related cases. As Andrew Ridenour explains, "The resulting body of jurisprudence has slowly expanded over the past twenty years to deal with an otherwise open area of law: civil remedies for certain violations of international law."[12]

Subsequent courts in the United States have generally followed the interpretation set out in *Filartiga*, holding that the ATCA not only provides jurisdiction, but also authorizes plaintiffs to base their substantive claims on international law norms.[13] Courts also have relied on this interpretation to suggest that plaintiffs do not have to base their causes of action on the municipal law of the forum or of the site of the tort.[14]

However, courts have debated whether the statute provides a cause of action against a party that has violated *international* law. One of the most difficult issues facing the courts has been that of determining what constitutes a violation of the law of nations. In *Tel-Oren v. Libyan Arab Republic*, the District Court for the District of Columbia reasoned that

> the law of nations never has been perceived to create or define the
> civil actions to be made available by each member of the community
> of nations; by consensus, the states leave that determination to their
> respective municipal laws. . . . In consequence, to require international
> accord on a right to sue, when in fact the law of nations relegates deci-
> sions on such questions to the states themselves, would be to effectively
> nullify the "law of nations" portion of [ATCA].[15]

That is, the law of nations itself does not provide rights of action, thus Congress must have intended for ATCA to grant a cause of action to a foreign national to remedy a violation of the law of nations by another party. Yet, as the District Court pointed out, this raises a further issue: how are the courts to derive from an amorphous entity (i.e., the law of nations) standards of liability that are applicable in concrete situations? The *Tel-Oren* court proposed an alternative approach to that of the *Filartiga* court. While ATCA can provide federal court jurisdiction to aliens alleging torts framed as a violation of the law of nations, the substantive right on which this action is based must be found in the domestic tort law of the United States.

In 1991, the U.S. Congress passed the Torture Victim Protection Act (TVPA) with the intention of augmenting the *Filartiga* approach and extending it to citizens of the United States.[16] The TVPA states that

> an individual who, under actual or apparent authority, or color of law,
> of any foreign nation, subjects an individual to torture shall, in a civil
> action, be liable for damages to that individual; or subjects an individual
> to extra judicial killing shall, in a civil action, be liable for damages
> to the individual's legal representative, or to any person who may be a
> claimant in an action for wrongful death.[17]

Since Congress passed this statute, courts have held that regardless of the original intent that Congress may have had in adopting ATCA, the TVPA demonstrates a contemporary legislative intent that ATCA does create a private cause of action for violations of international law.[18] In other words, the TVPA gave new meaning to the law of nations, permitting nonstate actors to be sued under ATCA for violations of international law, provided that the tort represents the violation of a norm that is universal, specific, and obligatory.

In 1995, the Court of Appeals for the Second Circuit Court drew upon Congress's explicit intention in passing the TVPA to hold that certain forms of conduct violate the law of nations whether undertaken by those acting under the auspices of a state or only as private individuals.[19] This in turn opened ATCA to being used to sue private individuals—not just states and their agents—who violate the law of nations. Even "private" individuals, i.e., individuals who are *not* acting as agents of the state per se, but those who are found to be acting in cooperation with government officials or significant government aid when they allegedly committed a violation of the law of nations, were also within U.S. court jurisdiction under the ATCA.[20]

Thus, it is the intersection of ATCA, which is almost as old as the Republic, with recent developments in the domestic appropriation of international law that created the legal opportunity, or critical discursive space, for suing the Unocal Corporation. The activist attorneys representing the Doe plaintiffs pushed the argument further. They asserted that as private actors, corporations are capable of being held liable for violations of *jus cogens* norms, a class of international norms that have increasingly been recognized as universal and nonderogable.

The Human Rights Regime and Corporate Personhood

An important factor that has influenced the changing relationship between state sovereignty and the law of nations is the development of the international human rights regime. As Sarah Cleveland has cogently argued, this regime has been

> enunciated through a loose network of general treaties promulgated
> by the United Nations; rights-specific regimes which are promoted by
> intergovernmental entities and international organizations [e.g., the
> International Labor Organization]; regional regimes of conventions

and oversight; and universal customary prohibitions that have evolved through treaties, the practices of states, and the efforts of nongovernmental and private actors.[21]

Emerging from these efforts has been an unevenly developed global system of normative rules relating to human rights. Not all human rights are equal before the law. Comprising this global system of rules are two tiers of human rights: (1) jus cogens norms ("compelling laws") and (2) treaty rights and customary obligations *erga omnes* ("toward all").[22] This has implications for those filing suits under the Alien Tort Claims Act.

Treaty rights, of course, are detailed in the formal instrument of the human rights regime. These international treaty obligations cover a wide range of protections for human rights by creating binding obligations between party states. A state that accedes to these conventions becomes obligated to every other state to uphold the promises of the treaty and "submit[s] its performance to scrutiny and to appropriate, peaceful action by other parties."[23] It should be noted that Myanmar is a member of both the United Nations and the International Labor Organization.[24]

Beyond those human rights formally expressed in these treaties, the law of nations recognizes certain rights to be universally accepted and binding on all sovereign states as either jus cogens or erga omnes principles of customary international law. Jus cogens norms hold the highest hierarchical position among all other norms and principles.[25] In 1969, the Vienna Convention on the Law of Treaties first defined jus cogens norms as principles "accepted and recognized by the international community of States as a whole as a norm from which no derogation is permitted and which can be modified only by a subsequent norm of general international law having the same character."[26] They represent the higher of the two tiers of human rights to which I previously alluded. As a consequence of this standing within the law of nations, nearly all courts around the world (including U.S. courts) deem jus cogens norms to be "peremptory" and "nonderogable." In other words, jus cogens norms are norms of international law from which derogation by States, including between treaties bilaterally, are not permissible. Any international agreement that would violate them would be void.[27] Any jus cogens violation, therefore, is also, by definition, a violation of the law of nations. The legal literature discloses that the following are broadly recognized rights that no state officially claims the right to violate and may be considered jus cogens principles of the human rights system: aggression, genocide, crimes against humanity, war crimes, torture, piracy, and slavery and slavery-related practices.[28]

Human rights obligations that enjoy the status of erga omnes norms share with jus cogens norms their universal character and are binding on all states. However, unlike jus cogens norms, erga omnes norms are not peremptory norms that prevail over all other rules of customary law. Thus, we can think of treaty rights and erga omnes norms together as comprising the lower of the two tiers of human rights.

In the summer of 2004, the U.S. Supreme Court held in the case of *Sosa v. Alvarez-Machain* that only a human rights violation of the highest and most agreed upon magnitude qualifies for consideration under ATCA. In other words, only ATCA claims based on violations of jus cogens norms qualify.[29] This institutionalization of jus cogens presupposes that some laws are inherent and inalienable, reflecting the notion that there are ultimately fundamental moral choices, and thus that there are noneconomic boundaries that market participants should not be permitted to transgress; for example, that slavery is immoral. This case illustrates how transnational legal space mediates the process through which global markets become embedded in morality. This case also highlights discursive contention around a statute that confers jurisdiction in a U.S. federal court, but which does not create a substantive right. Yet the ambiguity of this statute is powerful when combined with jus cogens.

The U.S. Supreme Court ruled that ATCA can be used to confer jurisdiction in the case of jus cogens violations. But the question raised in *Doe v. Unocal* was whether a party could sue a corporation for these jus cogens violations. As discussed in the previous chapter, U.S. courts have increasingly granted corporations the rights of personhood over the course of the nineteenth and twentieth centuries, allowing them to be treated legally as private individual persons, separately from the individuals who own or operate them, and providing them with the same rights to due process under the law enjoyed by human persons.[30] Foreshadowing the same transnationalist discourse that Free Burma activists deployed in their campaign to revoke Unocal's corporate charter, the plaintiffs in *Doe v. Unocal* essentially argued that with the rights of personhood also come responsibilities. Thus, they argued, corporate violations should be held liable under the ATCA for jus cogens violations in the same way that individuals are, rather than as "vicariously liable" as agents of the state. (After all, Unocal was not an agent of Myanmar's state.)

The district court ruled that the plaintiffs in *Doe v. Unocal* had a legitimate cause of action and agreed to hear the case. However, what remained at issue was whether Unocal should be held liable for the jus cogens violations suffered by the peasants. But Unocal, after years of litigation, settled the suit in March 2005, before this question was ever decided by the courts, and it remains to this day a central question for ATCA claims against corporations.[31]

Discursive Ambivalence

This transnational legal space has been significantly shaped by a transnationalist discourse on human rights. But the struggle to give this space meaning has also generated discursive ambivalence among some of the very actors who have voiced support for human rights within this space. In particular, corporations and states have diluted human rights discourse by combining it with others meant to protect corporations from being held accountable for their abusive human rights practices and to minimize the state's vulnerability to international legal standards.

The Discursive Ambivalence Created by Corporations

Corporations have deliberately created discursive ambivalence on two fronts: first, by resisting attempts to subject corporations in general to an enforceable legal framework; and second, by actively consolidating a self-regulatory regime of "corporate social responsibility" that is based on a host of voluntary and unenforceable instruments.

For example, in its effort to have *Doe v. Unocal* dismissed, Unocal deployed two main discourses: one relating to corporations' liability for human rights abuses and the other relating to the United States' present foreign policy toward Burma. Unocal consistently proclaimed its support for human rights. At issue, it argued, was whether it should be held liable for the abusive human rights practices of the Myanmar junta. First, Unocal argued that it had a civil right to freely contract,[32] and that holding it "vicariously liable" for the actions of its state partners would interfere with that right. Unocal fought for the use of a weaker domestic standard of liability (based on direct and active participation) rather than the more stringent standard (based on aiding and abetting abusive human rights practices) that is used in international law.

Furthermore, they asserted that "Unocal is not [even] vicariously liable for the Myanmar military's torts because the pipeline was constructed by a separate corporation," namely, the Gas Transportation Company, and because "there is no basis to pierce the corporate veils of the [Unocal Pipeline Corporation] or [the Unocal Offshore Company]."[33] In other words, Unocal argued that its partnership with the Myanmar military, as well as its own corporation, is a transnational nexus of contracts linking separate corporate persons, each one of whom is independently responsible for (and thus exclusively liable for) separate duties and operations, the boundaries of which have been contractually delineated. Moreover, each possesses its own right to freely contract. In short, Unocal Corporation cannot control the actions and contractual bargaining of its subsidiary corporations that, after all, each have separate shareholders, employees, clients, and agents to whom they must answer.[34]

Appreciation for Unocal's argument that it is a "nexus of contracts" and thus cannot be held liable for the human rights violations committed by the SLORC government begins with understanding just how complex is the structure of ownership in this project. Shortly after the SLORC began ruling Burma in 1988, it established a state-owned company, Myanmar Oil and Gas Enterprise (MOGE), to produce and sell the nation's oil and gas resources. It was not long before the transnational oil and gas corporations of the very same Western countries that had condemned the Myanmar military's violent crackdown on the pro-democracy movement fell in line to establish billion-dollar joint venture enterprises with MOGE. At the front of the line was French oil giant Total S.A. (Total). In 1992, MOGE licensed Total to produce, transport, and sell natural gas from deposits in the Yadana Field, located off the coast of Burma. For this purpose, Total set up a corporate subsidiary called Total Myanmar Exploration and Production (Total Myanmar). Thus, initially, the contractual structure of ownership in this overall gas pipeline project in Yadana consisted of four main partners: the SLORC, MOGE, Total, and Total Myanmar. This was only the beginning.

The Yadana Project was divided into two parts. One part consisted of a Gas Production Joint Venture, which was responsible for extracting the natural gas from the Yadana Field, and another part consisted of a Gas Transportation Company, which was responsible for constructing and operating a pipeline to transport the natural gas from the coast of Burma through the interior of the country to Thailand. Later in 1992,

Unocal Corporation and its wholly owned subsidiary Union Oil Company of California, which I collectively refer to below as Unocal, acquired a 28 percent interest in the Project from Total.

The structure of Unocal's investment in the partnership is complex and shifts among various corporate subsidiaries of Unocal between 1992 and 1999. (See Figure 17.) Unocal Oil Company of California itself had a wholly owned subsidiary corporation (chartered in Delaware) called the Unocal International Corporation. The Unocal International Corporation originally set up a wholly owned subsidiary, the Unocal Myanmar Offshore Oil Company (the Unocal Offshore Company), as a holding company for its 28 percent interest in the Gas Production Joint Venture part of the Yadana Project. Similarly, Unocal International Corporation set up another wholly owned subsidiary, the Unocal International Pipeline Corporation, to hold Unocal's 28 percent interest in the other part of the Yadana Project, the Gas Transportation Company. The structure of Unocal's ownership of the Yadana Project remained this way until 1998.

Although there is no causal evidence to suggest that the Unocal charter revocation campaign or this lawsuit exercised any influence on Unocal's decision, it is interesting to note that in 1998, as the Unocal petition was being filed, and as Unocal Oil Corporation (the parent corporation) was preparing its new legal strategy for the District Court (after the Appeals Court sent it back to the lower court), the Unocal International Corporation transferred its ownership of the Unocal International Pipeline Corporation (and thus, ownership of its 28 percent "holding" interest in the Gas Transportation Company of the Yadana Project) to Unocal Global Venture, Ltd. (Unocal Global). Unocal Global is a Bermuda corporation and a wholly owned subsidiary of the Unocal International Corporation. In 1999, still during the discovery period in the District Court trial, Unocal International Corporation also transferred its ownership of the Unocal Offshore Company to Unocal Global, explaining to their shareholders that the move was made to achieve tax and cash management efficiencies. By 1999, therefore, Unocal Global was left holding the 28 percent interest in both parts of the Yadana Project, the Gas Production Joint Venture, and the Gas Transportation Company—and doing so while enjoying the tax-haven status permitted by Bermuda and the U.S. Federal Burma Law's exemption for corporations that were already operating in Burma before 1997.

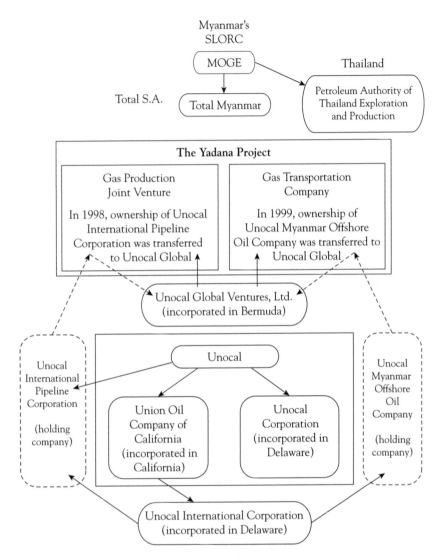

Figure 17. The Yadana Project's transnational network of business partnerships, including Unocal's subsidiaries and holding companies.

There were other partners in the Yadana Project as well. MOGE and a Thai government entity, the Petroleum Authority of Thailand Exploration and Production (PTT), also acquired interests in the project.[35] Total Myanmar was appointed operator of both the Gas Production Joint Venture and the Gas Transportation Company. As the operator, Total Myanmar was responsible for "determin[ing] . . . the selection of . . . employees [and] the hours of work and the compensation to be paid to all . . . employees" in connection with the Yadana Project.

Despite Unocal's complex organizational structure, dispersed ownership, and differentiation of responsibilities, the Ninth Circuit Court of Appeals rejected Unocal's argument that its corporation is actually a contractual network of separate corporate persons' obligations and responsibilities. The Court ruled:

> We initially observe that there is evidence allowing a reasonable factfinder to conclude that the Unocal Pipeline Corp. and the Unocal Offshore Co. were the alter egos of Unocal, and that any actions by the Unocal Pipeline Corp. or the Unocal Offshore Co. are therefore attributable to Unocal. This evidence includes the Unocal Pipeline Corp. or the Unocal Offshore Co.'s undercapitalization and the direct involvement in and direction of the Unocal Pipeline Corp.'s and the Unocal Offshore Co.'s business by Unocal President Imle, Unocal CEO Beach, and other Unocal officers and employees.
>
> More importantly, we do not address—and neither did the District Court—whether a reasonable factfinder could hold Unocal "*vicariously liable* for the Myanmar military's torts." . . . Rather, we find that there is sufficient evidence to hold Unocal liable based on its own actions and those of its alter ego subsidiaries which aided and abetted the Myanmar military in perpetrating forced labor.[36]

Unocal asserted that it could both profit from doing business with a repressive regime and promote human rights. Moreover, Unocal has maintained that only continued trade and investment in Burma will restore democracy. However, this case presents a difficult challenge to the general proposition asserted by "free trade" economists—that is, the proposition that trade liberalization policies promote economic growth and are therefore beneficial to countries that embrace them. Unocal argued that its presence in Burma and partnership with the Myanmar state was ultimately a positive force because it was providing greater wealth for the country and jobs for Burmese citizens. They also argued that such economic growth would ultimately contribute to the democratization of

Burma and empower its citizens to demand from its political institutions greater adherence to human rights norms.

However, this discursive ambivalence reveals a kind of disingenuous support for human rights in Burma. As Aung San Suu Kyi pointed out repeatedly, the vast percentage of wealth generated by foreign investment is not used to improve the economic conditions of Burma's citizens, but only to strengthen the military whose primary enemies are the economic minorities and pro-democracy activists within their country. It is also unclear how Unocal's use of slave labor in the construction of its $1.5 billion gas pipeline project is providing "jobs" for Burma's citizenry in any meaningful sense. Nor is it clear how such corporate practices—despite the economic "growth" that they might create—would ultimately contribute to Burma's democratization, much less promote human rights.

Indeed, the National Foreign Trade Council (NFTC), an association of more than 680 transnational corporations (chartered in the United States), argued in support of Unocal that the federal court should not hold Unocal liable because it could deter companies from economic engagement with the oppressive regime.[37] Although Unocal repeatedly claimed to support human rights, they have continued to aid and abet the Myanmar state's use of coerced labor and intentionally exploited the situation for profit.

Unocal argued before the district court that granting jurisdiction over the *Doe v. Unocal* suit would interfere with the United States' present policy on Burma, which Unocal stated was to refrain "from taking precipitous steps, such as prohibiting all American investment that might serve only to isolate the [Myanmar state] and actually hinder efforts toward reform."[38] In short, Unocal claimed that any court decision that might threaten the existence of such a previously established partnership (like that established between Unocal and the Myanmar government) is an inappropriate intrusion by the court into U.S. foreign policy.

The Discursive Ambivalence Created by States

The state too has shown discursive ambivalence with respect to human rights. The federal court refused all requests to dismiss the *Doe v. Unocal* case. Indeed, in response to Unocal's claim that it has a civil right to freely contract, the Ninth Circuit Court pointed out that it has a civil obligation to uphold the Thirteenth Amendment as well, which includes forced labor in its prohibition against slavery. "The fact that the Thirteenth Amendment reaches private action," explained the court in its written decision, "in turn supports the view that forced labor by private actors gives rise to liability under [the] ATCA."[39]

The federal court also explained that because forced labor is a jus cogens violation, not only can a private party be held liable, but they should be subject to the stronger international, not the weaker domestic, civil standard of liability, namely, "aiding and abetting" rather than "direct and active participation."[40] Under the international standard of aiding and abetting a jus cogens violation, the test for whether Unocal is liable is based not on its exercise of "control" over the Myanmar military's actions, but rather on whether Unocal could, or should, have been able to foresee a reasonable likelihood of the Myanmar military's using the material support and information that Unocal provided them to commit a jus cogens violation.[41]

As evidence of Unocal's "aiding and abetting" the Myanmar military's policy of forced labor in connection with the pipeline, it pointed to the testimony from numerous witnesses, including several of the plaintiffs themselves, that they were forced to clear the right of way for the pipeline and to build helipads for the project before construction of the pipeline began, which were then used by Unocal to visit the pipeline during the planning stages, as well as to ferry their executives and materials to the construction site. In terms of Unocal's practical assistance, Unocal hired the Myanmar military to provide security and build infrastructure along the pipeline route in exchange for money and food. Unocal also provided the Myanmar military with photos, maps, and surveys in daily meetings to show them where to provide the security and build the infrastructure that Unocal had hired them to do.[42]

The court further pointed to admissions made by Unocal representatives in two separate contexts that support the conclusion that Unocal's assistance had a "substantial effect on the perpetration of forced labor, which most probably would not have occurred in the same way without someone hiring the Myanmar military to provide security, and without someone showing them where to do it." The first admission was that of Unocal on-site representative Joel Robinson to the U.S. Embassy in Rangoon (in the once-classified "Robinson cable" that was forwarded to the U.S. State Department), which read: "Our assertion that [the

Myanmar military] has not expanded and amplified its usual methods around the pipeline on our behalf may not withstand much scrutiny."[43]

The second admission was that of then Unocal president Imle who, when confronted by Free Burma and human rights activists in January 1995 at Unocal's headquarters in Los Angeles, acknowledged to them that the Myanmar military might be using forced labor in connection with the project by saying that "people are threatening physical damage to the pipeline," that "if you threaten the pipeline there's gonna be more military," and that "if forced labor goes hand and glove with the military, yes, there will be more forced labor."[44] Notably, the court observed that on the basis of the same evidence, Unocal could even be shown to have met the standard of "active participation" erroneously applied by the District Court.[45]

Responding to Unocal's claim that this ATCA suit represents an unconstitutional intrusion by the judiciary into the United States' foreign policy toward Burma, the district court disagreed with Unocal's argument. First of all, instead of interpreting the State Department's foreign policy intentions for itself, the court asked the State Department directly to clarify its foreign policy position regarding Burma. In the "Statement of Interest of the United States," the State Department wrote that "at this time the adjudication of claims based on allegations of torture and slavery would not prejudice or impede the conduct of U.S. foreign relations with the current government of Burma."[46]

Second, the court reasoned that, even if Unocal is correct in drawing upon the Congressional debates over whether to impose sanctions on Burma as a valid indicator of the Congressional and executive foreign policy position, that debate revolved around how to *improve* conditions in Burma by asserting *positive* pressure on the SLORC through investment in Burma.[47] Yet this lawsuit did not question this foreign policy. Instead, the court explained,

> the [Doe] Plaintiffs essentially contend that Unocal, rather than encouraging reform through investment, is knowingly taking advantage of and profiting from [the] SLORC's practice of using forced labor and forced relocation, in concert with other human rights violations, including rape and other torture, to further the interests of the Yadana gas pipeline project. Whatever the Court's final decision in this action may be, it will not reflect on, undermine or limit the policy determinations made by the coordinate branches with respect to human rights violations in Burma.[48]

Figure 18. Nae Moe seeks safety on April 1, 2002, at Ler Per Her Internally Displaced People's Camp near the Thailand/Burma border. Moe is one of hundreds of thousands of ethnic Karen who are internally displaced in Burma because of brutal repression by the Burmese military regime. Photograph copyright 2002 D. Ngo/ZUMA Press.

In other words, the District Court asserted that the foreign policy of the United States, regardless of its position on the influence of corporate investment in Burma, does not intend to protect corporate activity that violates human rights. The District Court rejected Unocal's argument to have the suit dismissed on the grounds that it represented an impediment to the federal government's foreign policy.[49]

However, we have also seen how the U.S. Supreme Court has sought in *Sosa v. Alvarez-Machain* to contain the extent to which international human rights law might become enunciated within the federal court system. Furthermore, the executive and legislative branches of the federal government have been exercising additional power to delimit ATCA. For example, bowing to the political pressure of corporations, Congress could easily create limitations on the use of ATCA. In October 2005, California senator Dianne Feinstein, while serving on the Senate Energy and Natural Resource Committee, introduced S. 1874, a bill to reform the Alien Tort Claims Act. Human rights groups like EarthRights International (ERI) were quick to denounce the bill as the "Torturer's Protection Act."[50]

Figure 19. Meela Po Hta Internally Displaced People's camp near the
Thailand border. Photograph copyright 1999 D. Ngo/ZUMA Press.

The bill prohibited any suit where a foreign government is responsible for the abuse within its own territory. ERI pointed out that this
alone would eliminate most ATCA cases. The bill excluded from lawsuits war crimes, crimes against humanity, forced labor, terrorism, and
cruel, inhuman, and degrading treatment. It also required that the defendant be a "direct participant" in the abuse. In essence, it argued that
courts should use civil rather than international standards (of "aiding
and abetting" the abuse) in assessing liability. Also, as ERI correctly
warned, "Feinstein's bill gives the [Bush] Administration a blank check
to interfere [in court cases] and have any case it chooses dismissed."[51]

Among the corporate beneficiaries would have been Chevron, which
had donated $30,800 to Feinstein's senatorial campaigns since 1989, ac-
cording to the Center for Responsive Politics.[52] Also noteworthy is that
Unocal maintained its headquarters in California since 1890, until it
merged with Chevron Texaco (now Chevron) on August 10, 2005. Unocal
is now a wholly owned subsidiary of Chevron Corporation. However,
this did not mean that the bill's passage was a foregone conclusion.

Only one week after introducing S. 1874, Feinstein submitted a formal letter to the chair of the Senate Committee on the Judiciary, Arlen
Specter, requesting that he not proceed with the legislation at this time.

She cited concerns raised by human rights advocates as the impetus behind her action. Feinstein's letter explains:

> The legislation in question is designed to address concerns about the clarity of the existing Alien Tort Claim statute in light of the recent Supreme Court decision *Sosa v. Alvarez-Machain*, 542 U.S. 692 (2004). However, I believe that the legislation in its present form calls for refinement in light of concerns raised by human rights advocates, and thus a hearing or other action by the Committee on this bill would be premature.[53]

Although several California corporations would have benefited from S. 1874, these corporations, at least on this legislative battlefront, ultimately did not wield more influence over Senator Feinstein than human rights advocates.

There are, however, also pressures from the executive branch bearing on the future application of ATCA. The federal court's decision to hear *Doe v. Unocal* prompted other transnational activist networks to help file more such ATCA suits against corporations—particularly, though not exclusively, oil corporations.[54] Chevron soon became a defendant in one ATCA lawsuit relating to its complicity in the killing of peaceful protestors by the Nigerian military.[55] An ATCA suit also was filed in New York by the family of late Ogoni activist playwright Ken Saro-Wiwa against Royal Dutch (Shell) Petroleum alleging that the corporation had conspired with the military tribunal in Nigeria that hanged Wiwa, along with eight other activists who were organizing opposition to Royal Dutch Shell operations in their native Ogoniland on the delta of the Niger River.[56] Also, in 2001, eleven plaintiffs from the Aceh province of Indonesia's Sumatra Island, with the help of the International Labor Rights Fund, filed a suit using the ATCA against the Exxon Mobil Corporation in a suit titled *Doe v. Exxon Mobil*.[57]

Yet it is not clear whether these cases strengthened ATCA as a tool for addressing human rights abuses against corporations or simply provided legal fodder that enabled the Supreme Court to justify narrowing the spectrum of human rights abuses committed by corporations for which the federal district courts may serve as a venue in ATCA suits. As the ATCA case against Unocal lumbered through the appellate court, the swifter decisions in these other ATCA cases provided useful discursive resources for Unocal's struggle to influence the courts to decide these legal conflicts in its favor. This became a significant factor after the Bush administration (with its strong ties to the oil industry) began to discursively redefine its foreign policy around "counterterrorism." In early August 2002, the U.S. State Department warned the District Court of the District of Columbia that the *Doe v. Exxon Mobil* case "would hinder the war on terrorism and jeopardize U.S. foreign investment in a key ally [Indonesia]." The *Financial Times* reported that "a former State Department official" had stated that the department's legal affairs office "saw an irresistible opportunity to strike a blow against the Alien Tort Claims Act."[58] Yet the official also reported that the State Department's letter came "after a heated debate inside the agency, with its human rights bureau arguing that U.S. intervention in the case would mar U.S. credibility on issues of corporate social responsibility," while other officials were "worried that the spate of court cases is angering US allies and interfering with the government's foreign policy authority."[59] Publicly, however, the government issued a statement that claimed, "Letting the case go to trial would harm the national interest, including the war on terrorism, and efforts to improve the Indonesian military's record of human rights abuses."[60] During the same week, Unocal lawyers asked California State Superior Court Judge Victoria Chaney, who was presiding over a California unfair business practices claim in a case based on the same facts as *Doe v. Unocal*, to seek a similar government opinion, asserting that many of the arguments in the *Doe v. Exxon Mobil* case were "equally applicable" to the *Doe v. Unocal* case.

Subsequently, the U.S. Supreme Court in June 2008 refused to intervene, turning away an Exxon Mobil appeal that said the suit might interfere with U.S. foreign policy. But in August 2008, the District Court denied a motion by Exxon and ExxonMobil Oil Indonesia to dismiss the suit, saying there was evidence that Indonesian security forces under contract with the companies committed atrocities.[61]

These examples also highlight how economic globalization and the transnational legal space for regulating it are always subject to politics. This law, interpreted by a court and subject to amendment by a federal congress, reminds us of the vital role that states play in the process of globalization. All of these dimensions of state action (legislative, administrative, and judicial) remain crucial to the unfolding struggle over the rules and institutional arrangements of economic globalization.

Because human rights discourse is so often invoked as a political, legal, and moral resource for addressing (and diffusing contentious challenges to) the dehumanizing consequences of economic globalization, it is important to focus on its many forms of practice. Included are the discursively ambivalent practices of corporate and state agents that combine human rights discourse with others that are meant to protect corporations from being held accountable for their abusive human rights practices, as well as those that are meant to minimize the state's vulnerability to international legal standards. Transcending the particularities of any specific lawsuit under the ATCA, we may therefore speak of a strategy that employs powerful discursive, ideological, and practical devices designed to stabilize this transnational legal space around voluntary and legally nonbinding practices of social responsibility.

Discursive Ambivalence and Human Rights

ATCA is a potentially useful tool for furthering human rights. But it is also one that, when combined with other countervailing discourses, may become so diluted or declawed that it fails to retain the power or scope to reach some of the most egregious violators and violations of human rights. The struggle over ATCA illustrates the ambivalence and discursive dilemmas of foreign policy conservatives who have appropriated the language of international human rights for their own purposes. The consequence is that they are in an awkward position in trying to draw a line that immunizes U.S. firms from complicity in such abuses. Yet, I have argued, even in the current political environment there are reasons to believe that this transnational legal strategy, using ATCA to hold liable corporations that aid and abet human rights violations, has legs.

This legal strategy represents one of the most significant efforts of the past century to rein in the power of transnational corporations. The case of *Doe v. Unocal* dramatically demonstrates the potential for using transnational legal action to challenge neoliberal understandings of globalization. Rather than allowing the proponents of neoliberal globalization to dismiss human rights concerns as "artificial obstacles to free trade," the federal courts have been providing a venue for discussing corporations' responsibilities and liabilities with regard to human rights. By shaping the moral boundaries within which corporations compete for profits, these venues have provided an important institutional mechanism and discursive resource for further discussion of how and why global markets are not self-regulating, but rather are (and must always be) institutionally constructed through and embedded in politics, law, and morality.

Despite the ambivalent discursive practices of both corporate and state actors who have donned the mantle of human rights, we should resist insisting that human rights discourse itself is necessarily hegemonic. Doing so serves ultimately to further empower those who seek to instrumentally subordinate human rights norms to the control of markets and particular nation states. Rather we must focus on the ways that competing social actors, including corporations and states, draw upon human rights discourse and combine it with diverse configurations of multiple discourses to insert their own networks' social arrangement of power, practice, and meaning. Human rights discourse is not oppressive; but *how* we institutionalize the legal arrangement of human rights in practice can be.

This case, therefore, speaks not only to the discursive ambivalence of human rights practice, but also to what Goodale and Merry refer to as the "betweenness" of human rights discourse,

> the ways in which human rights discourse unfolds ambiguously, without a clear spatial referent, in part through transnational networks, but also, equally important, through the projection of the moral and legal imagination by social actors whose precise locations—*pace* Keck and Sikkink—within these networks are (for them) practically irrelevant.[62]

An approach highlighting transnational legal discourse is important precisely because the state's legal discourse and norms are so often hegemonic. Appreciation for the success of these transnational legal campaigns begins not with an accounting of victory or defeat in the court, or on the floor of the legislature, nor merely with an assessment of their direct role in transforming existing international law or global norms, but rather with the capacity of their participants to create an alternative discursive space in the legal records of the transnational struggles that take place in these institutions of the state.

These records, combined with the experiences of allied movement participants supporting the campaigns from outside the legal institutional arena, provide critical resources for sustaining the kind of public collective memory that future transnational campaigns and movements will have to draw upon in the inevitably incremental struggle for democratic global change. Transnational discursive strategies help us to reconceptualize the relations within which we institutionalize economic globalization, as well as the way that we imagine the possibilities of participating in its institutionalization.

Conclusion

Where Do We Go from Here?

I have argued that, contrary to the perspective of most scholars, the pro-democracy movement in Burma did not start down a path of inevitable decline after 1990. Instead, it reincarnated itself as the Free Burma movement through its transnational legal action. After nearly fifteen years, the movement is alive and well.

Nevertheless, predicting the future of democracy in Burma is difficult. Democracy in Burma will likely not come on the back of a social movement alone. More powerful states in the international community (e.g., China and the United States) will certainly play a role in determining Burma's political course. As I argued in chapter 1, this has been the case since Burma's independence and, along with the member states of ASEAN, this continues to be the case. While the pariah status of the Myanmar military throughout the international community is well deserved, the ritualized discourse among the international community emphasizing it masks an important truth about the possibilities for democratic change in Burma. It leads us to believe that the most powerful states in the international community would like to see the Myanmar military replaced or reformed by democratic leadership. Yet this book documents how the United States and many of its partners in the international community lack the political will to exercise the kind of democratic influence that could contribute to such reform. In the short term, this does not bode well for the future of democracy in Burma.

As we saw in chapter 3, federal sanctions against Burma, enacted in 1997, allowed Unocal Oil Company to continue with its construction of the Yadana gas pipeline (now owned by Chevron). It represented a shift away from existing, effective, local sanctions with real teeth to a policy that blended sanctions with "constructive engagement." After the 2007 Saffron Revolution, President George W. Bush and the U.S. Congress implemented several tougher, "smart sanctions" that targeted the Burmese generals' assets and bank accounts, as well as the importation of key "conflict" gems, like jade and rubies. So, taken together, the U.S. sanctions policy has not been consistent and at times has included some economic engagement. It is this particular mix of carrots and sticks that represents the failed U.S. policy toward Burma, not, as Virginia senator Jim Webb (and U.S. Secretary of State Hillary Clinton) argued throughout 2009, sanctions in general.

Despite the differences between policies of constructive engagement and economic sanctions, what both proclaim to share is the goal of promoting tripartite dialogue among Burma's generals, Aung San Suu Kyi's National League for Democracy Party, and leaders of the ethnic and nationalist minority groups. However, these policies, as practiced, have never really come close to achieving this goal. President Barack Obama's new policy of "direct engagement," which his administration began pursuing in October 2009, attempts to rethink and recalibrate the balance of carrots and sticks that it might use to promote such tripartite dialogue. "Direct," as opposed to "constructive," engagement is meant to emphasize first and foremost diplomacy and dialogue with Burma's ruling regime, rather than the formation of business ventures with them.

What form has this direct engagement taken so far in the run-up to the scheduled 2010 elections in Myanmar? President Obama's meeting with Burmese prime minister Thein Sein at the U.S.–ASEAN Summit in November 2009 was meant to signal that the United States is completely committed to direct political engagement with Myanmar's military leaders. It was not merely a temporary gesture in a more instrumental effort to shore up U.S.–ASEAN trade relations. Despite General Than Shwe's comments during the preceding week depicting the efforts of Secretary of State Clinton and Assistant Secretary of State for East Asian and Pacific Affairs Kurt Campbell as neocolonial interference in

Myanmar's affairs, it seems significant that he allowed his prime minister to meet with Obama afterward.

As I am writing this in February 2010, the Obama administration seems poised to begin making some concessions, possibly including the easing of sanctions, if Than Shwe is able to orchestrate the "free and fair" elections that he claims are his intentions. For the Obama administration, "free and fair" means also "credible"; that is, elections that would include the participation of the winner of the previous democratic elections in 1990 whom the State Law and Order Restoration Council (SLORC) prevented from taking office and placed under house arrest. It also includes the many political prisoners who were punished for representing or supporting the views of the winning National League for Democracy Party.

However, this is not the whole picture. The Obama administration is also signaling, albeit more ambivalently, that it wants to see "democratic reform" in Burma before it begins translating political engagement into economic engagement with Myanmar. Democratic reform is more than free and fair and credible elections. It is a signal that the Obama administration is also aware of the grossly undemocratic constitution that Than Shwe's administration has drafted and that would be fully implemented in the wake of the 2010 elections.

This raises a key question: Can democratic elections, even with the international community's stamp of approval, produce a democratic outcome in Myanmar when the new constitution that it would legitimate is structured to retain military rule with no significant checks and balances? We should remember that the elections in 1990 were also free and fair and credible. This is how we came to know that Daw Aung San Suu Kyi won by a landslide. Yet this was not enough to prevent the SLORC from stopping democratic reform in its tracks. The difference between the elections of 2010 and those of 1990 is that were Than Shwe's party to honor the election results this time, he would have the new constitutional authority to do so simply by declaring a "state of emergency."

However, in the long term, the Free Burma movement has been contributing critical resources to the kind of democratic groundwork influencing civil society both within and outside of Burma that would be necessary for any possible future political transition to democracy in Burma. If Burma does experience such a transition, then this study will help us to understand an important aspect of how the change occurred.

Figure 20. U Bo Kyi stands in front of the walls of his office located near the Thailand/Burma border. He is joint secretary of the Assistance Association for Political Prisoners, which documents the incarceration and release of political prisoners by the Myanmar military regime. When this photograph was taken in May 2009, there were more than 2,200 political prisoners under the custody of the regime. Photograph by author.

If Burma's political development runs the course of civil war, or becomes a perpetual client state of China or Western "coalition forces," we should be able to claim on the basis of this study that such a direction was certainly not inevitable.

Lessons from the Free Burma Movement

There are at least five important lessons that we can glean from the transnational legal action of the Free Burma movement.

Lesson 1: States Have the Power but Not the Will to Control Corporations

The first lesson is that states are still critical and powerful actors in shaping the unfolding institutionalization of globalization. The corporations that Free Burma activists confronted claimed that the practice of human rights is the business of states, not market participants, suggesting that markets can be disembedded from the practice of human rights. In the extreme version of this claim, corporations equate human rights protections with artificial barriers to free trade. Thus, if we allow free trade to flourish, markets will solve most of our abusive human rights practices. The Free Burma movement challenged such claims. It picked up the thread in political economy that markets are always embedded in politics, law, and morality, and that states have the power, although not usually the political will, to control corporations through their legislative, administrative, and judicial action. States claim that they are powerless to control corporations. Yet these transnational legal campaigns showed states how to do it and that, in fact, states choose not to control their corporations.

Moreover, these campaigns demonstrate how a layer of neoliberalism shapes these discussions and blinds them to the ways in which they can exercise substantial control to rein in corporations that undermine democracy and facilitate or engage in abusive human rights practices. They taught us that states in a globalizing world are not inevitably disempowered to enforce human rights. Instead, states—even democratic ones, as demonstrated by the United States' toothless foreign policy toward Myanmar—are complicit in the perpetuation of abusive human rights practices.

Lesson 2: Transnational Discourse Provides an Alternative to Neoliberal Globalization

The second lesson of the Free Burma movement is that transnationalist discursive strategies can empower and increase the effectiveness of movements. As I explained in the Introduction, transnational discursive strategies help us to reconceptualize the relations through which we institutionalize economic globalization, as well as the way that we imagine the possibilities of participating in its institutionalization.

This book presents a case study of the Free Burma movement to demonstrate the potentially transformative movement politics of transnational legal action. This movement incrementally forged through a series of campaigns a set of transnationalist discourses that, when taken together, provides an alternative to neoliberal globalization. An approach highlighting transnational *legal* discourse is important precisely because the state's legal discourse and norms are so often hegemonic. Appreciation for the success of these legal campaigns begins not with an accounting of victory or defeat in the court or on the floor of the legislature, nor merely with an assessment of their direct role in transforming existing international law or global norms, but rather in the capacity of their participants to create an alternative discursive space in the legal records of the transnationalist struggles that take place in these institutions of the state. These records, combined with the experiences of allied movement participants supporting the campaigns from outside the legal institutional arena, provide critical resources for sustaining the kind of public collective memory that future transnational campaigns and movements will have to draw upon in the inevitably incremental struggle for democratic global change.

The transnationalist discursive approach shows us how these campaigns exploit the legal contradictions and disjunctures arising between different spatial scales of market regulation as the United States has exercised a disproportionately influential role in constructing institutional arrangements for global investment and trade. This approach also helps us to identify how each campaign highlights a different dimension— legislative, administrative, and judicial—of the processes through which the United States institutionalizes rules and arrangements facilitating and constraining global markets. These campaigns illustrate how global markets become embedded in politics, law, and morality. They do so in a way that challenges the neoliberal economic notion that the state's economic regulation, when based on politics, law, and morality, produces artificial barriers to the development of global markets.

Methodologically, the transnationalist discursive approach is useful when combined with those of the political process approach. I have not employed it as a method unto itself, but rather to complement my study where most studies of collective action have neglected to tread: namely, within the existing political institutional channels of the state. I traced a single movement's development, focusing on its strategies and targets of collective action. I noticed how its collective action became increasingly focused on giving voice to the people and conditions of Burma through legal campaigns in the United States. As I examined the legal briefs and transcripts of the resulting suits, comparing them to the movement's ongoing discourse outside the courts, I began to identify the movement's deliberate effort to reframe the sources of its oppression. I then began to trace the elements of transnationalist discourse in these legal campaigns that the movement used, both within and outside the existing political institutional channels of the state, to increasingly develop the narrative representation of the relations and processes affecting the conditions in Burma. I observed how they drew upon the legal discursive contention arising from legal battles in one campaign to elaborate subsequently in concurrent legal battles of the other campaigns the transnational representations that they were developing.

It was through this method that I began to first notice how the movement's discourse and strategies of collective action had shifted radically from a state-centered to a transnational social movement. This shift had a tremendously effective impact on the movement's ability to mobilize support outside of Burma. It also effectively mobilized sudden and massive opposition from transnational corporations whose interests in Burma had only now become threatened. It was in many ways this overwhelming countermobilization by transnational corporations that drew the serious attention of the media and unleashed the transnationalist representations of the Free Burma movement from the confines of the court records, catapulting them into the public eye.

An important part of the transnationalist discursive approach is to challenge the binary distinction between globalization and the nation-state by insisting on the continuing significance of borders, state policies, and national identities even as these often are transgressed by transnational communication circuits and social practices. My effort to trace the state's role in shaping the outcome of these Free Burma campaigns has yielded some methodological lessons as well.

First, it is fruitful to differentiate and examine the state's various dimensions of action: legislative, administrative, and judicial. We should also seek to identify how each of these dimensions of state action may be operating (even simultaneously) at a variety of spatial scales: municipal/local; regional; federal/national; international (i.e., state-to-state interaction); and transnational (i.e., a state's interaction with nonstate actors that are situated or operating outside the state's own national territorial boundaries). Doing so reveals how the state's action is always potentially contradictory and rarely uniform or coherent. States rarely speak with one voice. They often speak with multiple voices simultaneously. Failing to examine these various dimensions and scales of action would lead us to mistakenly see the state either as uniformly in support of the Free Burma movement's campaigns or as uniformly opposed to them at different periods of time with regard to each legal campaign. However, the transnationalist discursive approach teaches us that the state acting at multiple scales simultaneously may hold contradictory positions vis-à-vis the movement—not only varying from one legal campaign context to the next, but also varying within the same legal campaign context.

Second, there is a tendency among some social movement scholars to equate a cultural analysis of social movements with an abandoning of traditional social movement theory's emphasis on "objective" political structures in favor of social movement participants' "subjective" perceptions and valuations of political structures. This thinking reflects an unwarranted assumption that political structures are objective, but that culture is always nonstructural and subjective. The methodological lesson that my book advances is different. My discursive approach emphasizes cultural structures, particularly discourses and narratives—including those of the state, which ultimately must enforce global norm structures. I am suggesting that we should probe the (objective) resources and constraints generated by the cultural dimensions of political structures. To the extent that states continue to institutionalize rules and policies driven by the norms and discursive logic of neoliberal economic "free trade," thus devolving the state's regulatory power to the interests of transnational corporations, we need progressive, transnational discourses that can effectively speak to this discourse (i.e., this cultural structural dimension of state action) and offer alternative ways of making sense of the process through which we can embed global trade, production, and investment in law, politics, and morality.

It is worth recognizing that under conditions in which states, particularly democratic states, participate in shaping the global institutionalization of the rules and regulations of trade and investment, many of their own existing domestic laws and policies will become inconsistent with these rules and regulations. This legal or regulatory disjuncture between the domestic laws of democratic states and those of global governing institutions offers political opportunities for transnational social movements that can identify and successfully reframe these domestic legal principles in progressive transnationalist terms. This is not to suggest that there is a high likelihood that transnational social movements will effectively shape the outcome of these global rules and regulations. For such legal disjuncture in democratic states affords the same opportunities and organizational space to the movement's more powerful and resource-rich opponents. But such legal struggles produce new cultural resources and activate existing (even dormant) ones for ongoing normative contestation within the broader institutions of civil society.

Lesson 3: Corporations, Like Governments, May Violate Human Rights

The third lesson that we should take from the transnational legal campaigns of the Free Burma movement is that transnational corporations, as much as governments, may also be significant violators of human rights. In some cases, transnational corporations may even work together with states in violating them. Moreover, the *Doe v. Unocal* litigation, as well as other lawsuits filed against both corporate and state violators of human rights under the Alien Tort Claims Act, reflects a transnational legal space created by the Free Burma movement's transnational legal action, where individuals and groups from other human rights struggles outside the United States may well find recourse within the judicial arenas of the U.S. District Court. That is, the domestic state in which human rights victims hold their citizenship does not necessarily have a monopoly on their access to a judicial arena. The Free Burma movement has helped us to create (or, at least, to consider the possibility of creating) a more transnational system of human rights regulation that is potentially more effective at holding corporate actors accountable for abusive human rights practices, and that reduces the opportunity for "regulatory capture" by domestic repressive forces in states like Myanmar that have a policy of impunity with regard to enforcing human rights.

Lesson 4: The Lack of Democracy Contributes to Authoritarianism

The fourth lesson that the Free Burma movement has taught us is that the lack of political democracy in Myanmar stems in part from the lack of political democracy in the United States. It is not only the U.S. government, but also the citizens of the United States, who have demonstrated an astonishing lack of democracy. And this lack of democracy in the United States has contributed directly to Myanmar's authoritarianism.

In this book, we have seen that U.S. foreign policy toward Burma, both in the past and present, has contributed directly to supporting an authoritarian military regime. In chapter 1, we saw that the Eisenhower administration and the CIA organized through covert policies an invasion of Burma territory to provide military support to Chinese anticommunist troops of the KMT during the Chinese civil war, indirectly pushing the Burmese military toward authoritarianism. Shortly afterward, we also saw how the United States, through overt policies, bypassed the democratic civilian government of Burma to organize sales of arms and weapons directly to the Burmese military, thereby contributing to the military's strength vis-à-vis the democratic civilian government. These undemocratic foreign policies toward Burma motivated and helped to strengthen the military's capacity to overthrow the democratic government of Burma in 1962.

In Part II of this book, we saw how recent U.S. foreign policy toward Burma has essentially served to sustain large-scale U.S. corporate ventures in Burma, even grandfathering in the largest U.S. corporate ventures, despite enacting economic sanctions. The result of this policy has been to provide badly needed foreign investment to the Myanmar military, with whom these corporations forged their business ventures, and in turn strengthen the military's capacity to continue diverting its revenues to repressing the pro-democracy movement in Burma. Another result of this policy has been to sustain U.S. corporations' abusive human rights practices in Burma, like the aiding and abetting of (and profiting from) forced labor.

We have also seen that civil society in the United States has not been exercising its democratic power vis-à-vis its own state. The Free Burma movement, as we saw in chapter 4, has taught us that civil society in the United States has slowly given over to the state its responsibility to participate in decision-making processes that shape corporate accountability. Indeed, U.S. citizens have been doing it for so long now that they have forgotten that they even have the power, much less responsibility, to engage in corporate accountability. Worse still, many U.S. citizens have come to believe that corporations will behave in their best interests if they get out of the way and allow corporations to regulate their own conduct. The Free Burma movement has taught us that this has cost both them and U.S. citizens their democracy.

Lesson 5: Human Rights Are Part Law, Part Ideology

The Free Burma movement has also taught us a fifth lesson: human rights are more than law, despite what international lawyers tell us about human rights. Human rights are also norms, ideology, practices (including discursive ones), and, in part, a social movement. To the extent that we can examine how the meaning of human rights is created through our practices, and within specific relational contexts, we can speak of the production of human rights. We can also examine how we organize the production of human rights. Is it possible to further democratize the production of human rights? What difference does it make if we produce human rights through relations and practices of inequality?

Transnational movements that focus on influencing domestic policies in democracies are not necessarily less effective in enhancing representation of groups suffering under authoritarian rule, but they can be. To the extent that we can democratize the production of human rights, there are *limits* to the strategy of using transnational legal action to pursue human rights—at least as it has been practiced within the Free Burma movement to date. But it might be possible to improve on this strategy.

As I suggested above, the Free Burma movement illustrates how groups suffering under authoritarian rule may be repressed by not only the domestic policies of authoritarian states, but also by the domestic policies of democratic states that facilitate the undemocratic practices of the transnational corporations that they charter and which collaborate with authoritarian states in repressing for profit groups that live there. When we pay closer attention to these transnational connections between democratic and authoritarian states, their domestic policies, and their citizens, as well as the corporate practices and partnerships that span the boundaries of democratic and authoritarian states, it blurs the binary conceptual distinction between them. This provides the first step toward creating new possibilities for imagining effective transnational legal action that challenges the hegemonic relations and discourses that sustain such a reified conceptual distinction between democratic and authoritarian states. This has been one of the strengths of the Free Burma movement's transnational legal action.

However, in this book, I have not given sufficient attention to the hegemonic relations that may exist within the Free Burma movement itself. The Free Burma movement's transnational legal action ultimately relies on the transnational solidarity that the movement has forged between activists in the global North and activists in Burma (within the global South). I have argued throughout this book that the movement's hope, and quite possibly its fate, has become woven into the transnational web of relations that its participants have been spinning under the banner of the Free Burma movement for nearly two decades now.

But what is the character of the social relations that have produced this transnational solidarity?

Critics have raised general concerns about the hegemonic relations between NGOs of the global North and South[1] and the repressive and exclusionary politics of representation that play out through transnational human rights advocacy and litigation.[2] They point to a transnational solidarity that is produced through socially "thin" relations and raise questions about the durability and potential of its agency for social change, as well as the practices of human rights and democracy that they are locally routinizing within civil society.

As Fuyuki Kurasawa argues, the possibilities for an alternative cosmopolitan process of engagement depend on how and to what extent civic associations, nongovernmental organizations, social movement organizations, transnational advocacy networks, and other progressive agents of civil society enact the social labor required to counter the sources of structural and situational violence and injustice as well as produce a new social order.[3] This is no less true for the Free Burma movement. How are Free Burma activists working to "thicken" their social relations within the movement? How are they practicing among themselves the social justice, democracy, and human rights that they promote? That is, aside from the relations between civil societies, states, and markets that they project within the discourses that they have struggled to institutionalize within national and international legal systems, what kinds of relations within and between civil societies are they producing or, perhaps unintentionally, reproducing in their quest for social change?

Burma's military argues that it is the only force that can keep a lid on the bubbling cauldron of fractious, interethnic, nationalist rivalries within the country. If the leaders of Burma's pro-democracy movement were to successfully gain control of the state, would civil society in Burma unravel? What do democracy and human rights mean in practice to the people inside Burma who are chanting (or whispering) these words?

The limits of the strategy of transnational legal action that the Free Burma movement has deployed stem from the hegemony of dominant human rights practices that many NGOs, particularly those from the United States that specialize in legal advocacy, reinforce within the movement. However, there are also many NGOs of the global North working in support of the Free Burma movement that have self-consciously sought to democratize the production of the meaning of human rights.

Figure 21. Meela Po Hta Internally Displaced People's (IDP) camp near the
Thailand border. Photograph copyright 2000 D. Ngo/ZUMA Press.

I am currently exploring how they engage in these democratizing practices, especially in light of the fact that the movement not only engages
at a grassroots level but also attempts to harness powerful institutions to
promote democracy and human rights in Burma. How do they struggle
to create conceptions of human rights and justice that are grounded in
the grassroots and yet are recognized by powerful external institutional
actors (e.g., the UN, the International Criminal Court, U.S. federal
courts, the U.S. Congress, etc.)?

    In 2009, activists began organizing a transnational campaign to har-
ness the power of the United Nations and indict before the International
Criminal Court (ICC) General Than Shwe, the effective dictator in
Burma, for war crimes and crimes against humanity. As a first step, they
have called for a UN Commission of Inquiry to send an international
monitoring team to investigate their allegations against the general.
Securing such an inquiry requires the support of only one permanent
member of the UN Security Council. That is, the United States as a
permanent member of the UN Security Council has the power to initiate a UN Commission of Inquiry without unanimous consensus of the
other four permanent members (which include China, which certainly

represents a potential challenger of this Commission of Inquiry). The idea is to pressure the United States or the United Kingdom to initiate the UN Commission of Inquiry without facing the veto power of China.

This strategy focuses more squarely on the Myanmar state than on its transnational relations with corporate partners. Such a campaign can be morally founded upon the UN's recently developed international human rights norm that emphasizes the international community's "Responsibility to Protect" (or "R2P," as some refer to it). When a state refuses, fails, or demonstrates an inability to protect its civilians from fundamental human rights abuses, it is the responsibility of the international community to then protect that state's civilians. Additionally, unlike the Alien Tort Claims Act strategy, this one focuses on individual criminal, rather than individual civil, accountability and therefore seeks to imprison Myanmar's generals, rather than force corporations to pay damages to victims.

This, however, is when the real work for human rights NGOs inside and along the borders of Burma would begin. In May 2009, I attended a conference in Bangkok, along with representatives of scores of NGOs and civic associations supporting the Free Burma movement, which was organized by the International Federation of Human Rights and the Burma Lawyers' Council. The conference was titled "Advancing Human Rights and Ending Impunity in Burma: Which External Leverages?" Many Burmese and ethnic minority groups attending expressed concern about participating in the upcoming 2010 elections. The dominant sentiment was that a boycott of the elections was necessary. It is ironic, yet perfectly understandable, that pro-democracy activists find themselves in the position of denouncing these democratic elections. Most of the attendees argued that the new constitution drafted by the military regime was so grossly undemocratic in substance and structure that no (even internationally monitored) free and fair elections could produce a democratic outcome in Burma's civil society if they were to lend legitimacy to this constitution and cement the military's rule along the lines it authorizes.

Concern was also expressed over the proposed campaign for a UN Commission of Inquiry. Some NGOs, especially those in and along Burma's borders, were concerned about the kinds of risks to which they might be subject were Than Shwe not successfully extradited in the wake of an International Criminal Court indictment—which, at least initially, was the intended result of this campaign. In other words, they were concerned that, just as al-Bashir in the Sudan avoided extradition following the International Criminal Court's indictment of him, Than Shwe might well be able to do the same. Al-Bashir then systematically began forcing NGOs in the Sudan to cease their operations.

The greatest concern voiced at the conference was the timing of the campaign. The main focus of the NGOs in Burma and along the borders was on the 2010 elections, and they did not want to drain energy from this focus. In the end, however, most agreed that this campaign for a UN Commission of Inquiry, regardless of whether it ultimately resulted in a UN referral to the International Criminal Court for an indictment of Than Shwe, had the advantage of creating a UN investigation into war crimes and crimes against humanity in Burma—and thus potentially of setting up a UN monitoring mechanism during the run-up to the 2010 elections, when increased violent state repression was likely.

Still, others noted the contradictions in calling for the generals in Burma to engage in tripartite dialogue, on the one hand, and, on the other, attempting to indict them before the International Criminal Court. This raises an equally challenging question for the Obama administration. Can the U.S. effectively initiate a UN Commission of Inquiry into war crimes and crimes against humanity in Burma as it simultaneously seeks to initiate and influence "direct engagement" with Burma's generals? Would not their doing so send mixed messages to the Regime?

Perhaps the Obama administration only intends to initiate a UN Commission of Inquiry as a stick to be used if the generals fail to engage in tripartite dialogue. But the message that the administration has been sending is that direct engagement is about "free and fair and credible elections" as a first step toward democratic change in Burma. What if the generals are only seeking a stamp of legitimacy from the international community for their elections, with no concern for dialogue beyond that point? This, after all, is why the military held "free and fair" elections in 1990. To reiterate, the difference of the 2010 elections and from previous elections is that if the military again flexes its power, they can point to their new constitutional authority to do so.

Resorting only at that point to a UN Commission of Inquiry raises again all of the appropriate concerns regarding risks voiced by NGOs inside and along Burma's borders. Will Burma be another Sudan? These are difficult but decisive times for Burma, the international community, and advocacy as well. The Free Burma movement, as much as the Obama administration, has to carefully consider the precise nature *and timing* of their "direct engagement." Although the NGOs in Burma and along the borders have been documenting human rights abuses for years, the UN would be looking for evidence that meets the specific litigation standards of the International Criminal Court. These NGOs have already been questioning each other about their methods of interviewing survivors and documenting evidence of human rights abuse and the relational context in which the abusive practices and conflict occurred. Many NGOs of the global North are pushing NGOs working in and around Burma who are compiling the evidence to remain cognizant of the kinds of evidentiary description that would be actionable in a legal case of this nature. No one doubts that there is ample human rights abuse to justify the case against Than Shwe, but how the evidence is obtained, and how the abuse is represented, matters. Will this pressure to frame the abuse within preexisting, institutionalized human rights discourse hinder the efforts of more progressive NGOs that have been trying to identify local meanings of human rights and injustice that are not internationally institutionalized and legally actionable?

This raises a battery of related questions. How are these NGOs organizing their relations with grassroots participants in these programs to discuss, interpret, and identify local meanings of human rights and democracy? How do these grassroots training programs work in practice? How do trainers know a "local meaning of human rights" when they see or hear one? And what do they do with one once they have identified it? How do the NGOs and participants in their training programs understand their role in the international human rights movement and in the pro-democracy movement in Burma? What does a democratically organized process of producing meanings of "human rights" practice look like? Do conflicts over these meanings arise? And if so, how are they resolved? What forms do these conflicts and their resolution take? What effects do they have on the relations between and among NGO trainers and program participants?

I also want to examine how these human rights and democracy training programs are working to develop new identities and discourses of transnational solidarity across lines of ethnic (national) difference within

Figure 22. In January 2000, a Karen woman in Ki Toh Hta village worries about the future of her family and her village. Located hours from the Thailand border in eastern Burma, Ki Toh Hta village is one of the lucky few protected from the Burmese military (SPDC) by Karen guerilla resistance. Photograph copyright 2000 D. Ngo/ZUMA Press.

Burma. Is such training influencing the practice of human rights among North-South and South-South relations in ways that promote the social thickening of civil society? Is it affecting the grassroots program alumni's practices of identifying and documenting human rights abuses? Is it influencing their practice of creating protest campaigns to protect human rights and defend against human rights abuses?

This research on the transnational and democratic production of human rights within the relational context of actors in civil society builds on the transnational legal action approach that I have taken in this book. It does not abandon the emphasis on a politics of influence that transnational movements attempt to exercise vis-à-vis states and other institutions of governance. Rather, it focuses on the transnational activists relations linking Burma's civil society with others and examines how they organize their social relations of transnational solidarity to produce shared, complementary, or even conflicting understanding of human rights.

The next step is to trace how, the extent to which, and with what effect these local meanings travel (and transform) through the movement's transnational networks of meaning and practice, and to examine whether and how they influence NGO campaigns for political-legal institutional change, giving particular attention to the ongoing campaign to indict General Than Shwe before the ICC on charges of war crimes and crimes against humanity. My hunch is that most will be lost in translation, but it is the process of how this happens, and why, that we should be exploring. If the Free Burma movement's activists can find ways to democratize their social relations of transnational solidarity and practice of human rights in ways that inform their strategies of transnational legal action, then they will have charted a truly alternative and progressive course for change—not only for Burma, but for all of us.

Acknowledgments

This book has been a long time in the making. I owe thanks and more to a long list of people. First and most important, I thank my wife and closest companion, Daniela Kraiem. She lived with this project from start to finish, debating the twists and turns in my interpretation all the way. She invested countless hours helping me edit and conceptualize this book. She was supportive when I grew weary and made tremendous sacrifices that enabled me to spend the time, effort, and resources ultimately necessary to bring it to completion. She may be the only person more pleased than I to see this book finally in print.

I am deeply indebted to many people from Burma and Thailand, presently or formerly, who volunteered their time and effort, shared their food and homes, and in some cases took significant risks to assist me in collecting data. To many of them, I have promised confidentiality. To other generous and courageous individuals I offer my humble respect and gratitude, especially to Zaw Min, Ko Kyaw Kyaw, Teddy Buri, Aung Myo Min, Dr. Sein Win, Bo Hla-Hint, Win Hlaing, Ah Moe Zoe, Zaw Zaw Htun, Min Min Oo, U Bo Kyi, Bo Thakhin Sa, Lu Maw, Saw Cit Oo, Soe Aung, Myat Thu, Sitthipong Kalayanee, Htet Khai, Moe Zaw

Oo, Aung Din, Khin Omar, and many brave friends in Karen State, Shan State, Rangoon (Yangon), and Mandalay. I benefited greatly from discussions and interviews with many individuals dedicated to the transnational struggle for democracy and human rights in Burma, including Debbie Stothard, Max Ediger, Faith Doherty, Lyndal Barry, Jack Dunford, Sally Thompson, Kevin Heppner, Jackie Pollock, Veronika Martin, Peter Halford, Pippa Curran, Matthew Smith, Roshan Jason, Alison Tate, Dr. Guy Morineau, Dr. Yuval Ginbar, Antoine Madelin, Chris Kennel, Dave Mathieson, Mark Farmaner, Jeanne Hallacy, Benedict Rogers, Amy Alexander, Justin Sherman, and Annette Kunigagon.

Outside Burma and Thailand, more individuals and organizations than I have space to list provided me with critical assistance. I must thank Burma Centre Nederlands for allowing me liberal access to its archives in Amsterdam. In the United States, I am grateful to Simon Billenness, Robert Benson, and Jeremy Woodrum for offering me substantial insight into their work on transnational and international legal campaigns that have contributed to the Free Burma movement. Mike Haack at U.S. Campaign for Burma kindly helped me to locate and use many of the photographs that appear in this book. Additionally, D. Ngo graciously permitted me to use many personal photographs of protests and internally displaced and forcibly relocated persons inside Burma.

The University of California–Davis provided invaluable funding during the research and writing of my dissertation manuscript, from which this book derives. Especially generous were the mentors and colleagues there who critically influenced my thinking about the politics of globalization and human rights, social movements, and transnationalism. Fred Block deserves special acknowledgment for his unwavering support, intellectual nurturing, professional guidance, and warm friendship. Jack Goldstone, Michael Peter Smith, and David Kyle also greatly influenced the development of this research. All four provided insightful comments on earlier drafts of this work.

I also extend thanks to Andy Nathan and my other coparticipants in the Seminar on Human Rights in an Age of Globalization, supported by the National Endowment for the Humanities and hosted by Columbia University during the summer of 2005. Mark Goodale, Sally Engle Merry, and Balakrishnan Rajagopal offered valuable comments and encouragement as I revised my work on the *Doe v. Unocal* case.

Notes

Preface

1. Arturo Escobar, "Power and Visibility: Development and the Intervention of Management in the Third World," *Cultural Anthropology* 3, no. 4 (1988): 428–43.

2. Michael Burawoy, ed., *Global Ethnography: Forces, Connections, and Imaginations in a Transnational World* (Berkeley: University of California Press, 1999), 65.

Introduction

1. The ruling military regime of Myanmar changed its name from the State Law and Order Restoration Council (SLORC) to the State Peace and Development Council in November 1997. Despite the change in name and a reshuffling of leadership within the government, there was no significant change in the military's governance.

2. Daniel Mato, "On Global and Local Agents and the Social Making of Transnational Identities and Related Agendas in Latin America," *Identities* 4, no. 2 (1997): 171.

3. Sarah A. Radcliffe, "Development, the State, and Transnational Political Connections: State and Subject Formations in Latin America," *Global Networks* 1, no. 1 (2001): 1936.

4. See Robert I. Rotberg, ed., *Burma: Prospects for a Democratic Future* (Washington, D.C.: Brookings Institution Press, 1998), especially the following chapters: John J. Brandon, "The State's Role in Education in Burma: An Overview";

Mark Mason, "Foreign Direct Investment in Burma: Trends, Determinants, and Prospects"; Marvin C. Ott, "From Isolation to Relevance: Policy Considerations"; and Andrew Selth, "The Armed Forces and Military Rule in Burma."

5. See Mya Than, "Economic Transformation in Southeast Asia: The Case of Myanmar," in *Burma/Myanmar toward the Twenty-first Century: Dynamic of Continuity and Change*, ed. John J. Brandon (Bangkok, Thailand: T.K. Printing, 1997).

6. Bertril Lintner, "Arrested Development: Is the Opposition Doomed to Irrelevance?" *Far Eastern Economic Review* (March 2, 1995): 28–29.

7. Tin Maung Maung Than, "Myanmar Democratization: Punctuated Equilibrium or Retrograde Motion?" in *Democratization in Southeast and East Asia*, ed. Anek Laothamatas (Singapore: Silkworm Books, 1997).

8. See Mary P. Callahan, "On Time Warps and Warped Time: Lessons from Burma's 'Democratic Era'" and Joseph Silverstein, "The Evolution and Salience of Burma's National Political Culture," both in *Burma*, ed. Rotberg.

9. See, for example, Sidney Tarrow, *Power in Movement: Social Movements, Collective Action, and Politics* (New York: Cambridge University Press, 1994); and Doug McAdam et al., "Introduction: Opportunities, Mobilizing Structures, and Framing Processes—Toward a Synthetic, Comparative Perspective on Social Movements," in *Comparative Perspectives on Social Movements: Political Opportunities, Mobilizing Structures, and Cultural Framings*, ed. Doug McAdam, John D. McCarthy, and Mayer N. Zald (New York: Cambridge University Press, 1996). For a useful typology of state-centered analyses (state autonomy, state capacity, political opportunity, and state constructionist) and a lucid discussion of the strengths and limitations of each type of state-centered approach to revolutions (and collective action in any of its forms), see Jeff Goodwin, "State-centered Approaches to Social Revolutions: Strengths and Limitations of a Theoretical Tradition," in *Theorizing Revolutions*, ed. John Foran (London: Routledge, 1997).

10. Sanjeev Khagram, Kathryn Sikkink, and James V. Riker, *Restructuring World Politics: Transnational Social Movements, Networks, and Norms* (Minneapolis: University of Minnesota Press, 2002), 8; and Tarrow, *Power in Movement*, 184.

11. For a fuller treatment of this case, see John Dale, "Transnational Conflict between Peasants and Corporations in Burma: Human Rights and Discursive Ambivalence under the U.S. Alien Tort Claims Act," in *The Practice of Human Rights: Tracking Law between the Global and the Local*, ed. Mark Goodale and Sally Engle Merry (Cambridge, UK: Cambridge University Press, 2007), 285–319.

12. U.S. Alien Tort Claims Act, 28 U.S.C. § 1350.

13. Khagram, Sikkink, and Riker, *Restructuring World Politics*, 7.

14. An INGO is a private, voluntary, nonprofit association whose chief aim is to influence publicly some form of social change. It has legal status and tends to be professionally staffed and more formally organized than a social movement. In general, this is true of all nongovernmental organizations, domestic as well as international. Indeed, both may have aims that are cross-national or international in scope. Yet INGOs also have a decision-making structure with vot-

ing members from multiple countries. Examples include Oxfam International, Mercy Corps, World Vision International, and Save the Children Alliance. An INGO may be founded through private philanthropy, such as the Carnegie, Ford, MacArthur, or Gates foundations, or as adjunct to existing international organizations, such as the Catholic Church's INGO Catholic Relief Services.

15. Transnational advocacy networks are configurations of nonstate actors, based usually on informal contacts and linked across nation-state boundaries that share common values, discourses, and a dense exchange of information. The exchange and use of information is the hallmark of the transnational advocacy network. See Margaret E. Keck and Kathryn Sikkink, *Activists beyond Borders: Advocacy Networks in International Politics* (Ithaca, N.Y.: Cornell University Press, 1998).

16. The Myanmar state had held these elections in the belief that it would win the vast majority of votes through intimidation, but it lost in a landslide victory to Aung San Suu Kyi's National League for Democracy party.

17. New social movement theory is largely an identity-oriented paradigm that rejected both neoclassical assumptions regarding social actors and the anemic conception of the role of civil society and culture in forging, shaping, and sustaining the "new" social movements that were emerging in the 1960s. New social movement theorists tend to see the modernization of society as a process that has entailed the state's gradual institutional colonization and domination of civil society. They therefore tend to shun a politics of reform in favor of what they perceive to be the only true course of emancipation: revolution. The aim of a social movement, from the perspective of new social movement theory, is not to influence the political process, but rather to transcend the structural limits of the current system and transform it along more democratic lines.

"New" social movements were those (1) for which identity was important, (2) that engaged in new forms of politics (e.g., innovative, direct action tactics), and (3) that contributed to new forms of sociability. Examples include indigenous, ethnic, ecological, gay, women's, and human rights movements. A politics of identity entails a war of interpretation and representation—a struggle to make visible or create space for individual and collective identities, to redefine cultural norms and appropriate social roles, and to channel or transform discursive practices.

18. New social movement theory suggests that movement actors choose political strategies that generate or conform to ways of organizing that are nonhierarchical and democratic and that encourage wide participation. The organizational means matters. Undemocratically organized movements will not produce democratic change.

19. Michael Peter Smith, *Transnational Urbanism: Locating Globalization* (Oxford, UK: Blackwell Publishers, 2001), 3–4.

20. Glenn Jordan and Chris Weedon, *Cultural Politics: Class, Gender, Race, and the Postmodern World* (Oxford, UK: Blackwell, 1995), 8.

21. William H. Sewell Jr., "A Theory of Structure, Duality, Agency, and Transformation," *American Journal of Sociology* 98 (1992): 1–29.

22. See Ann Swidler, "Culture in Action: Symbols and Strategies," *American Sociological Review* 51 (1986): 273–86; Eviatar Zerubavel, *The Fine Line: Boundaries and Distinctions in Everyday Life* (New York: Free Press, 1990); Anne E. Kane, "Theorizing Meaning Construction in Social Movements: Symbolic Structures and Interpretation during the Irish Land War, 1879–1882," *Sociological Theory* 15, no. 3 (1997): 249–76; Anne E. Kane, "Reconstructing Culture in Historical Explanation: Narratives as Cultural Structure and Practice," *History and Theory* 39 (2000): 311–30; and John R. Hall, *Cultures of Inquiry: From Epistemology to Discourse in Sociohistorical Research* (Cambridge, UK: Cambridge University Press, 1999).

23. Francesca Polletta, "Culture Is Not Just in Your Head," in *Rethinking Social Movements: Structure, Meaning, and Emotion*, ed. Jeff Goodwin and James M. Jasper (Lanham, Md.: Rowman and Littlefield, 2004), 99.

24. David A. Snow and Robert D. Benford, "Master Frames and Cycles of Protest," in *Frontiers in Social Movement Theory*, ed. Aldon D. Morris and Carol McClurg Mueller (New Haven, Conn.: Yale University Press, 1992); Robert D. Benford, "An Insider's Critique of the Social Movement Framing Perspective," *Sociological Inquiry* 67 (1997): 409–30; Mario Diani, "Linking Mobilization Frames and Political Opportunities: Insights from Regional Populism in Italy," *American Sociological Review* 61 (1996): 1053–1069; Bert Klandermans, *The Social Psychology of Protest* (Oxford, UK: Blackwell, 1996); and Doug McAdam, "Culture and Social Movements," in *New Social Movements: From Ideology to Identity*, ed. Enrique Laraña, Hank Johnston, and Joseph R. Gusfield (Philadelphia, Pa.: Temple University Press, 1994); McAdam, McCarthy, and Zald, *Comparative Perspectives on Social Movements*.

25. See, e.g., McAdam, "Culture and Social Movements" in *New Social Movements*. See also Sewell, "A Theory of Structure, Duality, Agency, and Transformation"; Mustafa Emirbayer and Jeff Goodwin, "Network Analysis, Culture, and the Problem of Agency," *American Journal of Sociology* 99, no. 6 (1994): 1411–454; Sharon Hays, "Structure and Agency and the Sticky Problem of Culture," *Theory and Society* 12 (1994): 57–72; and Polletta, "Culture Is Not Just in Your Head."

26. Francesca Polletta, "Snarls, Quacks, and Quarrels: Culture and Structure in Political Process Theory," *Sociological Forum* 14, no. 1 (1999): 64; see also Francesca Polletta, "Culture and Its Discontents: Recent Theorizing on the Cultural Dimensions of Protest," *Sociological Inquiry* 67 (1997): 431–50; and Mabel Berezin, "Politics and Culture: A Less Fissured Terrain," *Annual Review of Sociology* 23 (1997): 361–83.

27. See Emirbayer and Goodwin, "Network Analysis, Culture, and the Problem of Agency," 1440; and contrast, e.g., Alison Brysk, *From Tribal Village to Global Village: Indian Rights and International Relations in Latin America* (Stanford, Calif.: Stanford University Press, 2000), 42–44.

28. Sonia E. Alvarez, Evelina Dagnino, and Arturo Escobar, "Introduction," in *Cultures of Politics, Politics of Cultures: Re-Visioning Latin American Social*

Movements, ed. Sonia E. Alvarez, Evelina Dagnino, and Arturo Escobar (Boulder, Colo.: Westview Press, 1998), 6.

29. Karl Polanyi, *The Great Transformation: The Political and Economic Origins of Our Time*, 2nd Beacon Paperback edition, with a foreword by Joseph E. Stiglitz and new introduction by Fred Block (Boston: Beacon Press, [1944] 2001).

30. Polanyi, *The Great Transformation*, 143–44.

31. Fred Block and Margaret Somers, "Beyond the Economistic Fallacy: The Holistic Social Science of Karl Polanyi," in Theda Skocpol, ed., *Vision and Method in Historical Sociology* (Cambridge, UK: Cambridge University Press, 1984), 47–84; see also Alan Scott, "Introduction: Globalization: Social Process or Political Rhetoric," in *The Limits of Globalization: Cases and Arguments*, ed. Alan Scott (New York: Routledge, 1997).

32. Fred L. Block, *The Origins of International Economic Disorder: A Study of United States International Monetary Policy from World War II to the Present* (Berkeley: University of California Press, 1977); Peter Evans, "Fighting Marginalization with Transnational Networks: Counter-Hegemonic Globalization," *Contemporary Sociology* 2, no. 1 (2000): 230–41, 238.

33. Fred Block, *Postindustrial Possibilities: A Critique of Economic Discourse* (Berkeley: University of California Press, 1990); Fred Block, *The Vampire State: And Other Myths and Fallacies about the U.S. Economy* (New York: The New Press, 1996); Philip McMichael, *Development and Social Change: A Global Perspective*, 2nd edition (Thousand Oaks, Calif.: Pine Forge Press, 2000); Michael Peter Smith, "Transnationalism and the City: From Global Cities to Transnational Urbanism," in *The Urban Moment*, ed. Sophie Body-Gendrot and Robert A. Beauregard (Thousand Oaks, Calif.: Sage, 1998); and Evans, "Fighting Marginalization with Transnational Networks," 230–32.

34. Polanyi, *The Great Transformation*, 262.

35. See Smith, *Transnational Urbanism*, ch. 3; and J. K. Gibson-Graham, *The End of Capitalism (As We Knew It): A Feminist Critique of Political Economy* (Malden, Mass.: Blackwell Publishers, 1996), ch. 5 and ch. 6.

36. Smith, *Transnational Urbanism*, 3.

37. Saskia Sassen, *A Sociology of Globalization* (New York: W. W. Norton, 2007), 6.

38. Evans, "Fighting Marginalization with Transnational Networks," 231.

39. Ibid., 230.

40. Ibid.

41. Roberto Mangabeira Unger, *Free Trade Reimagined: The World Division of Labor and the Method of Economics* (Princeton, N.J.: Princeton University Press, 2007), 2.

42. This concept troubles legal positivist conceptions of law that dismiss the notions of legal pluralism. For further elaboration on this, see John G. Dale and Tony Roshan Samara, "Legal Pluralism within a Transnational Network of Governance: The Extraordinary Case of Rendition," in "Legal Pluralism,"

special issue, *Law, Social Justice, and Global Development* 12, no. 2 (2008), at http://www2.warwick.ac.uk/fac/soc/law/elj/lgd/.

43. See Evans, "Fighting Marginalization with Transnational Networks."

44. Keck and Sikkink, *Activists beyond Borders*, 12.

45. Ibid.

46. Ibid.

47. For a fuller treatment of this case, see Dale, "Transnational Conflict between Peasants and Corporations in Burma."

48. Emphasis mine. The law of nations is "the law of international relations, embracing not only nations but also . . . individuals (such as those who invoke their human rights or commit war crimes)." *Black's Law Dictionary*, 7th ed. (1999), 822. This is the same definition of the law of nations that the Ninth Circuit Court of Appeals used in *Doe v. Unocal*. According to the *Random House Compact Unabridged Dictionary*, special 2nd ed. (1996), the term "law of nations" first came into use sometime between A.D. 1540 and 1550.

49. See Robert Benson, *Challenging Corporate Rule: A Petition to Revoke Unocal's Charter as a Guide to Citizen Action* (New York: Apex Press, 1999).

1. Burma's Struggle for Democracy and Human Rights before 1988

1. See Basil Katz, "U.N. Assembly Condemns Myanmar Rights Record," *Reuters*, December 24, 2009 (accessed February 9, 2010) at http://www.reuters.com/article/idUSTRE5BN2GO20091224. Also see International Human Rights Clinic at Harvard Law School, *Crimes in Burma* (May 2009).

2. "Daw" is not part of her name, but is an honorific title similar to "madam" that people in Burma use for older, revered women. It literally means "aunt."

3. See, for example, Kyaw Zaw Win, "The Asian Socialist Conference in 1953 as Precursor to the Bandung Conference in 1955." Paper presented at the 15th Biennial Conference of the Asian Studies Association of Australia, in Canberra, June 29–July 2, 2004.

4. The term "Third World" did not yet carry the negative connotation of marginalization, but rather was embraced as an identity that signified an emerging new force in geopolitics. See Odd Arne Westad, *The Global Cold War: Third World Interventions and the Making of Our Times* (Cambridge, UK: Cambridge University Press, 2007), 2–3.

5. Also participating in the conference were delegations from Afghanistan, Cambodia, Ceylon (now Sri Lanka), Democratic Republic of Vietnam, Egypt, Ethiopia, Gold Coast (now Ghana), Iran, Iraq, Japan, Jordan, Laos, Lebanon, Liberia, Libya, Nepal, Pakistan, People's Republic of China, Philippines, Saudi Arabia, South Vietnam, Sudan, Syria, Thailand, Turkey, and Yemen.

6. See Roland Burke, "The Compelling Dialogue of Freedom": Human Rights at the Bandung Conference," *Human Rights Quarterly* 28, no. 4 (2006): 947–65. Burke points out that colonialism, including the cold war neocolonialism of the United States and the Soviet Union, was the defining issue of the

conference. Yet the question of colonialism was in many respects a question about human rights.

7. Altogether the country's total land area is 261,970 square miles, or roughly equivalent to the size of the state of Texas in the United States.

8. Thanks to Nehginpao Kipgen, general secretary of the U.S.-based Kuki International Forum and expert on political conflicts in modern Burma, for this information on the subgroups of the major ethnic nationality groups.

9. Although the Burman account for roughly two-thirds of the country's total population of more than fifty million people, ethnic minorities occupy roughly two-thirds of the country's total land area.

10. The seven divisions of present-day Myanmar are Ayeyarwady, Bago, Magway, Mandalay, Sagaing, Tanintharyi, and Yangon.

11. In late 2005, Myanmar's government officials suddenly and mysteriously designated Naypyidaw as the country's new capital city. Much farther inland than the former capital of Yangon (Rangoon), it was built ex nihilo near the site of the country's largest military academy.

12. The seven states of Myanmar are Chin, Kachin, Kayah, Kayin, Mon, Rakhine, and Shan.

13. Thant Myint-U, *The Making of Modern Burma* (Cambridge, UK: Cambridge University Press, 2001), 6.

14. Myint-U, *The Making of Modern Burma*, 7.

15. Ibid.

16. Martin Smith, *Burma: Insurgency and the Politics of Ethnicity* (London: Zed Books, 1991), 44.

17. Christina Fink, *Living Silence: Burma under Military Rule* (New York: Zed Books, 2001), 21.

18. Fink, *Living Silence*, 21–22.

19. Joseph Silverstein, *Burmese Politics and the Dilemma of National Unity* (New Brunswick, N.J.: Rutgers University Press, 1980), 108.

20. Smith, *Burma*, 79.

21. Silverstein, *Burmese Politics and the Dilemma of National Unity*, 155.

22. Smith, *Burma*, 82.

23. Ibid.

24. Ibid., 258–62.

25. Ibid., 220 and 259.

26. Hazel Lang, *Fear and Sanctuary: Burmese Refugees in Thailand* (Ithaca, N.Y.: Southeast Asia Program Publications, Southeast Asia Program, Cornell University, 2002).

27. Mary P. Callahan, *Making Enemies: War and State Building in Burma* (Ithaca, N.Y.: Cornell University Press, 2003), 223.

28. See the International Human Rights Clinic at Harvard Law School, *Crimes in Burma* (May 2009), 37–76.

29. Westad, *The Global Cold War*, 128.

30. Callahan, *Making Enemies*, 155; Robert Taylor, *Foreign and Domestic Consequences of the KMT Involvement in Burma* (Ithaca, N.Y.: Cornell University

Press, 1973), 15–16; Smith, *Burma*, 120; Fink, *Living Silence*, 24; Tim Weiner, *Legacy of Ashes: The History of the CIA* (New York: Doubleday, 2007), 60–61; and Westad, *The Global Cold War*, 128.

31. Weiner, *Legacy of Ashes*, 60.
32. Smith, *Burma*, 120.
33. Callahan, *Making Enemies*, 159.
34. Ibid.
35. Ibid., ch. 7.
36. Westad, *The Global Cold War*, 103.
37. Wendell L. Minnick, "Target: Zhou Enlai. Was America's CIA Working with Taiwan Agents to Kill Chinese Premier?" *Far Eastern Economic Review* (July 13, 1995): 54–55. See also Joseph J. Trento, *The Secret History of the CIA* (New York: Carroll and Graph Publishers [2001], 2005), 94; and Steve Tang, "Target Zhou Enlai: The Kashmir Princess' Incident of 1955," *China Quarterly* 139 (September 1994).
38. Minnick, "Target: Zhou Enlai," 54.
39. Ibid.
40. Callahan, *Making Enemies*, 18.
41. Ibid.
42. See Smith, *Burma*, ch. 1; and Bertril Lintner, *Outrage: Burma's Struggle for Democracy* (London: White Lotus, 1990), ch. 1.
43. Smith, *Burma*, 2.
44. But see David I. Steinberg, *Burma: The State of Myanmar* (Washington, D.C.: Georgetown University Press, 2001), 8. Steinberg suggests that "the best evidence available indicates that Ne Win was probably serious in his suggestion of a multi-party election, but perhaps solely to shake up the lethargy and bureaucracy of the party itself, with which he had become disillusioned, perhaps by the economic problems exacerbated by the suffocation deaths, and fully expecting that a vote would return a reformed BSPP to power."
45. When former dictator General Ne Win died on December 5, 2002, at the age of ninety-two, he was the wealthiest person in Burma. After formally resigning from the chairmanship of the BSPP in July 1988, Ne Win rarely appeared in public. Yet he remained active behind the scenes, influencing the military's top cadre of generals and state officials who had changed the name of the BSPP to the State Law and Order Restoration Council (SLORC) and then again in 1997 to its current name, the State Peace and Development Council (SPDC). Most people believed that he remained the most powerful person in Burma until March 2002, when he was placed under house arrest following the imprisonment of several family members who were accused of plotting a coup against the country's military junta. No charges were brought against Ne Win, but he remained under house arrest until his death.
46. The founding parties and organizations of the NDF included the Arakan Liberation Party (ALP); the Kachin Independence Organization (KIO); the Karen National Union (KNU); the Karenni National Progressive Party (KNPP); the Lahu National Progressive Party (LNUP); the Union Pa-O National Orga-

nization (UPNO); the Palung State Liberation Organization (PSLO); the Shan
State Progressive Party (SSPP); and the Kayan New Land Party (KNLP).

47. Smith, *Burma*, 17.

48. Callahan, *Making Enemies*, 223.

49. Ibid., 224.

2. Locating Power in the Free Burma Movement

1. See Lintner, *Outrage*; Bertril Lintner, "Drugs, Insurgency, and Counter-
insurgency in Burma," in *Burma/Myanmar Towards the Twenty-first Century:
Dynamic of Continuity and Change*, ed. John J. Brandon (Bangkok, Thailand:
T.K. Printing, 1997), 210; and Stan Sesser, *The Lands of Charm and Cruelty:
Travels in Southeast Asia* (New York: Vintage Departures, 1994), 219.

2. See Lintner, *Outrage*; Smith, *Burma*; Mya Maung, *Totalitarianism in Burma:
Prospects for Economic Development* (New York: Paragon House, 1992); and Kurt
Schock, "People Power and Political Opportunities: Social Movement Mobilization and Outcomes in the Philippines and Burma," *Social Problems* 46, no. 3
(1999): 355–75.

3. The term "disappeared" is widely interpreted by civilians in Burma to be
a euphemism used by the military to suggest that the arrested person has been
executed by the military. Use of the term, however, allows the military to simultaneously signal a threat to any civilians who may clandestinely participate in
or affiliate with oppositional political parties and avoid accepting legal responsibility or providing official justifications for executing civilians challenging the
military's rule.

4. See Yawnghwe, "Burma: The Depoliticization of the Political," in
Political Legitimacy in Southeast Asia: The Quest for Moral Authority, ed. Muthiah
Alagappa (Stanford, Calif.: Stanford University Press, 1995); and Robert H. Tay-
lor, "Political Values and Political Culture in Burma," in *Burma: Prospects for a
Democratic Future*, ed. Robert I. Rotberg (Washington, D.C.: Brookings Institu-
tion Press, 1998).

5. See Verta Taylor, "Social Movement Continuity: The Women's Movement in Abeyance," *American Sociological Review* 54 (1989): 761–75; and David S.
Meyer, "Tending the Vineyard: Cultivating Political Process Research," *Sociological Forum* 14, no. 1 (1999): 79–92.

6. Zarni and May Oo, "Common Problems, Shared Responsibilities: Citizens' Quest for National Reconciliation in Burma/Myanmar: Report of a Citizen
Exiles Group" (Free Burma Coalition, October 2004).

7. See Schock, "People Power and Political Opportunities."

8. See Lintner, "Arrested Development," 28–29; David I. Steinberg, "The
Burmese Political Economy: Opportunities and Tensions," in *Burma/Myanmar
Towards the Twenty-first Century: Dynamic of Continuity and Change*, ed. John J.
Brandon (Bangkok, Thailand: T.K. Printing, 1997); and these chapters in Rob-
ert I. Rotberg, ed., *Burma: Prospects for a Democratic Future* (Washington, D.C.:
Brookings Institution Press, 1998): David Steinberg, "The Road to Political

Recovery: The Salience of Politics in Economics," Tin Maung Maung Than, "Myanmar Democratization"; Callahan, "On Time Warps and Warped Time"; Mason, "Foreign Direct Investment in Burma"; Ott, "From Isolation to Relevance"; Selth, "The Armed Forces and Military Rule in Burma"; and Silverstein, "The Evolution and Salience of Burma's National Political Culture."

9. Sidney Tarrow, "States and Opportunities: The Political Structuring of Social Movements," in *Comparative Perspectives on Social Movements: Political Opportunities, Mobilizing Structures, and Cultural Framings*, ed. Doug McAdam, John D. McCarthy, and Mayer N. Zald (New York: Cambridge University Press, 1996), 53 (emphasis added).

10. Jeff Goodwin and James M. Jasper, eds., *The Social Movements Reader: Cases and Concepts* (Malden, Mass.: Blackwell, 2003), 4.

11. Doug McAdam, *Political Process and the Development of Black Insurgency, 1930–1970* (Chicago: University of Chicago Press, 1982); McAdam et al., "Introduction: Opportunities, Mobilizing Structures, and Framing Processes," in *Comparative Perspectives on Social Movements*; and Doug McAdam, Sidney Tarrow, and Charles Tilly, *Dynamics of Contention* (Cambridge, UK: Cambridge University Press, 2001).

12. Tarrow, *Power in Movement*; and McAdam, "Culture and Social Movements," in *New Social Movements*.

13. See "Mini-Symposium on Social Movements," *Sociological Forum* 14, no. 1 (March 1999): 27–136.

14. Doug McAdam has pointed out that state repression is not a consensual dimension of the political opportunity structure. Some political process theorists consider state repression to be "more an expression of the general receptivity or vulnerability of the political opportunity structure, rather than an independent dimension of the same." See, e.g., Donatella della Porta, *Social Movements, Political Violence, and the State: A Comparative Study of Italy and Germany* (New York: Cambridge University Press, 1995). Yet, McAdam argues, such a position "blind[s] us to the unpredictable nature of repression and the complex social processes that structure its operation" (*Comparative Perspectives on Social Movements*, 28). Thus, he includes state repression as an independent variable of the political opportunity structure. See also Charles D. Brockett, "A Protest-Cycle Resolution of the Repression/Popular-Protest Paradox," in *Repertoires and Cycles of Collective Action*, ed. Mark Traugott (Durham, N.C.: Duke University Press, 1995). I have included it here because Lintner emphasizes the role that state repression played in fueling the movement, as I discuss below. Although both McAdam and Lintner see state repression as an independent variable in relation to explaining movement emergence, they interpret the relationship between the two in different ways, which, as I explain, are instructive.

15. Other analysts also have emphasized the events of the March Affairs as marking the movement's emergence. See Smith, *Burma*; Mya Maung, *Totalitarianism in Burma*; and Michael Fredholm, *Burma: Ethnicity and Insurgency* (Westport, Conn.: Praeger Publishers, 1993).

16. Sidney Tarrow, "Struggle, Politics, and Reform: Collective Action, Social Movements and Cycles of Protest," Cornell University, Western Societies Paper no. 21, 1989.

17. John Walton, *Reluctant Rebels: Comparative Studies of Revolution and Underdevelopment* (New York: Columbia University Press, 1984); Jack A. Goldstone, "Deterrence in Rebellions and Revolutions," in *Perspectives on Deterrence*, ed. P. Stern, R. Axelrod, R. Jervis, and R. Radner (New York: Oxford University Press, 1989); Goodwin, "State-Centered Approaches to Social Revolutions," in *Theorizing Revolutions;* and Brockett, "A Protest-Cycle Resolution of the Repression/Popular-Protest Paradox."

18. Goodwin, "State-Centered Approaches to Social Revolutions," 19.

19. Ibid., 13–14.

20. While Lintner explains how state action unintentionally contributes to the process by which it becomes the target of the radicalizing social movement, he also explains several instances in which the state attempted to *intentionally* facilitate collective action among particular movement sectors as part of a divide-and-conquer strategy. For example, see Lintner, *Outrage*, 79–81, where he describes how authorities attempted to exploit existing tensions between sectors of different ethnic and religious identities, targeting Chinese and Muslim communities. But note that such state actions were committed precisely for the purpose of deflecting the movement's attempts to frame existing grievances in a way that suggested that their resolution was only possible through the radical reorganization of the state. More important, note how these state efforts also backfired.

21. For Lintner, this also marks the beginning of a new cycle of conflict, one in which Burma's struggle for democracy becomes an international issue.

22. Lintner, *Outrage*, 82–83, 86.

23. Ibid., 86.

24. Ibid., 90.

25. Goodwin, "State-Centered Approaches to Social Revolutions," 17 (emphasis added).

26. Lintner, *Outrage*, 108.

27. Smith, *Burma*, 4 and 402; Mya Maung, *Totalitarianism in Burma*, 48; Fredholm, *Burma*, 61–63.

28. Lintner, *Outrage*, 11, 70, 73, 79, 95, and 108.

29. Ibid., 90–92 and 117–19.

30. Ibid., 76–77 and 114.

31. Ibid., 90.

32. Ibid., 9.

33. Ibid.

34. Lintner, *Outrage*, 73 and 81–82.

35. Quintan Wiktorowicz, *The Management of Islamic Activism: Salafis, the Muslim Brotherhood, and State Power in Jordan* (Albany: State University of New York Press, 2001), 8–9.

36. See Lintner, *Outrage*; Smith, *Burma*; Mya Maung, *Totalitarianism in Burma*; and Fredholm, *Burma*.

37. See Goldstone, "Deterrence in Rebellions and Revolutions"; Brockett, "A Protest-Cycle Resolution of the Repression/Popular-Protest Paradox"; and Goodwin, "State-Centered Approaches to Social Revolutions."

38. Schock, "People Power and Political Opportunities," 357.

39. Ibid., 365–70.

40. McAdam, McCarthy, and Zald, "Introduction," 23–40; and Tarrow, *Power in Movement*, 85–89.

41. Schock, "People Power and Political Opportunities," 370.

42. See Charles C. Ragin, *The Comparative Method: Moving beyond Qualitative and Quantitative Strategies* (Berkeley: University of California Press, 1987).

43. Remember that foreign correspondents were not permitted in Burma. The following descriptions of Christopher Gunness come from Lintner, *Outrage*. Lintner is a freelance journalist who regularly contributes to the *Far Eastern Economic Review*. He has established himself as a leading authority on insurgency in Burma and has written several books and innumerable articles on the subject. He is married to a woman who grew up in Burma and fought as a sergeant and cipher clerk for six years in the Shan State Army. Although banned from Burma, he has been known to make occasional journalistic forays (one of which lasted eighteen months) inside Burma's insurgent-occupied areas.

44. Lintner, *Outrage*, 82–90; Sesser, *The Lands of Charm and Cruelty*, 208.

45. Quoted in Lintner, *Outrage*, 90.

46. Leaders of the military-state certainly listened to the broadcasts. See *Skyful of Lies—B.B.C. [and] V.O.A.—Their Broadcasts and Rebuttals to Disinformation* (Yangon, Myanmar: Ministry of Information, 1990). If they had had the technology to "scramble" these broadcasts at the time, one might assume that they would have. On the other hand, the state may well have considered such broadcasts to have been informative.

47. Quoted in Lintner, *Outrage*, 91.

48. Ibid.

49. Lintner, *Outrage*, 92; also personal interview with Trans U, 1998.

50. Lintner, *Outrage*, 91.

51. Ibid., 92.

52. Mya Maung, *Totalitarianism in Burma*, 60.

53. Ibid.

54. *Skyful of Lies—B.B.C. [and] V.O.A.—Their Broadcasts and Rebuttals to Disinformation*, 19.

55. Lintner, *Outrage*, 92. Lintner does not make the connection between the timing of the monks' protest and the date of the broadcast, nor, of course, between the interpretation of Mya Maung and the monks' joining the protest when they did.

56. Alison Brysk, "'Hearts and Minds': Bringing Symbolic Politics Back In," *Polity* 27, no. 4 (1995): 561.

57. Tarrow, *Power in Movement;* and McAdam, Tarrow, Tilly, *Dynamics of Contention.*

58. Alberto Melucci, *Challenging Codes: Collective Action in the Information Age* (New York: Cambridge University Press, 1996), 115.

59. Emirbayer and Goodwin, "Network Analysis, Culture, and the Problem of Agency," 1411–454.

60. Joseph Silverstein, *Burma: Military Rule and the Politics of Stagnation* (Ithaca, N.Y.: Cornell University Press, 1977).

61. Schock, "People Power and Political Opportunities," 365.

62. Bruce Matthews, "Buddhism under a Military Regime: The Iron Heel in Burma," *Asian Survey* 33 (1993): 408–23; Robert H. Taylor, *The State in Burma* (Honolulu: University of Hawaii Press, 1987); and Tin Maung Maung Than, "The *Sangha* and *Sasana* in Socialist Burma," *Sojourn* 3 (1988): 26–61.

63. Lintner, *Outrage.*

64. Matthews, "Buddhism under a Military Regime"; and David I. Steinberg, *The Future of Burma: Crisis and Choice in Myanmar* (Lanham, Md.: University Press of America, 1990).

65. Schock, "People Power and Political Opportunities," 366.

66. Brysk, "'Hearts and Minds'"; and Jeff Goodwin and James M. Jasper, "Caught in a Winding, Snarling Vine: The Structural Bias of Political Process Theory," *Sociological Forum* 14 (1999), no. 1: 27–54.

67. Emirbayer and Goodwin, "Network Analysis, Culture, and the Problem of Agency."

68. Tarrow, *Power in Movement,* ch. 7; Klandermans, *The Social Psychology of Protest.*

69. Mustafa Emirbayer and Jeff Goodwin, "Symbols, Positions, Objects: Situating 'Culture' within Social Movement Theory." Paper presented at the annual meeting of the American Sociological Association, New York, N.Y., 1996.

70. Goodwin and Jasper, "Caught in a Winding, Snarling Vine," 34.

71. Schock, "People Power and Political Opportunities," 369.

72. Ibid., 370.

73. Kathryn Sikkink, "Human Rights, Principled Issue Networks, and Sovereignty in Latin America," *International Organization* 47, no. 3 (1993): 411–41; Jackie Smith, Charles Chatfield, and Ron Pugnucco, eds. *Transnational Social Movements and Global Politics: Solidarity beyond the State* (Syracuse, N.Y.: Syracuse University Press, 1997); Keck and Sikkink, *Activists beyond Borders.*

74. Schock, "People Power and Political Opportunities," 370.

75. Ulrich Beck, *Power in the Global Age: A New Global Political Economy* (Cambridge, UK: Polity Press, 2005), 22–34.

76. Schock, "People Power and Political Opportunities," 369.

77. Ibid. (emphasis mine).

78. See, e.g., Lyn H. Lofland, *A World of Strangers: Order and Action in Urban Public Space* (New York: Basic Books, 1973); and Claude S. Fischer, *To Dwell among Friends: Personal Networks in Town and City* (Chicago: University of Chicago Press, 1982).

79. Gerard Clarke, "Non-Governmental Organizations (NGOs) and Politics in the Developing World," *Papers on International Development* 20 (Swansea, Wales: Center for Development Studies, 1996); John Boli and George M. Thomas, *Constructing World Culture: International Nongovernmental Organizations since 1975* (Stanford, Calif.: Stanford University, 1999); Louis Kriesberg, "Social Movements and Global Transformation," in *Transnational Social Movements beyond the State*, ed. Jackie Smith, Charles Chatfield, and Ron Pugnucco (New York: Syracuse University Press, 1997).

80. William F. Fisher, "Doing Good? The Politics and Antipolitics of NGO Practices," *Annual Review of Anthropology* 26 (1997): 439–64.

81. Michael Edwards and David Hulme, "Too Close for Comfort? The Impact of Official Aid on Nongovernmental Organizations," *World Development* 24, no. 6 (1996): 961–73.

82. Albert O. Hirschman, *Rival Views of Market Society and Other Recent Essays* (Viking: New York, 1986); and Bishwaspriya Sanyal, *Cooperative Autonomy: The Dialectic of State-NGOs Relationship in Developing Countries*, Research Series 100 (Geneva: International Institute for Labor Studies, 1994).

83. Fisher, "Doing Good?" 452.

84. Clifford Bob, *Marketing Rebellion: Insurgents, Media, and International Activism* (Cambridge, Mass.: Cambridge University Press, 2005).

85. Naomi Chazan, "Africa's Democratic Challenge," *World Policy Journal* 9, no. 2 (1992): 279–307; Alan Fowler, "NGOs as Agents of Democratization: An African Perspective," *Journal of International Development* 5, no. 3 (1993): 325–29; Stephen N. Ndegwa, *The Two Faces of Civil Society: NGOs and Politics in Africa* (West Hartford, Conn.: Kumarian, 1996); Orin Starn, "To Revolt against Revolution: War and Resistance in Peru's Andes," *Cultural Anthropology* 10, no. 4 (1995): 547–80; Kriesberg, "Social Movements and Global Transformation"; Fisher, "Doing Good?" 439–64; and Wiktorowicz, *The Management of Islamic Activism*.

86. In 1995, the SLORC temporarily released Suu Kyi after six years of house arrest. Almost immediately, she was arrested again for resuming the political organizing of her NLD party. She was released once more, briefly in 1998, but then rearrested for the same reason. In June 2002, she was released again, but continued to organize for the NLD. When released in 2010, she had been under house arrest for fifteen out of twenty-one years and was barred from participating in the 2010 general elections, the first elections held since her victory in 1990.

87. It should be noted, however, that in recent years a younger generation of democracy activists in Burma has been criticizing the NCGUB's leadership, which comprises mostly the older, 1988 generation of democracy activists, some of whom are approaching their eighties. Criticism has focused largely on the NCGUB's relatively conservative attitude toward risky protest tactics and steadfast refusal to participate in the 2010 elections, which would nullify the results of the 1990 elections, in which many of the NCGUB's leaders had won. In an

interview that I conducted with NCGUB prime minister Sein Win in June 2009, he explained that the NCGUB welcomed new, young leaders taking the reins, but that this should happen only after the dust settles (and maybe blood dries) from the military's effort to force an undemocratic constitution on the people of Burma by way of new, putatively democratic elections.

88. Tiffany Danitz and Warren P. Strobel, "Networking Dissent: Cyber Activists Use the Internet to Promote Democracy in Burma," in *Networks and Netwars: The Future of Terror, Crime, and Militancy,* ed. John Arquilla and David Ronfeldt (Washington, D.C.: RAND, 2002).

89. See Albert O. Hirschman, *The Passions and the Interests: Political Arguments for Capitalism before Its Triumph* (Princeton, N.J.: Princeton University Press, 1977), 28–31, 56–66; and Arthur O. Lovejoy, *Reflections on Human Nature* (Baltimore, Md.: Johns Hopkins University Press, 1961), 46–65.

3. Free Burma Laws

1. In June 1996, Massachusetts enacted *An Act Regulating State Contracts with Companies Doing Business with or in Burma (Myanmar)*, ch. 130, 1996 Mass. Acts 239 (codified at Mass. Gen. Laws), ch. 7, §§ 22G-22M, 40F (West Supp. 1998) ("Massachusetts Burma Law"). "Doing business with Burma" is defined by § 22G as (a) having a principal place of business, place of incorporation, or its corporate headquarters in Burma (Myanmar) or having any operations, leases, franchises, majority owned subsidiary licensee or franchise[e] of such a person; (b) providing financial services to the government of Burma (Myanmar), including providing direct loans, underwriting government securities, providing any consulting advice or assistance, providing brokerage services, acting as a trustee or escrow agent, or otherwise acting as an agent pursuant to a contractual agreement; (c) promoting the importation or sale of gems, timber, oil, gas or other related products, commerce in which is largely controlled by the government of Burma (Myanmar) or from Burma (Myanmar); (d) providing any goods or services to the government of Burma (Myanmar). The law allows exceptions for entities "with operations in Burma (Myanmar) for the sole purpose of reporting the news, or solely for the purpose of providing goods or services for the provision of international telecommunications." Ibid. § 22H(e). The law also exempts firms whose business in Myanmar "is providing only medical supplies." Ibid. § 22I.

2. See, e.g., the Commonwealth of Massachusetts Operational Services Division. "How to Do Business with the Commonwealth of Massachusetts: A Guide for Manufacturers and Suppliers of Environmentally Preferable Products (EPPs)," May 2005, p. 1. "Every year, the Commonwealth of Massachusetts spends more than $2 billion on purchases of goods and services. Out of that, in Fiscal Year 2004, state agencies spent over $140 million specifically on recycled and environmentally preferable products (EPPs). All of these purchases were made from awarded state contractors."

3. See John G. Dale and Tony Roshan Samara, "Legal Pluralism within a Transnational Network of Governance: The Extraordinary Case of Rendition," *Law, Social Justice, and Global Development* 12, no.2 (2008; Special Issue on "Legal Pluralism"), http://www2.warwick.ac.uk/fac/soc/law/elj/lgd/.

4. On "transnationalist discourse," see Chapter 1. I also further discuss this below.

5. Desmond Tutu, "Burma as South Africa," *Far Eastern Economic Review* (September 16, 1993), 23.

6. Public speech delivered by Aung San Suu Kyi in front of her home in September 1996 while under house arrest. The speech was videotaped, and the videotape was smuggled out of Burma and mass produced and distributed by a Thailand-based NGO.

7. See Bernard Krisher, "Conversing with the Voice of Democracy: An Interview with Aung San Suu Kyi," *Harvard Asia Pacific Review* (Summer 2000), available at http://www.hcs.harvard.edu/~hapr/summer00_tech/aung.html.

8. Founded in 1982, this corporation subsequently changed its name to Trillium Assets Management. At the time, it managed more than $400 million for individuals, religious institutions, labor unions, charitable foundations, progressive corporations, and nonprofits. Simon Billenness was its senior analyst and volunteered as a leader of the New England Burma Roundtable, a member organization of the Free Burma Coalition. He went on to work for the AFL-CIO and Sierra Club and currently is a board member of U.S. Campaign for Burma and Amnesty International.

9. Interview with Simon Billenness, October 27, 1999.

10. In 1990, Pepsi entered Burma through a joint venture with Myanmar Golden Star Company, owned by former Myanmar military officer and bean exporter Thein Tun. Pepsi's bottling operation in Rangoon grew from 800,000 bottles per day to 5 million and added a new plant in Mandalay. See Michael Hirsh and Ron Moreau, "Making It in Mandalay," *Newsweek* (June 19, 1995), 24.

11. See Tiffany Danitz and Walter P. Strobel, "Networking Dissent: Burmese Cyberactivists Promote Nonviolent Struggle Using the Internet," in *Networks and Netwars: The Future of Terror, Crime, and Militancy*, ed. John Arquilla and David Ronfeldt (Arlington, Va.: RAND, 2001), 129–58.

12. Simon Billenness claims that he simply retyped verbatim the South Africa selective purchasing legislation enacted in Massachusetts, except where he replaced "South Africa" with "Burma." He then submitted his slightly modified version to Rushing, who introduced it to the Massachusetts State Legislature. See *Investing for a Better World: A Publication of Trillium Asset Management* 15, no. 7 (Winter 2000–2001): 4.

13. See Lynn Berat, "Undoing and Redoing Business in South Africa: The Lifting of the Comprehensive Anti-Apartheid Act of 1986 and the Continuing Validity of State and Local Anti-Apartheid Legislation," 6 *Conn. J. Int'l L.* 7, 8–11 (1990); see also Minter, William, "South Africa: Straight Talk on Sanctions," *Foreign Policy* 65 (1986): 43–63; and generally, e.g., Note, "Federal Preemption and the South African Sanctions: A Survival Guide for States and

Cities," 10 *Loyola L.A. Int'l & Comp. L.J.* 693 (1988); Lewis, "Dealing with South Africa: The Constitutionality of State and Local Divestment Legislation," 61 *Tulane L. Rev.* 469 (1987); Note, "Anti-South Africa Action as an Intrusion upon the Federal Power in Foreign Affairs," 72 *Virginia L. Rev.* 813 (1986); Note, "State and Municipal Governments React against South African Apartheid: An Assessment of the Constitutionality of the Divestment Campaign," 54 *U. Cincinnati L. Rev.* 543 (1985); Note, "The Constitutionality of State and Local Governments' Response to Apartheid: Divestment Legislation," 13 *Fordham Urb. L.R.* 763 (1985).

14. Carey Goldberg, "After Defeat, Campaign for 'Free Burma' Begins Anew," *New York Times* (June 24, 2000), http://www.nytimes.com/2000/06/24/us/after-defeat-campaigner-for-free-burma-begins-anew.html.

15. Mass. Gen. Laws ch. 7, § 22J. Massachusetts and its agencies, according to the law, are permitted to contract with companies on the restricted purchase list in only three situations: when procurement of the bid is essential and there is no other bid or offer, when the Commonwealth of Massachusetts is purchasing certain medical supplies, or when there is no other "comparable low bid or offer." Mass Gen. Laws ch. 7, § 22H. The law defines a "comparable low bid or offer" as equal to or less than 10 percent above a low bid from a company on the restricted purchase list. Ibid. § 22G.

16. Mass. Gen. Laws ch. 7, § 22H.

17. *NFTC v. Natsios*, 181 F.3d 38, 46 (1st Cir. 1999), *aff'd*, 530 U.S. 363 (2000). See also Meg Vaillancourt, "Massachusetts Becomes First State to Boycott Burma Business," *Boston Globe* (June 26, 1996), 27.

18. Defs. Mem. of Points and Authorities, 16.

19. See Cal. AB 888 1997 (authorizing the prohibition of state government contracts with companies doing business with Burma); COLO. S.R. 5 1997 (same); CONN. HB 6354 1997 (same); N.C. SB 1067 1997 (same); TEX. HB 2960 1997 (same).

20. Field notes from interview with Australian activists in Rangoon, Burma, on February 26, 1998. See http://lists.essential.org/1998/shell-nigeria-action/mss00317.html. New England Burma Roundtable, "Background Article" (May 1, 1998); and http://www.geocities.com/CapitolHill/3018/bsp_list.html. "Free Burma Laws Outside the U.S." (January 20, 2001). At the time, there were several Web sites that tracked this legislation and that contained links to the individual resolutions. See, for example, http://archives.usaengage.org/archives/news/status.html.

21. James Jasper, *The Art of Moral Protest: Culture, Biography, and Creativity in Social Movements* (Chicago: University of Chicago Press, 1997), 267.

22. Ibid., 264.

23. Ibid., 265.

24. Ibid., 264–65.

25. Ibid., 265.

26. Ibid., 258.

27. Ibid., 259 (emphasis mine).

28. Ibid., 262, 265.

29. Ulrich Beck, *Power in the Global Age: A New Global Political Economy* (Cambridge, UK: Polity, 2005), 7.

30. See, for example, Theo Emery, "Motorola, HP to cut ties to Burma: Cite Massachusetts law barring business in nation." *Boston Globe* (November 29, 1996), B11.

31. According to Burmese dissident Zar Ni, who was one of the original founders, the FBC relied on an e-mail list provided by the University of Wisconsin at Madison and a Web site developed by Alex Turner, one of his fellow graduate students at Wisconsin.

32. *Foreign Operations, Export Financing, and Related Programs Appropriations Act,* 1997, § 570, 110 Stat. 3009–166 through 3009–167 (enacted by the *Omnibus Consolidated Appropriations Act 1997,* Pub. L. No. 104–208, § 101 (c), 110 Stat. 3009–121 through 3009–172 (1996). See Section 570 (a).

33. In 1997, the State Law and Order Restoration Council changed its name to its present one, the State Peace and Development Council (SPDC).

34. Ibid., at § 570 (c).

35. Ibid., at § 570 (a) (1); §570 (a) (2); and §570 (a) (2), (3).

36. Ibid., at § 570 (b).

37. See Exec. Order No. 13,047, 62 Fed. Reg. 28,301 (1997); see also 31 C.F.R. Pt. 357 (1998).

38. This fact became a significant point of contention within the courts as the Commonwealth of Massachusetts argued that the failure of Congress to preempt the state act demonstrates implicit permission to allow it to remain in effect. The U.S. Supreme Court ultimately challenged Massachusetts's argument, ruling instead that "a failure to provide for preemption expressly may reflect nothing more than the settled character of implied preemption doctrine that courts will dependably apply, and in any event, the existence of conflict cognizable under the supremacy clause does not depend on express congressional recognition that federal and state law may conflict. The state's inference of congressional intent is unwarranted here, therefore, simply because the silence of Congress is ambiguous." See *Crosby, Secretary of Administration and Finance of Massachusetts, et al. v. National Foreign Trade Council,* 530 U.S. 363, 387 to 388 (2000).

39. At the time that the formal complaint was filed, Massachusetts's blacklist had grown to about 255 businesses, 205 of which were foreign-based firms. Burma News Update No. 35, June 29, 1997, 1. The "Massachusetts Restricted Burma Purchasing List" for this period was obtained from the fax archives of XminY Solidarity Fund and the Burma Centre Nederlands, two Dutch NGOs based in Amsterdam, The Netherlands.

40. Nelson Pichardo, "The Power Elite and Elite-Driven Counter-Movements: The Associated Framers of California during the 1930s," *Sociological Forum* 10, no. 1 (March 1995): 21–49.

41. In its complaint, the European Commission alleged that the Massachusetts Burma law violates U.S. obligations under the WTO Agreement on Government Procurement Article VIII (b), given that the statute "imposes

conditions on a tendering company which are not essential to ensure the firm's capability to fulfill the contract; Article X, as it imposes qualification criteria based on political rather than economic considerations, and Article XIII, to the extent that the statute allows the award of contracts to be based on political rather than economic considerations." Japan's complaints cited the same provisions, in addition to Article III §2 of the Agreement on Government Procurement, which prohibits WTO members from discriminating against "locally established suppliers on the basis of the country of production of the good or service being supplied." See Price and Hannah (1998), 445 fn.7 and 8.

42. *Agreement on Government Procurement*, Apr. 15, 1994. See http://www.wto.org/english/tratop_E/gproc_e/gp_gpa_e.htm, "Text of the Agreement on Government Procurement."

43. See, e.g., Yves Dezalay and Bryant G. Garth, *Dealing in Virtue: International Commercial Arbitration and the Construction of a Transnational Legal Order* (University of Chicago Press, 1996).

44. William Greider, "Sovereign Corporations," *The Nation* (April 30, 2001), 5–6.

45. Copy of letter, dated February 3, 1997, obtained from the archives of Burma Centre Nederlands, in Amsterdam, The Netherlands.

46. The crux of the matter concerns U.S. Code 3512, Sections (a) and (b), which gives the federal government the power to bring action against conflicting state laws: "The United States shall have the burden of proving that the law that is the subject of the action, or the application of that law, is inconsistent with the agreement in question." But according to Jay Ziegler, then the spokesperson for U.S. trade representative Charlene Barshefsky, the federal government is not obligated to sue states that pass legislation in opposition to federal treaties. See Danitz and Strobel, "Networking Dissent," par. 7.

47. The European Institute is a public policy organization based in Washington, D.C., and devoted to transatlantic affairs. It promotes itself as a specialist in helping to resolve policy disputes that arise between the United States and Europe by providing a "back channel" for negotiations. See http://www.europeaninstitute.org.

48. See http://www.citizen.org/trade/article_redirect.cfm?ID=1709, "The European Union and Japan v. The Selective Purchasing Law of the Commonwealth of Massachusetts."

49. See http://www.nftc.org. "Board of Directors." The NFTC's board of directors consists of such noteworthy heavyweights as AIG, Amoco, ARCO, AT&T International, Bank of America, Boeing, Caterpillar, Chevron, Chrysler, Citibank, Colgate-Palmolive, Eastman Kodak, General Electric, General Motors, Halliburton, IBM, Johnson & Johnson, Mobil, Monsanto, PepsiCo, Pfizer, Procter & Gamble, Texaco, W. R. Grace, and Westinghouse Electric.

50. Based on the NFTC's own profile in 2001, http://www.nftconline.org/profile.html (June 18, 2001).

51. *Crosby, Secretary of Administration and Finance of Massachusetts, et al. v. National Foreign Trade Council*, 530 U.S. 363 (2000) at § II (a) (1).

52. Based on the NFTC's own profile in 2001, http://www.nftconline.org/profile.html (18 June 2001). This is reiterated in its 2010 Statement of Goals and Priorities, http://www.nftc.org/?id=233.

53. Field notes from presentation given by Bill Lane, chair of USA*Engage, at a conference on "Unilateral Economic Sanctions and U.S. Foreign Policy," on November 5, 1998, at the Hyatt Regency Embarcadero, San Francisco, Calif. The conference was cosponsored by USA*Engage, the World Affairs Council, the Commonwealth Club, the California Council for International Trade, and the NFTC.

54. Brief for respondent at 10, *Crosby v. National Foreign Trade Council*, 530 U.S. 363 (2000) (No. 99–474).

55. See http://www.usaengage.org/news/nftcsummary.html. "Summary of the NFTC Lawsuit," § 2 (March 3, 2000). See also http://www.usaengage.org/lawsuit/memo.html. "Memorandum of Points and Authorities in Support of Plaintiff's Motion for Preliminary Injunction or, Alternatively, for Consolidation and Expedited Consideration of the Merits," § 3. (May 14, 2001).

56. Go to http://www.usaengage.org/background/members.html (June 18, 2001).

57. See http://www.usaengage.org (June 18, 2001); and http://www.usaengage.org/why.html (June 18, 2001), "USA*Engage Promotes US Engagement in the World," par. 5.

58. Specifically, USA*Engage has been lobbying for unilateral sanctions to be evaluated on the basis of three criteria: (1) whether they achieve their intended results; (2) the costs imposed upon U.S. workers in terms of lost jobs and reduced incomes; and (3) the potential sacrifice of other national interests. See http://usaengage.org/background/principles.html (June 18, 2001), "Coalition Principles." For their letter to Senators Trent Lott and Tom Daschle encouraging their support for the Sanctions Reform Act, S.757, introduced by Senators Lugar, Kerrey, and Hagel, see http://www.usaengage.org/legislative/Ceoletter_Sep-99.html (November 25, 1999). Moreover, this action has produced a more recent discourse on "smart sanctions." However, it is not clear how "smart sanctions" means anything more than sanctions that provide legal loopholes for corporations that wish to continue doing business with the actor that is being targeted by the sanctions, and thus representing a circular argument that seeks to legitimate preexisting corporate interests rather than to serve as an improved means for assessing whose (or what combination of) interests may be the most rational ones upon which to construct foreign policy.

59. See *International Longshoreman's Association, AFL-CIO v. Allied International, Inc.*, 456 U.S. 212, 214–15 (1982).

60. Ibid., 224.

61. Kane, "Reconstructing Culture in Historical Explanation," 311–30.

62. For some exemplary collections of this kind of scholarship, see Philip Smith, ed., *The New American Cultural Sociology* (Cambridge, UK: Cambridge University Press, 1998); Michele Lamont and Marcel Fournier, eds., *Cultivating Differences: Symbolic Boundaries and the Making of Inequality* (Chicago: Univer-

sity of Chicago Press, 1992); and Victoria Bonnell and Lynn Hunt, eds., *Beyond the Cultural Turn* (Berkeley: University of California Press, 1999).

63. Kane, "Reconstructing Culture in Historical Explanation," 315.

64. Ibid.

65. See Marc W. Steinberg, "Talk and Back Talk in Contention: A Dialogic Perspective of Collective Action Discourse and Culture," *American Journal of Sociology* 105, no. 3 (November 1999): 336–80.

66. Kane, "Reconstructing Culture in Historical Explanation," 315.

67. Ibid.

68. Ibid., 315–16.

69. Margaret R. Somers and Gloria D. Gibson, "Reclaiming the Epistemological Other: Narrative and the Social Constitution of Identity," in *Social Theory and the Politics of Identity,* ed. Craig Calhoun (London: Blackwell Publishing, 1994); and Margaret R. Somers, "The Privatization of Citizenship: How to Unthink a Knowledge Culture," in *Beyond the Cultural Turn: New Directions in the Study of Society and Culture,* ed. Victoria E. Bonnell and Lynn Hunt (Berkeley: University of California Press, 1999).

70. Eric Rambo and Elaine Chan, "Text, Structure, and Action in Cultural Sociology," *Theory and Society* 19 (1990): 635–48.

71. *NFTC v. Baker,* 26 F. Supp. 2d 287, 290 n5 (D. Mass. 1998), *aff'd,* 530 U.S. 363 (2000).

72. Although not a "multilateral" movement, the Burma laws—both local and federal—have encouraged other countries to legislate sanctions. During 1998, as concerns about Burma's forced labor practices were increasingly voiced by the International Labor Organization, Amnesty International, and Human Rights Watch Asia, all of whom had been working informally with the Free Burma Coalition, the European Community chose to revoke Burma's tariff preferences. Furthermore, the European Parliament passed a resolution the same year, noting that the communities' "common position" had included a "ban on entry visas" and an "embargo on sales of arms, munitions, and military equipment, and the suspension of non-humanitarian aid or development programmes." Consequently, Japan, along with Canada and Australia, joined the EU in enacting sanctions against Burma. Each enacted an arms embargo, and Japan also limited itself to providing only humanitarian aid. See Shawn W. Crispin, "Business Decision: U.S. Court Strikes Down Burma-Boycott Law," *Far Eastern Economic Review* (July 8, 1999), 22; and http://www.usaengage.org/background/lawsuit/nftcmemo.html (30 Oct 1998), at § "Sanctions Imposed on Burma by Other Countries."

73. *NFTC v. Baker,* 26 F. Supp. 2d 287, 292 (D. Mass. 1998), *aff'd,* 530 U.S. 363 (2000).

74. NFTC brief, p. 23, filed in the Supreme Court of the United States (emphasis mine).

75. *NFTC v. Natsios,* 181 F.3d 38, 000 (1st Cir. 1999), *aff'd,* 530 U.S. 363 (2000).

76. Simon Billenness, "Upholding Local Democracy," *Investing for a Better World: A Publication of Trillium Asset Management* 15 (Winter 1999–2000): 3.

77. See Crosby, *Secretary of Administration and Finance of Massachusetts, et al. v. National Foreign Trade Council,* 530 U.S. 363 (2000).

78. Massachusetts had submitted amicus briefs from seventy-eight members of Congress, nine states, and twelve municipalities, as well as the American Federation of Labor and Congress of Industrial Organizations (AFL-CIO), Consumer's Choice Council, American Lands Alliance, Preamble Center, Institute for Agriculture and Trade Policy, Friends of the Earth, Humane Society of the United States, Defenders of Wildlife, Rainforest Relief, the Center for Constitutional Rights, Citizens for Participation in Political Action, the International Labor Rights Fund, the New England Burma Roundtable, the Unitarian Universalist Service Committee, and EarthRights International, a nonprofit human rights and environmental organization based in the United States and Thailand, which provided information concerning the relationship between human rights abuses and foreign investment in Burma to state legislators. [Citations for all amici curiae].

79. Somers, "The Privatization of Citizenship," 125.

80. NFTC v. Baker, 98-CV-10757-JLT (Plntfs. Mem. of Points and Authorities), 10.

81. Somers, "The Privatization of Citizenship," 137.

82. NFTC v. Baker, 98-CV-10757-JLT (Plntfs. Mem. of Points and Authorities), 11.

83. Somers, "The Privatization of Citizenship."

84. "Defendant's Memorandum in Support of Their Motion for Summary Judgment," IV, D, at § 3. Presented to the U.S. District Court of Massachusetts, July 27, 1998, by attorneys Scott Harshbarger and Thomas Barnico for their defendants Charles D. Baker, Secretary of Administration and Finance of the Commonwealth of Massachusetts, and Philmore Anderson III, State Purchasing Agent for the Commonwealth of Massachusetts, 23 (emphasis mine).

85. Ibid.

86. "Defendant's Memorandum in Support of Their Motion for Summary Judgment," IV, D, at § 3. Presented to the U.S. District Court of Massachusetts, July 27, 1998, by attorneys Scott Harshbarger and Thomas Barnico for their defendants Charles D. Baker, Secretary of Administration and Finance of the Commonwealth of Massachusetts, and Philmore Anderson III, State Purchasing Agent for the Commonwealth of Massachusetts, 26.

87. Ibid.

88. Ibid.

89. See Crosby, *Secretary of Administration and Finance of Massachusetts, et al. v. National Foreign Trade Council,* 530 U.S. 363 (2000), 375–76.

90. Ibid., 377.

91. Ibid., 376.

92. Ibid., 378.

93. Ibid., 379.

94. Ibid.

95. Ibid., 380.

96. Ibid., 378.
97. Ibid., 380.
98. Ibid., 381.
99. For a complete list of current U.S. sanctions against Burma, see U.S. Department of the Treasury, Office of Foreign Assets Control, "An Overview of the Burmese Sanctions Regulations Title 31 Part 537 of the U.S. Code of Federal Regulations." Available at http://www.treas.gov/offices/enforcement/ofac/programs/burma/burma.shtml.
100. See, e.g., Jim Webb, "We Can't Afford to Ignore Myanmar," *Washington Post* (August 26, 2009), Op-Ed, A23.

4. Corporate "Death Penalty"

1. In 1988, under Ne Win's dictatorship, the military reconsolidated power when it violently repressed a domestic pro-democracy movement that was deploying "people power" tactics in an effort to end the military's rule. In the wake of international condemnation for its action, the Burmese military's ruling party, the State Law and Order Restoration Council (SLORC), initiated a series of measures intended to sublimate any collective memory of the illegitimate means by which it had secured its political domination over the state. One of the first measures that SLORC took was to rename the country that it ruled, from Burma to Myanmar.
2. *Doe v. Unocal Corp.*, 963 F. Supp. 880 (C.D. Cal. 1997).
3. See Beate Andrees and Patrick Besler, eds., *Forced Labor: Coercion and Exploitation in the Private Economy* (Geneva, Switzerland: International Labor Organization, 2009).
4. For more on the NFTC's constitutional challenge to the state of Massachusetts's power to conduct foreign policy, see Chapter 3.
5. The following organizations supported the first petition of the Unocal Charter Revocation Campaign: Action Resource Center; Alliance for Democracy of USA; Alliance for Democracy of Austin, Texas; Alliance for Democracy of San Fernando Valley, Calif.; Amazon Watch; Asian/Pacific Gays and Friends; Burma Forum Los Angeles; Democracy Unlimited of Humboldt County, California; Earth Island Institute; Feminist Majority Foundation; Free Burma Coalition; Free Burma: No Petro-Dollars for SLORC; Global Exchange; National Lawyers Guild USA; National Lawyers Guild of Los Angeles, San Diego, Santa Clara Valley, and San Francisco; National Organization for Women; National Organization for Women, California; Program on Corporations, Law and Democracy (POCLAD); Project Maje; Project Underground; Rainforest Action Network; Surfers' Environmental Alliance; and the Transnational Resource and Action Center.
6. Benson, *Challenging Corporate Rule*, 96–106.
7. Ibid., 110–15.
8. Ibid., 107–9.
9. Ibid., 123–29.

10. Ibid., 4.

11. Russell Mokhiber, "The Death Penalty for Corporations Comes of Age," *Business Ethics* (November 1, 1998), quoting Robert Benson. See http://www.corpwatch.org/issues.

12. See http://www.burmaforumla.org.

13. See http://www.burmaforumla.org/activism/activism.htm and http://ga0.org/campaign/olympics.

14. See http://www.irn.org.

15. See http://www.ibiblio.org/freeburma at "oil companies."

16. Benson, *Challenging Corporate Rule*, 35 (emphasis mine).

17. Ronnie Dugger, "Foreword," in Benson, *Challenging Corporate Rule*, vii–viii.

18. Benson, *Challenging Corporate Rule*, 41.

19. Naomi R. Lamoreaux, "How Corporations Acquired Legal Personhood: Language and Economics in the Late-Nineteenth-Century United States." Paper presented at the University of California, Davis Center for History, Society, and Culture, May 4, 2000, 19.

20. This was in part due to the hard lessons learned by the English crown from its experience with the East India Company and with the South Sea Company during the early eighteenth century. For a brief yet cogent overview of the responses of the English crown and Parliament during this period of corporate development, see Dan Bennett, "What Are Corporations? Where Did They Come from? How Did They Become So Powerful?" (September 6, 2002), http://www.corporatewatch.org.uk. For a more complete history of the development of the East India Company as a corporation, and the efforts of the English crown and Parliament to regulate this process, see Ramkrishna Mukherjee, *The Rise and Fall of the East India Company: A Sociological Appraisal* (New York: Monthly Review Press, 1974). For a more complete history of the development of the South Sea Company as a corporation, the stock market crash (or "Bubble Crisis") in 1711 that it engendered, and the reasons for the British government's subsequent enactment of the "Bubble Act" of 1720, see John Carswell, *The South Sea Bubble* (Gloucestershire, UK: Sutton Publishing, 2002).

21. David Millon, "The Ambiguous Significance of Corporate Personhood," *Agora* 2, no. 1 (2002): 42, http://www.law.stanford.edu/agora.

22. Lamoreaux, "How Corporations Acquired Legal Personhood," 19.

23. Richard L. Grossman and Frank T. Adams, *Taking Care of Business: Citizenship and the Charter of Incorporation* (Cambridge, Mass.: Charter, Ink, 1993), http://www.ratical.com/corporations/TCoB.html. As Grossman (1993) notes, "Side by side with these legislative controls, citizens experimented with various forms of enterprise and finance. Artisans and mechanics owned and managed diverse businesses. Farmers and millers organized profitable cooperatives, shoemakers created unincorporated business associations. None of these enterprises had the rights and powers of modern corporations."

24. Millon, "The Ambiguous Significance of Corporate Personhood," 42.

25. Lamoreaux, "How Corporations Acquired Legal Personhood," 14.

26. See Grossman and Adams, *Taking Care of Business*.

27. Millon, "The Ambiguous Significance of Corporate Personhood," 42.

28. As Grossman and Adams (1993) point out, "States limited corporate charters to a set number of years. Citizen authority clauses dictated rules for issuing stock, for shareholder voting, for obtaining corporate information, for paying dividends and for keeping records. They limited corporate capitalization, debts, land holdings and sometimes profits. They required a company's books to be turned over to a legislature upon request. . . . The power of large shareholders was limited to scaled voting, so that large and small investors have equal voting rights. Interlocking corporation directorates were outlawed. Shareholders had the right to remove directors at will."

29. Millon, "The Ambiguous Significance of Corporate Personhood," 43.

30. Lamoreaux, "How Corporations Acquired Legal Personhood," 14. For a summary of such constitutional provisions, see George Herberton Evans Jr., *Business Incorporation in the United States, 1800–1943* (New York: National Bureau of Economic Research, 1948), 11. On the democratization process more generally, see Pauline Maier, "The Revolutionary Origins of the American Corporation," *William and Mary Quarterly* 50 (1993): 51–84.

31. Lamoreaux (2000: 14–15) reports that between 1800 and 1817, the New England states chartered about 850 corporations; between 1844 and 1862, they chartered more than 3,500 (over 70 percent of them by means of special legislation). Between 1826 and 1835, New Jersey authorized on average 11 corporations per year using a special charter system; between 1846 and 1855, it granted on average 45 charters per year through a combination of special and general incorporation; between 1866 and 1875, 145 per year under a similar combination; and between 1876 and 1885, 202 per year using general incorporation alone.

32. Morton Horwitz, *The Transformation of American Law, 1870–1960: The Crisis of Legal Orthodoxy* (London: Oxford University Press, 1992).

33. See, e.g., Lamoreaux, "How Corporations Acquired Legal Personhood," and Millon, "The Ambiguous Significance of Corporate Personhood." The activists participating in the campaign to revoke Unocal's corporate charter have deployed a strategy to denaturalize the rights of corporations, even while essentializing the rights of human persons, as well as ignoring the more immediately sticky issue of how their own base of support—predominantly 501(c)(3) corporations (i.e., nonprofit organizations)—have a right to serve as signatories on a citizens' petition to mandate the attorney general to revoke a corporate charter. Thus, their own discursive efforts to denaturalize the discourse on corporate personhood at times rely upon it.

34. Millon, "The Ambiguous Significance of Corporate Personhood," 43.

35. Ibid., 44.

36. Benson, *Challenging Corporate Rule*, 43.

37. Ibid., 45.

38. Dugger, "Foreword," in Benson, *Challenging Corporate Rule*, viii–ix.

39. For a single compilation of these statutes, see Linzey Thomas, "Awakening a Sleeping Giant: Creating a Quasi-Private Cause of Action for Revoking

Corporate Charters in Response to Environmental Violations," *Pace Environmental Law Review* 13 (1995): 223, n15.

40. Benson, *Challenging Corporate Rule*, 52.

41. According to Benson, *Challenging Corporate Rule*, 53, "Judges have upheld revocation as a remedy for 'misuse' or 'nonuse' of the corporate charter, 'unlawful acts,' 'fraud,' 'willful abuse of chartered privileges,' 'usurpation of powers,' 'improper neglect of responsibility,' 'excess of power,' 'mistake in the exercise of an acknowledged power,' and 'failure to fulfill design and purpose.'"

42. Benson, *Challenging Corporate Rule*, 62. See *California Code of Civil Procedure* § 803.

43. Ibid., 33.

44. Ibid., 56. The Web site to which Benson refers is http://caag.state.ca.us/opinions/content/nature.htm. As Benson notes, "The pages emphasize the use of *quo warranto* against public officeholders, with barely a mention of its history or use against corporations."

45. *Citizens Utilities Co. of California v. Superior Court of Alameda County*, 56. Cal. App. 3d 399 (1976).

46. *People v. Council for Tobacco Research, U.S.A., Inc. and the Tobacco Institute, Inc.* (filed April 30, 1998, Supreme Court of New York, N.Y. Courts, Index No. 107479/98).

47. *William J. Wynn ex rel. State of Alabama v. Philip Morris et al.* (Circuit Court, Jefferson County, Case No. CY 98–3295, June 6, 1998). It would not be surprising to see a similar application of the quo warranto statute deployed to challenge fast-food corporations like McDonald's, in light of the recent efforts of individuals to sue them for liability on grounds similar to those argued in cases against cigarette manufacturers. See, for example, *Barber v. McDonald's Corp.* (filed July 24, 2002, Supreme Court of New York, N.Y. Courts, Index #23145/2002). See http://news.corporate.findlaw.com/hdocs/docs/mcdonalds/barbermcds72302cmp.pdf.

47. Richard Grossman, "Slaying Big Tobacco: Challenging the Authority under Which Tobacco Companies Operate in Alabama May Be Just the Way to Force Them Out," *Birmingham News*, September 6, 1998, 2C.

48. Benson, *Challenging Corporate Rule*, 36–37.

50. Ibid., 4.

51. *Citizens United v. Federal Election Commission*, 558 U.S. ___ (2010), No. 08–205.

52. See Charles Forelle, "Intel Cites Human Rights in EU Fight on Antitrust," *Wall Street Journal*, July 23, 2009, http://online.wsj.com/article/SB124826913522171933.html.

5. Alien Tort Claims

1. *Doe v. Unocal Corp.*, 963 F. Supp. 880 (C.D. Cal. 1997); 27 F. Supp. 2d 1174 (C.D. Cal. 1998); 67 F. Supp. 2d 1140 (C.D. Cal. 1999); 110 F. Supp. 2d 1294 (C.D. Cal. 2000); and 403 F.3d 708 (9th Cir. 2002).

2. Marc Lifsher, "Unocal Settles Human Rights Lawsuit over Alleged Abuses at Myanmar Pipeline; A deal ends a landmark case brought by villagers who said soldiers committed atrocities." *Los Angeles Times*, March 22, 2005, C1; and EarthRights International (April 5, 2005), "Common Questions and Answer for ERI: What are the terms of the settlement?" Accessed February 12, 2006, http://www.earthrights.org/news/unocalfaq.shtml.

3. See U.S. Alien Tort Claim Act, 28 U.S.C. §1350.

4. "The Peasants Versus Unocal," ABC *Nightline*, aired March 28, 2000, Item #N000328, p. 1. Transcript, http://abcnews.go.com/onair/nightline/transcripts/n1000328_trans_1html.

5. "The Peasants Versus Unocal," 2.

6. Ibid., 6.

7. Ibid.

8. See, e.g., Beate Andrees and Patrick Besler, eds., *Forced Labor: Coercion and Exploitation in the Private Economy* (Geneva, Switzerland, 2009); and Kevin Bales, *Disposable People: New Slavery in the Global Economy* (Berkeley: University of California Press, 1999), 235–40.

9. 28 U.S.C. §1350.

10. This is the definition of the law of nations that the Ninth Circuit Court of Appeals used in *Doe v. Unocal Corp.*, 395 F.3d 932, 944 n.12 (9th Cir. 2002).

11. 630 F.2d 876 (2d Cir. 1980). See also Andrew Ridenour, "*Doe v. Unocal Corp.*, Apples and Oranges: Why Courts Should Use International Standards to Determine Liability for Violation of the Law of Nations under the Alien Tort Claims Act," *Tulane Journal of International and Comparative Law* 9 (2001): 581–603, at n.21. As Ridenour explains, although plaintiffs had invoked the alien tort statute in numerous suits before 1980, only two suits had been successful under the statute (see *Abdul-Rahman Omar Adra v. Clift*, 195 F. Supp. 857 (D.Md. 1961), and *Bolchos v. Darrel*, 3 F. Cas. 810 (DSC 1795).

12. Ridenour, "*Doe v. Unocal Corp.*, Apples and Oranges," 584.

13. *In re Estate of Ferdinand E. Marcos Human Rights Litig.*, 25 F. 3rd 1467, 1475 (9th Cir. 1994), *cert. denied*, 513 U.S. 1126 (1995).

14. *Xuncax v. Gramajo*, 886 F. Supp. 162, 181–83 (D. Mass. 1995).

15. *Tel Oren v. Libyan Arab Republic*, 726 F.2d at 778 (D.C. Cir. 1984).

16. The U.S. House of Representatives stated, "The TVPA would establish an unambiguous and modern basis for a cause of action that has been successfully maintained under an existing law, section 1350 of the Judiciary Act of 1789 (the Alien Tort Claims Act), which permits Federal district courts to hear claims by aliens for torts committed 'in violation of the law of nations' . . . Judge Bork questioned the existence of a private right of action under the Alien Tort Claims Act, reasoning that separation of powers principles required an explicit—and preferably contemporary—grant by Congress of a private right of action before U.S. courts could consider cases likely to impact on U.S. foreign relations. . . . The TVPA would provide such a grant." H.R. *Report* No. 102-367, pt. 1, at 3–4 (1991).

17. *Torture Victim Protection Act of 1991*, 28 U.S.C. § 1350 *et seq.*, affirmed by *470 U.S. 1003* (1985).

18. See, e.g., *Xuncax v. Gramajo*, 886 F. Supp. 162, 179 (D. Mass. 1995).

19. *Kadic v. Karadzic*, 70 F. 3d 232, 241 (2d Cir. 1996).

20. Hon. John M. Walker Jr.,"Domestic Adjudication of International Human Rights Violations under the Alien Tort Statute," *Saint Louis University Law Journal* 41, no. 2 (Spring 1997): 543–49. In this case filed against Radnovan Karadzic following civil war in former Yugoslavia the court provided a reasoned analysis of the scope of the private individual's liability for violations of international law. The Second Circuit court disagreed with the proposition "that the law of nations, as understood in the modern era, confines its reach to state action. Instead, [the court held] that certain forms of conduct violate the law of nations whether undertaken by those acting under the auspices of a state or only as private individuals." *Kadic v. Karadzic*, 70 F. 3d at 239. While *international law* proscribes crimes such as torture and summary execution only when committed by state officials or under their legal authority, the *law of nations* has historically been applied to private actors for the crimes of piracy and slavery, and for certain war crimes. *Kadic v. Karadzic*, 70 F. 3d at 243 n4. Thus, individual liability may apply when torture or summary execution are perpetrated as a war crime. *Kadic v. Karadzic*, 70 F. 3d at 239.

21. Sarah H. Cleveland, "Norm Internalization and U.S. Economic Sanctions." *Yale Journal of International Law* 26 (2001): 1–92, at 20.

22. Ibid.

23. Louis Henkin, ed., *The International Bill of Rights: The Covenant on Civil and Political Rights* (New York: Columbia University Press, 1981), 1, 15.

24. The International Labor Organization (ILO), which is the international body responsible for defining and implementing international labor norms, has played a significant role in helping certain labor rights, including the prohibition against slavery and forced labor, to attain broad recognition among states as fundamental human rights. Its eight conventions explicitly setting forth "fundamental human rights" have been almost universally embraced, with the notable exception of the United States. The United States has, however, ratified the ILO's Convention No. 105 regarding the abolition of forced labor. In 1998, the ILO made further progress toward universalizing these norms by adopting its Declaration on Fundamental Principles and Rights at Work, which binds all ILO members to the core labor principles, regardless of whether the member has ratified the relevant conventions. Commitment to these core ILO principles is a condition of ILO membership. Moreover, the basic, nonspecific labor rights have been incorporated into foundational international human rights instruments, all of which have received nearly universal acceptance.

25. Cherif Bassiouni, "International Crimes: *Jus Cogens* and *Obligatio Erga Omnes.*" *Law and Contemporary Problems* 59 (Autumn 1996): 63–74, at 67.

26. *Vienna Convention of the Law on Treaties*, 1155 U.N.T.S. 331, 344, art. 53.

27. *Vienna Convention of the Law on Treaties*, 1155 U.N.T.S. 331, 347, art. 64.

28. Although identifying the international human rights principles that constitute jus cogens can be controversial, the Restatement (Third) of the Foreign Relations Law of the United States § 702 (1987) recognizes the following jus cogens norms: genocide; slavery or slave trade; summary execution or causing the disappearance of individuals; torture or other cruel, inhuman, or degrading treatment or punishment; prolonged arbitrary detention; systematic racial discrimination; and a consistent pattern or gross violations of internationally recognized human rights.

29. *Sosa v. Alvarez-Machain*, 542 U.S. 692 (2004).

30. Benson, *Challenging Corporate Rule*, and Naomi R. Lamoreaux, "How Corporations Acquired Legal Personhood: Language and Economics in the Late-Nineteenth-Century United States." Paper presented at the University of California, Davis Center for History, Society, and Culture, May 4, 2000.

31. Marc Lifsher, "Unocal Settles Human Rights Lawsuit over Alleged Abuses at Myanmar Pipeline," *Los Angeles Times*, March 22, 2005, http://articles.latimes.com/2005/mar/22/business/fi-unocal22/2.

32. District Court stated that the "plaintiffs' allegations of Unocal's complicity in forced labor do not meet the standard of liability used in U.S. civil proceedings." That is, the plaintiffs could not show that Unocal "actively participated" in the forced labor. In effect, the District Court ruled that because Unocal did not "actively and directly participate" in the alleged torts, they could not be held liable for those torts under the ATCA. Unocal subsequently asserted on its Web site that this ruling confirmed that they were not "vicariously liable" for the military's torts (Unocal Corporation 2002). On appeal, the attorneys and amici curiae for the *Doe*-plaintiffs successfully argued that the lower court had failed to properly use the international standard of "aiding and abetting" the alleged tort in testing Unocal's liability. *Doe v. Unocal Corp.*, 395 F.3d 932 (9th Cir. 2002).

33. *John Doe I v. Unocal Corp.*, Nos. 00–56603, 00–57197, 00–56628, 00–57195, 2002 U.S. App. 14187, 14222 (9th Cir. September 18, 2002).

34. The theory that a corporation is a "nexus of contracts" among all the participants in a corporation's activity can be found in Frank Easterbook and Daniel R. Fischel, *The Economic Structure of Corporate Law* (1991). For a concise overview, see Henry N. Butler, "The Contractual Nature of the Corporation," *George Mason Law Review* 11 (1989): 100. This theory downplays the notion of "corporate personhood" as a weak and unimportant fiction, in favor of the view that a corporation is a web of ongoing contracts (explicit or implicit) between various real persons. Rather than thinking of a corporation as simply an actor within a marketplace, it sees the corporation itself as also a market writ small.

35. The PTT joined with a 25 percent share. MOGE retained rights to 15 percent of the gas for a fertilizer and energy plant, providing the military with dividends and taxes of up to about (U.S.) $400 million per year. See EarthRights International and Southeast Asian Information Network, *Total Denial: A Report on the Yadana Pipeline Project in Burma* (1996), http://www.earthrights.org/

publication/total-denial-report-yadana-pipeline-project-burma; and U.S. Department of Labor, Bureau of International Labor Affairs, *Report on Labor Practices in Burma* (1998), "Chapter 2: Forced Labor and Forced Relocations."

36. *John Doe I v. Unocal Corp.*, Nos. 00–56603, 00–57197, 00–56628, 00–57195, 2002. U.S. App. 14187, 14222–14223 (9th Cir. September 18, 2002).

37. John Gilbert Dale, "Transnational Legal Space: Corporations, States, and the Free Burma Movement" (Ph.D. dissertation, University of California, Davis, 2003), 279–85.

38. *Doe v. Unocal Corp.*, 963 F. Supp. 880, 894 FN 17 (C.D. CA 1997).

39. *Doe v. Unocal Corp.*, 395 F.3d 932, 946 n18 (9th Cir. 2002).

40. The District Court incorrectly borrowed the "active participation" standard for liability from war crimes before Nuremberg military tribunals involving the role of German industrialists in the Nazi forced labor program during the Second World War. The military tribunals applied the "active participation" standard in these cases only to overcome the defendants' "necessity defense." In the present case, Unocal did not invoke—and could not have invoked—the necessity defense. The court notes that the tribunal had defined the necessity defense as follows: "Necessity is a defense when it has shown that the act charged was done to avoid an evil both serious and irreparable; that there was no other adequate means to escape; and that the remedy was not disproportionate to the evil." *Doe v. Unocal Corp.*, 395 F.3d 932, 948 n.21 (9th Cir. 2002).

41. "We require 'control' to establish proximate causation by private third parties only in cases . . . where we otherwise require state action. In other cases—including cases such as this one—where state action is *not* otherwise required, we require no more than 'foreseeability' to establish proximate causation. This requirement is easily met in the present case, where Unocal Vice President Lipman testified that even before Unocal invested in the Project, Unocal was aware that the 'option of having the [Myanmar] [M]ilitary provide protection for the pipeline construction . . . would [entail] that they might proceed in the manner that would be out of our control and not be in a manner that we would like to see them proceed,' i.e., 'going to excess.'" *Doe v. Unocal Corp.*, 395 F.3d 932, 954 n.32 (9th Cir. 2002).

42. *Doe v. Unocal Corp.*, 395 F.3d 932, 952–53 (9th Cir. 2002).

43. Ibid., 953 (9th Cir. 2002).

44. Ibid., 941 and 953 (9th Cir. 2002).

45. Ibid., 948 n.22 (9th Cir. 2002).

46. *Nat'l Coalition Gov't of the Union of Burma v. Unocal, Inc.*, 176 F.R.D. 329, 362 (C.D. Cal. 1997). Judge Paez initially authored the orders granting in part and denying in part refendants' motions to rismiss. See *Doe v. Unocal Corp.*, 963 F. Supp. 880 (C.D. Cal. 1997). Judge Lew later authored the order granting defendants' consolidated motions for summary judgment. See *Doe v. Unocal Corp.*, 110 F. Supp. 2d 1294 (C.D. Cal. 2000).

47. Statement of Sen. John McCain, 142 Cong. Rec. § 8755 (daily ed. July 25, 1996), quoted in *Doe v. Unocal Corp.*, 963 F. Supp. 880, 894 n.17 (C.D. Cal. 1997). As Paez stated in his published court opinion, "Even accepting the

Congressional and Executive decisions as Unocal frames them, the coordinate branches of government have simply indicated an intention to encourage reform by allowing companies from the United States to assert positive pressure on SLORC through their investments in Burma."

48. *Doe v. Unocal Corp.*, 963 F. Supp. 880, 895 (C.D. Cal. 1997).

49. *Nat'l Coalition Gov't of the Union of Burma v. Unocal, Inc.*, 176 F.R.D. 329, 354 n.29 (C.D. Cal. 1997). The Ninth Circuit Court stated, "We agree with the District Court's evaluation that 'Given the circumstances of the instant case, and particularly the Statement of Interest of the United States, it is hard to imagine how judicial consideration of the matter will so substantially exacerbate relations with [the Myanmar military] as to cause hostile confrontations." *Doe v. Unocal Corp.*, 395 F.3d 932, 959 (9th Cir. 2002).

50. EarthRights International (October 20, 2005), "Senator Feinstein Introduces Bill to Protect Perpetrators of Human Rights Abuses" (accessed February 14, 2006), http://earthrights.org/ news/saveatca.shtml.

51. Ibid.

52. David R. Baker,"Chevron Donates to Lawmakers against China Bid; politicians deny link to stance on oil firm's Unocal offer." *San Francisco Chronicle*, July 23, 2005, C1.

53. EarthRights International (October 25, 2005), "Senator Feinstein Puts the Brakes on the Anti-ATCA Bill S. 1874" (accessed February 9, 2010), http:// www.earthrights.org/campaigns/senator-feinstein-puts-breaks-anti-atca-bill-s-1874.

54. There have been other ATCA cases against corporations outside the oil industry. Coca-Cola, for example, has been sued under ATCA for its complicity in the murder and intimidation of union members from their Columbian factory. And, although the courts rejected their first ATCA claim in 1989, the new flurry of ATCA cases against corporations has encouraged a renewed effort by citizens in Bhopal, India, to hold Union Carbide liable for the 1989 gas-leak disaster that caused thousands of deaths and permanent health problems.

55. See *Bowoto v. Chevron Texaco Corp.*, 312 F. Supp. 2d 1229 (N.D. Cal. 2004). The suit, which the plaintiffs originally filed against a premerger Chevron, sought to hold the company responsible for both the deaths of protesters who occupied a Nigerian oil-drilling platform in 1998 and the attacks on residents of two Nigerian villages in 1999. The protesters were shot and killed by Nigerian security forces who were flown to the site in helicopters that were used by the joint venture that ran the platform. Both cases involved projects of companies that were Chevron Texaco's subsidiaries rather than the parent company itself. Attorneys and activists have asserted, however, that liability for these wrongdoings should rest with the parent corporation and be pursued in the country where that parent corporation is chartered.

56. See *Wiwa v. Royal Dutch Petroleum Co.*, 226 F. 3d 88 (2d Cir. 2000). The U.S. Supreme Court refused to hear arguments for the dismissal of the suit in March 2001 and did not address the merits of these arguments. Yet, in effect, this thwarted Royal Dutch/Shell's effort to end the litigation without a court ever hearing evidence of Shell's involvement in the abuses at issue. Also in March

2001, the plaintiffs sued Brian Anderson, the former managing director of the Royal Dutch/Shell subsidiary Shell Nigeria. On February 28, 2002, the district court denied Anderson's motions to dismiss. As EarthRights International describes the judge's findings, "The plaintiffs' allegations met the requirements for claims under the Alien Tort Claims Act, in that the actions of Royal Dutch/ Shell and Anderson constituted participation in crimes against humanity, torture, summary execution, arbitrary detention, cruel, inhuman, and degrading treatment, and other violations of international law. The court also found that Anderson could be sued under the Torture Victim Protection Act, which allows victims of torture to sue the perpetrators in federal court. Finally, the court found that the plaintiffs' RICO claims could proceed, because Royal Dutch/ Shell's actions in concert with the Nigerian military satisfied the racketeering requirements of the act and because they engaged in these acts in part to facilitate the export of cheap oil to the United States. The plaintiffs are now entitled to gather evidence by interviewing Anderson and other Royal Dutch/Shell employees, and by reviewing their documents." See EarthRights International, "Wiwa vs. Royal Dutch Shell Case History" (accessed February 9, 2010), http:// www.earthrights.org/about/news/wiwa-v-royal-dutch-shell-case-history.

57. See *Doe v. Exxon Mobil Corp.*, 393 F. Supp. 2d 20 (D.D.C. 2005). Exxon and Mobil merged in 1999. The International Labor Rights Fund is an advocacy organization dedicated to achieving just and humane treatment for workers worldwide, and the same organization that helped the National Coalition Government of Burma file their case against Unocal. The suit alleges that Exxon Mobil had been complicit in human rights violations committed by Indonesian military units who were hired to provide security for their natural gas field located in the Aceh province. Since 1975, the Indonesian military has had a history of violence and repression toward the Aceh ethnic minority and their Islamic separatist movement. While under contract with Exxon Mobil, allege the *Doe* plaintiffs, these military units committed widespread abuses, including murder, torture, rape, and kidnapping of the Aceh local population.

58. Edward Alden, "Unocal Wants Government to Assess Labour Lawsuit." *Financial Times*, August 9, 2002, 3.

59. Ibid.

60. Sonni Efron, "Judge Lets Unocal Ask State Dept. to Intervene in Myanmar Lawsuit." *Los Angeles Times*, August 9, 2002, C2.

61. See *Doe v. Exxon Mobil*, 01–1357, U.S. District Court, District of Columbia (Washington).

62. Mark Goodale and Sally Engle Merry, eds., *The Practice of Human Rights: Tracking Law between the Global and the Local* (Cambridge, Mass.: Cambridge University Press, 2007). See also Keck and Sikkink, *Activists beyond Borders*.

Conclusion

1. Inderpal Grewal and Caren Kaplan, eds. *Scattered Hegemonies: Postmodernity and Transnational Feminist Practices* (Minneapolis: University of Min-

nesota Press, 1994); William F. Fisher, "Doing Good?" The Politics and Anti-politics of NGO Practices," *Annual Review of Anthropology* 26 (1997): 439–64; Clifford Bob, *The Marketing of Rebellion: Insurgents, Media and International Activism* (New York: Cambridge University Press, 2005).

2. Benedict Kingsbury, "Representation in Human Rights Litigation," *Human Rights Dialogue* (Spring 2000): 3, http://www.cceia.org/resources/publications/dialogue/2_02/articles/611.html; Mark Bradley and Patrice Petro, eds., *Truth Claims: Representation and Human Rights* (New Bruswick, N.J.: Rutgers University Press, 2002); Balakrishnan Rajagopal, *International Law from Below: Development, Social Movements, and Third World Resistance* (New York: Cambridge University Press, 2003); Wendy S. Hesford and Wendy Kozol, *Just Advocacy? Women's Human Rights, Transnational Feminism, and the Politics of Representation* (New Brunswick, N.J.: Rutgers University Press, 2005).

3. See Fuyuki Kurasawa, *The Work of Global Justice: Human Rights as Practice* (New York: Cambridge University Press, 2007), 1–22; and John G. Dale, "A Review of Fuyuki Kurasawa's *The Work of Global Justice: Human Rights as Practice*," *Mobilization: An International Quarterly Review of Social Movements, Protest, and Contentious Politics* 1, no. 4 (December 2009): 517–18.

Select Bibliography of Key Legal Documents

These are the most relevant legal sources and concepts that shaped the three transnational legal campaigns discussed in this book.

Briefs

Appellants' Opening Brief, *Doe v. Unocal*, No. 00–56603 in the U.S. Court of Appeals for the Ninth Circuit, February 26, 2001.

Brief of Amici Curiae in Support of Plaintiffs-Appellants Urging Reversal, *Doe v. Unocal*, No. 00–56603, and *Roe v. Unocal*, No. 00–56628 in the U.S. Court of Appeals for the Ninth Circuit (submitted by Center for International Environmental Law, Global Exchange, Rainforest Action Network, Sierra Club), 2001.

Defendants/Appellees' Consolidated Answering Brief, *Doe v. Unocal*, No. 00-56603, and *Roe v. Unocal*, No. 00–56628 in the U.S. Court of Appeals for the Ninth Circuit, May 7, 2001.

"Defendants' Memorandum in Support of Their Motion for Summary Judgment," IV, D, at § 3. Presented to the U.S. District Court of Massachusetts, July 27, 1998, by attorneys Scott Harshbarger and Thomas Barnico for their defendants Charles D. Baker, Secretary of Administration and Finance of the Commonwealth of Massachusetts, and Philmore Anderson III, State Purchasing Agent for the Commonwealth of Massachusetts.

"Memorandum of Points and Authorities in Support of Plaintiff's Motion for Preliminary Injunction or, Alternatively, for Consolidation and Expedited Consideration of the Merits," § 3 (May 14, 2001).

"Summary of the NFTC Lawsuit," § 2 (March 3, 2000).

Government Documents

The Crackdown in Burma: Suppression of the Democracy Movement and Violations of Human Rights. Hearing and Markup before the Subcommittees on Human Rights and International Organizations and on the Asian and Pacific Affairs of the Committee on Foreign Affairs, House of Representatives, One Hundred First Congress, First Session on H. Con. Res. 185, September 13, 1989. Washington, D.C.: U.S. Government Printing Office, 1990.

Forced Labor in Myanmar (Burma). Report of the Commission of Inquiry appointed under article 26 of the Constitution of the International Labor Organization to examine the observance by Myanmar of the Forced Labor Convention, 1930 (No. 29). Geneva, 1998. See http://www.ilo.org/public/english/bureau/inf/pr/.

Memorandum of the Government of Myanmar on the Report of the Director-General to the Members of the Governing Body, May 1999. See http://www.ilo.org/public/english/standards/relm/gb/docs/gb276/gb-6-a2.htm.

Reports

142 Cong. Rec. § 8755 (daily ed. July 25, 1996).

H.R. Report No. 102–367, pt. 1 (1991).

Human Rights Documentation Unit (National Coalition Government of the Union of Burma) (1997), *Human Rights Yearbook: 1996 Burma.* Nonthaburi, Thailand.

Treaties

Agreement on Government Procurement, Apr. 15, 1994. See http://www.wto.org/english/tratop_e/gproc_e/agrmnt_e.htm, "Text of the Agreement on Government Procurement" (Aug. 17, 2001).

Vienna Convention on the Law of Treaties, May 23, 1969, 1155 U.N.T.S. 331, 344, art. 53; and 347, art. 64.

U.S. Cases

Abdul-Rahman Omar Adra v. Clift, 195 F. Supp. 857 (D.Md. 1961).

Bolchos v. Darrel, 3 F. Cas. 810 (DSC 1795).

Bowoto v. Chevron Texaco Corp., 312 F. Supp. 2d 1229 (N.D. Cal. 2004).

Citizens United v. Federal Election Commission, 558 U.S. ___ (2010). No. 08-205.

Crosby, *Secretary of Administration and Finance of Massachusetts, et al. v. National Foreign Trade Council*, 530 U.S. 363, 387 to 388 (2000).

Doe v. Exxon Mobil Corp., 393 F. Supp. 2d 20 (D.D.C. 2005).

Doe v. Unocal Corp., 963 F. Supp. 880 (C.D. Cal. 1997).

Doe v. Unocal Corp., 27 F. Supp. 2d 1174 (C.D. Cal. 1998).

Doe v. Unocal Corp., 67 F. Supp. 2d 1140 (C.D. Cal. 1999).

Doe v. Unocal Corp., 110 F. Supp. 2d 1294 (C.D. Cal. 2000).

Doe v. Unocal Corp., F.3d 915 (9th Cir. 2001).

Doe v. Unocal Corp., 395 F.3d 932 (9th Cir. 2002).

Doe v. Unocal Corp., 395 F.3d 978 (9th Cir. 2003).

Doe v. Unocal Corp., 403 F.3d 708 (9th Cir. 2005).

Filartiga v. Pena-Irala, 630 F. 2d 876 (2d Cir. 1980).

In re Estate of Ferdinand E. Marcos Human Rights Litig., 25 F. 3rd 1467, 1475 (9th Cir. 1994), *cert. denied*, 513 U.S. 1126 (1995).

International Longshoremen's Association, AFL-CIO v. Allied International, Inc., 456 U.S. 212, 214–215 (1982).

Kardic v. Karadzic, 70 F 3d 232 (2d Cir. 1995).

Nat'l Coalition Gov't of the Union of Burma v. Unocal, Inc., 176 F.R.D. 329 (C.D. Cal 1997).

NFTC v. Baker, 26 F. Supp. 2d 287, 290 n5 (D. Mass. 1998), *aff'd*, 530 U.S. 363 (2000).

NFTC v. Baker, 98-CV-10757-JLT (Plntfs. Mem. of Points and Authorities).

NFTC v. Natsios, 181 F.3d 38, 46 and 54 (1st Cir. 1999), *aff'd*, 530 U.S. 363 (2000).

Sosa v. Alvarez-Machain, 542 US 692 (2004).

Tel-Oren v. Libyan Arab Republic, 726 F.2d (D.C. Cir. 1984).

Tel-Oren v. Libyan Arab Republic, 470 U.S. 1003 (1985).

Xuncax v. Gramajo, 886 F. Supp.162 (D. Mass. 1995).

U.S. Constitution and Statutes

Abolition of Forced Labor Convention (ILO No. 105), 320 U.N.T.S. 291, entered into force Jan. 17, 1959.

Alien Tort Claims Act, 28 U.S.C. § 1350.

An Act Regulating State Contracts with Companies Doing Business with or in Burma (Myanmar), ch. 130, 1996 Mass. Acts 239 (codified at Mass. Gen. Laws ch. 7, §§ 22G-22M, 40F ("Massachusetts Burma Law").

Foreign Operations, Export Financing, and Related Programs Appropriations Act, 1997, § 570 ("Federal Burma Law").

Racketeer Influenced and Corrupt Organizations Act, 18 U.S.C. § 1961 *et seq.*

Torture Victim Protection Act of 1991, 28 U.S.C. § 1350 *et seq.*

Vienna Convention of the Law on Treaties, 1155 U.N.T.S. 331, entered into force Jan. 27, 1980.

Index

ABFSU. *See* All Burma Federation of Student Unions

ABSU. *See* All Burma Students' Union

accountability, 97, 138, 181, 193, 209; corporate, ix, 22, 26, 33, 114, 118, 123, 124, 131, 142, 143, 205

activists, 23, 103, 142, 144, 165–66, 176, 180, 188, 191, 199; photo of, 110; pro-democracy, 6, 11, 13, 27, 42, 43, 66, 71, 88–89, 90, 111, 209; role of, 52–56, 78; transnational, 22, 212

Adams, Frank, 156, 157–58

administrative discursive contention, 33–35

"Advancing Human Rights and Ending Impunity in Burma: Which External Leverages?" (conference), 209

AFL-CIO. *See* American Federation of Labor and Congress of Industrial Organizations

Agence France-Presse, xv

agency, 13; culture and, 16

Agreement on Government Procurement (WTO), 114–15, 235n41

Air India *Kashmir Princess:* bombing of, 51–52

Al-Bashir, 210

Alien Tort Claims Act (ATCA) (1789), 6, 10, 14, 28, 29, 35, 36, 178, 180, 187, 188, 189, 192, 204, 209, 243n16, 245n32, 247n54, 248n56; adoption of, 175; concerns about, 191; *Doe v. Unocal* and, 175–76; Exxon Mobil Corporation and, 191; *Filartiga v. Pena-Irala* and, 176, 177; human rights and, 175–76; law of nations and, 177; ruling on, 37; struggle over, 193; suing under, 171, 175–76, 179, 181; targets of, 36

All Burma Federation of Student Unions (ABFSU), 53, 54

All Burma Students' Union (ABSU), 53, 71, 76, 81

Alliance for Democracy, 154, 239n5

John G. Dale is assistant professor of sociology, affiliate faculty of the School of Conflict Analysis and Resolution, and associate faculty of the Center for Global Studies at George Mason University. He is co-author of *Political Sociology: Power and Participation in the Modern World*.